Building Serverless Applications on Knative

A Guide to Designing and Writing
Serverless Cloud Applications

Evan Anderson

Beijing · Boston · Farnham · Sebastopol · Tokyo

Building Serverless Applications on Knative

by Evan Anderson

Published by O'Reilly Media, Inc., 1005 Gravenstein Highway North, Sebastopol, CA 95472.

O'Reilly books may be purchased for educational, business, or sales promotional use. Online editions are also available for most titles (*http://oreilly.com*). For more information, contact our corporate/institutional sales department: 800-998-9938 or *corporate@oreilly.com*.

Acquisitions Editor: John Devins	**Indexer:** nSight, Inc.
Development Editor: Shira Evans	**Interior Designer:** David Futato
Production Editor: Clare Laylock	**Cover Designer:** Karen Montgomery
Copyeditor: Stephanie English	**Illustrator:** Kate Dullea
Proofreader: Sharon Wilkey	

November 2023:   First Edition

Revision History for the First Edition

2023-11-15:   First Release

See *http://oreilly.com/catalog/errata.csp?isbn=9781098142070* for release details.

978-1-098-14207-0

[LSI]

Table of Contents

Part I.   The Theory of Serverless

Part II.   Designing with Serverless

Part III.   Living with Serverless

Part IV.   A Brief History of Serverless

Preface

Serverless has become a major selling point of cloud service providers. Over the last four years, hundreds of services from both major cloud providers and smaller service offerings have been branded or rebranded as "serverless." Clearly, serverless has something to do with services provided over a network, but what is serverless, and why does it matter? How does it differ from containers, functions, or cloud native technologies? While terminology and definitions are constantly evolving, this book aims to highlight the essential attributes of serverless technologies and explain why the serverless moniker is growing in popularity.

This book primarily focuses on serverless *compute* systems; that is, systems that execute user-defined software, rather than performing a fixed-function system like storage, indexing, or message queuing. (Serverless storage systems exist as well, but they aren't the primary focus of this book!) With that said, the line between fixed-function storage and general-purpose compute is never as sharp and clear as theory would like—for example, database systems that support the SQL query syntax combine storage, indexing, and the execution of declarative query programs written in SQL. While the architecture of fixed-function systems can be fascinating and important to understand for performance tuning, this book primarily focuses on serverless compute because it's the interface with the most degrees of freedom for application authors, and the system that they are most likely to interact with day-to-day.

If you're still not quite sure what serverless is, don't worry. Given the number of different products on the market, it's clear that most people are in the same boat. We'll chart the evolution of the "serverless" term in "Background" on page x of the Preface and then lay out a precise definition in Chapter 1.

Who Is This Book For?

The primary audience for this book is software engineers[1] and technologists who are either unfamiliar with serverless or are looking to deepen their understanding of the principles and best practices associated with serverless architecture.

New practitioners who want to immediately dive into writing serverless applications can start in Chapter 2, though I'd recommend Chapter 1 for additional orientation on what's going on and why serverless matters. Chapter 3 provides additional practical material to develop a deeper understanding of the architecture of the Knative platform used in the examples.

The order of the chapters should be natural for readers who are familiar with serverless. Chapters 5 and 6 provide a checklist of standard patterns for applying serverless, while Chapter 8 and onward provides a sort of "bingo card" of serverless warning signs and solution sketches that may be handy on a day-to-day basis. Chapter 11's historical context also provides a map of previous technology communities to examine for patterns and solutions.

For readers who are more interested in capturing the big-picture ideas of serverless, Chapters 1, 4, and 7 have some interesting gems to inspire deeper understanding and new ideas. Chapter 11's historical context and future predictions may also be of interest in understanding the arc of software systems that led to the current implementations of scale-out serverless offerings.

For readers who are new not only to serverless computing, but also to backend or cloud native development, the remainder of this preface will provide some background material to help set the stage. Like much of software engineering, these areas move quickly, so the definitions I provide here may have changed somewhat by the time you read this book. When in doubt, these keywords and descriptions may save some time when searching for equivalent services in your environment of choice.

Background

Over the last six years, the terms "cloud native," "serverless," and "containers" have all been subject to successive rounds of hype and redefinition, to the point that even many practitioners struggle to keep up or fully agree on the definitions of these terms. The following sections aim to provide definitions of some important reference points in the rest of the book, but many of these definitions will probably continue to evolve—take them as general reference context for the rest of this book, but not as the one true gospel of serverless computing. Definitions change as ideas germinate and

---

1 Including operationally focused engineers like site reliability engineers (SREs) or DevOps practitioners.

grow, and the gardens of cloud native and serverless over the last six years have run riot with new growth.

Also note that this background is organized such that it makes sense when read from beginning to end, *not* as a historical record of what came first. Many of these areas developed independently of one another and then met and combined after their initial flowering (replanting ideas from one garden into another along the way).

Containers

Containers—either Docker or Open Container Initiative (OCI) format—provide a mechanism to subdivide a host machine into multiple independent runtime environments. Unlike virtual machines (VMs), container environments share a single OS kernel, which provides a few benefits:

Reduced OS overhead, because only one OS is running
This limits containers to running the same OS as the host, typically Linux. (Windows containers also exist but are much less commonly used.)

Simplified application bundles that run independently of OS drivers and hardware
These bundles are sufficient to run different Linux distributions on the same kernel with consistent behavior across Linux versions.

Greater application visibility
The shared kernel allows monitoring application details like open file handles that would be difficult to extract from a full VM.

A standard distribution mechanism for storing a container in an OCI registry
Part of the container specification describes how to store and retrieve a container from a registry—the container is stored as a series of filesystem layers stored as a compressed TAR (tape archive) such that new layers can add and delete files from the underlying immutable layers.

Unlike any of the following technologies, container technologies on their own benefit the running of applications on a single machine, but don't address distributing an application across more than one machine. In the context of this book, containers act as a common substrate to enable easily distributing an application that can be run consistently on one or multiple computers.

Cloud Providers

Cloud providers are companies that sell remote access to computing and storage services. Popular examples include Amazon Web Services (AWS), Microsoft Azure, and Google Cloud Platform (GCP). Compute and storage services include VMs, blob storage, databases, message queues, and more custom services. These companies rent access to the services by the hour or even on a finer-grained basis, making it easy for companies to get access to computing power when needed without having to invest and plan datacenter space, hardware, and networking investments up front.

Cloud Provider Economics

Major cloud providers make much of their money selling or multiplexing access to underlying physical hardware—for example, they might buy a server at (amortized) \$5,000/year, but then divide it into 20 slots, which they sell at \$0.05/hour. For a company looking to rent half a server for testing for a few hours, this means access to \$2,500+ of hardware for less than \$1.

Cloud providers are therefore attractive to many types of businesses where demand is not consistent day to day or hour to hour, and where access over the internet is acceptable. If the cloud provider can sell three-fourths of the machine (15 slots $\times$ \$0.05 = \$0.75/hour of income), they can make \$0.75 $\times$ 24 $\times$ 365 = \$6,570/year of income—not a bad return on investment.

While some cloud computing services are basically "rent a slice of hardware," the cloud providers have also competed on developing more complex *managed* services, either hosted on individual VMs per customer or using a *multitenant* approach in which the servers themselves are able to separate the work and resources consumed by different customers within a single application process. It's harder to build a multitenant application or service, but the benefit is that it becomes much easier to manage and share server resources among customers—and reducing the cost of running the service means better margins for cloud providers.

The serverless computing patterns described in this book were largely developed either by the cloud providers themselves or by customers who provided guidance and feedback on what would make services even more attractive (and thus worth a higher price premium). Regardless of whether you're using a proprietary single-cloud service or self-hosting a solution (see the next sections for more details as well as Chapter 3), cloud providers can offer an attractive environment for provisioning and running serverless applications.

Kubernetes and Cloud Native

While cloud providers started by offering compute as virtualized versions of physical hardware (so-called *infrastructure as a service*, or *IaaS*), it soon became clear that much of the work of securing and maintaining networks and operating systems was repetitive and well suited to automation. An ideal solution would use containers as a repeatable way to deploy software, running on bulk-managed Linux operating systems with "just enough" networking to privately connect the containers without exposing them to the internet at large. I explore the requirements for this type of system in more detail in "Infrastructure Assumptions" on page 50.

A variety of startups attempted to build solutions in this space with moderate success: Docker Swarm, Apache Mesos, and others. In the end, a technology introduced by Google and contributed to by Red Hat, IBM, and others won the day—Kubernetes. While Kubernetes may have had some technical advantages over the competing systems, much of its success can be attributed to the ecosystem that sprang up around the project.

Not only was Kubernetes donated to a neutral foundation (the Cloud Native Computing Foundation, or CNCF), but it was soon joined by other foundational projects including gRPC and observability frameworks, container packaging, database, reverse proxy, and service mesh projects. Despite being a vendor-neutral foundation, the CNCF and its members advertised and marketed this suite of technologies effectively to win attention and developer mindshare, and by 2019, it was largely clear that the Kubernetes + Linux combination would be the preferred infrastructure container platform for many organizations.

Since that time, Kubernetes has evolved to act as a general-purpose system for controlling infrastructure systems using a standardized and extensible API model. The Kubernetes API model is based on *custom resource definitions* (*CRDs*) and infrastructure *controllers*, which observe the state of the world and attempt to adjust the world to match a desired state stored in the Kubernetes API. This process is known as *reconciliation*, and when properly implemented, it can lead to resilient and self-healing systems that are simpler to implement than a centrally orchestrated model.

The technologies related to Kubernetes and other CNCF projects are called "cloud native" technologies, whether they are implemented on VMs from a cloud provider or on physical or virtual hardware within a user's own organization. The key features of these technologies are that they are explicitly designed to run on clusters of semi-reliable computers and networks and to gracefully handle individual hardware failures while remaining available for users. By contrast, many pre-cloud-native technologies were built on the premise of highly available and redundant individual hardware nodes where maintenance would generally result in planned downtime or an outage.

Cloud-Hosted Serverless

While a rush has occurred in the last five years to rebrand many cloud-provider technologies as "serverless," the term originally referred to a set of cloud-hosted technologies that simplified service deployment for developers. In particular, serverless allowed developers focused on mobile or web applications to implement a small amount of server-side logic without needing to understand, manage, or deploy application servers (hence the name). These technologies split into two main camps:

Backend as a service (BaaS)
> Structured storage services with a rich and configurable API for managing the stored state in a client. Generally, this API included a mechanism for storing small-to-medium JavaScript Object Notation (JSON) objects in a key-value store with the ability to send device push notifications when an object was modified on the server. The APIs also supported defining server-side object validation, automatic authentication and user management, and mobile-client-aware security rules. The most popular examples were Parse (acquired by Facebook, now Meta, in 2013 and became open source in 2017) and Firebase (acquired by Google in 2014).
>
> While handy for getting a project started with a small team, BaaS eventually ran into a few problems that caused it to lose popularity:
>
> - Most applications eventually outgrew the fixed functionality. While adopting BaaS might provide an initial productivity boost, it almost certainly guaranteed a future storage migration and rewrite if the app became popular.
> - Compared with other storage options, it was both expensive and had limited scaling. While *application developers* didn't need to manage servers, many of the implementation architectures required a single frontend server to avoid complex object-locking models.

Function as a service (FaaS)
> In this model, application developers wrote individual functions that would be invoked (called) when certain conditions were met. In some cases, this was combined with BaaS to solve some of the fixed-function problems, but it could also be combined with scalable cloud-provider storage services to achieve much more scalable architectures. In the FaaS model, each function invocation is independent and may occur in parallel, even on different computers. Coordination among function invocations needs to be handled explicitly using transactions or locks, rather than being handled implicitly by the storage API as in BaaS. The first widely popular implementation of FaaS was AWS Lambda, launched in 2014. Within a few years, most cloud providers offered similar competing services, though without any form of standard APIs.

Unlike IaaS, cloud-provider FaaS offerings are typically billed *per invocation* or *per second* of function execution, with a maximum duration of 5 to 15 minutes per invocation. Billing per invocation can result in very low costs for infrequently used functions, as well as favorable billing for bursty workloads that receive thousands of requests and are then idle for minutes or hours. To enable this billing model, cloud providers operate multitenant platforms that isolate each user's functions from one another despite running on the same physical hardware within a few seconds of one another.

By around 2019, "serverless" had mostly come to be associated with FaaS, as BaaS had fallen out of favor. From that point, the serverless moniker began to be used for noncompute services, which worked well with the FaaS billing model: charging only for access calls and storage used, rather than for long-running server units. We'll discuss the differences between traditional serverful and serverless computing in Chapter 1, but this new definition allows the notion of serverless to expand to storage systems and specialized services like video transcoding or AI image recognition.

While the definitions of "cloud provider" or "cloud native software" mentioned have been somewhat fluid over time, the serverless moniker has been especially fluid—a serverless enthusiast from 2014 would be quite confused by most of the services offered under that name eight years later.

One final note of disambiguation: 5G telecommunications networking has introduced the confusing term "network function as a service," which is the idea that long-lived network routing behavior such as firewalls could run as a service on a virtualized platform that is not associated with any particular physical machine. In this case, the term "network function" implies a substantially different architecture with long-lived but mobile servers rather than a serverless distributed architecture.

How This Book Is Organized

This book is divided into four main parts.[2] I tend to learn by developing a mental model of what's going on, then trying things out to see where my mental model isn't quite right, and finally developing deep expertise after extended usage. The parts correspond to this model—those in Table P-1.

---

2 The last part is one chapter because I couldn't resist adding some historical footnotes in Chapter 11.

Table P-1. Parts of the book

Part	Chapter	Description
Part I, "The Theory of Serverless"	Chapter 1	Definitions and descriptions of what serverless platforms offer.
	Chapter 2	Building by learning: a stateless serverless application on Knative.
	Chapter 3	A deep dive into implementing Knative, a serverless compute system.
	Chapter 4	This chapter frames the serverless movement in terms of business value.
Part II, "Designing with Serverless"	Chapter 5	With an understanding of serverless under our belt, this chapter explains how to apply the patterns from Chapter 2 to existing applications.
	Chapter 6	Events are a common patterns for orchestrating stateless applications. This chapter explains various patterns of event-driven architecture.
	Chapter 7	While Chapter 6 covers connecting events to an application, this chapter focuses specifically on building a serverless application that natively leverages events.
	Chapter 8	After four chapters of cheerleading for serverless, this chapter focuses on patterns that can frustrate a serverless application architecture.
Part III, "Living with Serverless"	Chapter 9	Following Chapter 8's warnings about serverless antipatterns, this chapter chronicles operational obstacles to serverless nirvana.
	Chapter 10	While Chapter 9 focuses on the spectacular meltdowns, this chapter covers debugging tools needed to solve regular, everyday application bugs.
Part IV, "A Brief History of Serverless"	Chapter 11	Historical context for the development of the serverless compute abstractions.

Conventions Used in This Book

The following typographical conventions are used in this book:

Italic

Indicates new terms, URLs, email addresses, filenames, and file extensions.

`Constant width`

Used for program listings, as well as within paragraphs to refer to program elements such as variable or function names, databases, data types, environment variables, statements, and keywords.

`Constant width bold`

Shows commands or other text that should be typed literally by the user.

`Constant width italic`

Shows text that should be replaced with user-supplied values or by values determined by context.

This element signifies a tip or suggestion.

 This element signifies a general note.

 This element indicates a warning or caution.

Using Code Examples

Supplemental material (code examples, exercises, etc.) is available for download at *https://oreil.ly/BSAK-supp*.

This book is here to help you get your job done. In general, if example code is offered with this book, you may use it in your programs and documentation. You do not need to contact us for permission unless you're reproducing a significant portion of the code. For example, writing a program that uses several chunks of code from this book does not require permission. Selling or distributing examples from O'Reilly books does require permission. Answering a question by citing this book and quoting example code does not require permission. Incorporating a significant amount of example code from this book into your product's documentation does require permission.

We appreciate, but generally do not require, attribution. An attribution usually includes the title, author, publisher, and ISBN. For example: *"Building Serverless Applications on Knative* by Evan Anderson (O'Reilly). Copyright 2024 Evan Anderson, 978-1-098-14207-0."

If you feel your use of code examples falls outside fair use or the permission given above, feel free to contact us at *permissions@oreilly.com*.

O'Reilly Online Learning

 For more than 40 years, *O'Reilly Media* has provided technology and business training, knowledge, and insight to help companies succeed.

Our unique network of experts and innovators share their knowledge and expertise through books, articles, and our online learning platform. O'Reilly's online learning platform gives you on-demand access to live training courses, in-depth learning paths, interactive coding environments, and a vast collection of text and video from O'Reilly and 200+ other publishers. For more information, visit *https://oreilly.com*.

How to Contact Us

Please address comments and questions concerning this book to the publisher:

O'Reilly Media, Inc.
1005 Gravenstein Highway North
Sebastopol, CA 95472
800-889-8969 (in the United States or Canada)
707-829-7019 (international or local)
707-829-0104 (fax)
support@oreilly.com
https://www.oreilly.com/about/contact.html

We have a web page for this book, where we list errata, examples, and any additional information. Access this page at *https://oreil.ly/BuildingServerlessAppsKnative*.

For news and information about our books and courses, visit *https://oreilly.com*.

Find us on LinkedIn: *https://linkedin.com/company/oreilly-media*.

Follow us on Twitter: *https://twitter.com/oreillymedia*.

Watch us on YouTube: *https://youtube.com/oreillymedia*.

Acknowledgments

This book has been at least three years in the making.[3] In many ways, it's also the result of my interactions with serverless users and builders, including authors of multiple serverless platforms as well as the broad and welcoming Knative community. This is the village that sprouted this book. This book would still be a sprout without the help of the many folks who've contributed to this finished product.

First are my editors at O'Reilly, who helped me through the process of actually publishing a book. John Devins first reached out to me in April 2022 about the possibility of writing a book and helped me through the early process of writing and polishing the initial proposal. Shira Evans was a patient and persistent partner as my development editor: helping me find the motivation to write and get unstuck when I slipped behind schedule, recommending additional content even when it pushed out the schedule, and providing constant optimism that this book would get done. Finally, Clare Laylock was my production editor, helping me see the book through to a finished product even after I'd read it a dozen times.

My technical reviewers provided incisive (and kind!) feedback on early drafts of this book. Without their perspectives, this book would be more tedious and less accurate. Even when the insight meant that I needed to write another section, I had the confidence that those were words that *mattered*. Celeste Stinger highlighted a number of security insights that had been given short shrift in my initial writing. Jess Males brought a strong sense of urgency and practical reliability thinking to refining my early drafts. And this book owes an immense debt to Joe Beda, both for having set me on the cloud native path that led me here as well as for forcing me to spell out more clearly the trade-offs of a number of exciting ideas and highlighting the parts that needed more celebration.

While the named contributors helped to make this book better, my family provided the support and motivation needed to stick with this effort. The idea of writing a book from my own experience was first kindled in my imagination by my father's work writing a linear algebra textbook he could enjoy teaching from. My son, Erik, and my daughter, Eleanor, have been exceptionally patient finding their own entertainment as I sit in common spaces typing away on the laptop "working on the book," and have made appreciative noises at how nice the preview PDFs look when I review them. Most of all, this book couldn't have happened without Emily, my wife and partner, who has been my first sounding board, a helpful distraction for the kids when I needed focus time, and realistic assessor of what I can get done when I say I want to do it all. And now here's one more thing I've gotten done.

---

3 Or six years if you count the start of my work on Knative. Or fourteen if we count my first use of Google App Engine in anger.

The Theory of Serverless

Welcome! The goal of the first part of this book is to give you a solid grounding in serverless computing, from both a theory (Chapters 1 and 4) and a practical point of view (Chapters 2 and 3). By the end of this part, you should be able to explain to an interested colleague why they should consider serverless for their next project, and show them some concrete examples of applications you can build with serverless.

## CHAPTER 1

What Is Serverless, Anyway?

Serverless has been hyped as a transformational technology, leveraged as a brand by various development platforms, and slapped as a label on dozens of services by the major cloud providers. It promises the ability to ship code many times per day, prototype new applications with a few dozen lines of code, and scale to the largest application problems. It's also been successfully used for production applications by companies from Snap (the main Snapchat app) to iRobot (handling communications from hundreds of thousands of home appliances) and Microsoft (a wide variety of websites and portals).

As mentioned in the Preface, the term "serverless" has been applied not only to compute infrastructure services, but also to storage, messaging, and other systems. Definitions help explain what serverless *is* and *isn't*. Because this book is focused on how to build applications using serverless infrastructure, many chapters concentrate on how to design and program the computing layers. Our definition, however, should also shine a light for infrastructure teams who are thinking about building noncompute serverless abstractions. To that end, I'm going to use the following definition of serverless:

> Serverless is a pattern of designing and running distributed applications that breaks load into independent units of work and then schedules and executes that work automatically on an automatically scaled number of instances.

In general,[1] the serverless pattern is to automatically scale the number of compute processes based on the amount of work available, as depicted in Figure 1-1.

---

[1] In "Task Queues" on page 134, we will talk briefly about scaling work over time rather than instance counts.

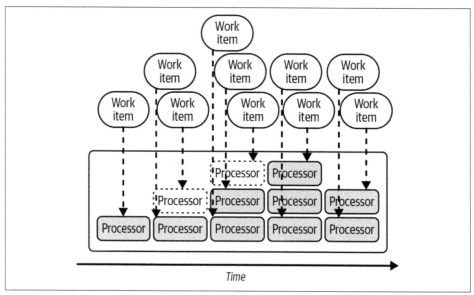

Figure 1-1. The serverless model

You'll note that this definition is quite broad; it doesn't cover only FaaS platforms like AWS Lambda or Cloudflare Workers, but could also cover systems like GitHub Actions (build and continuous integration [CI] actions), service workers in Chrome (background threads coordinating between browser and server), or even user-defined functions on a query platform like Google's BigQuery (distributed SQL warehouse). It also covers object storage platforms like Amazon Simple Storage Service, or S3 (a unit of work is storing a blob), and could even cover actor frameworks that automatically scaled the number of instances managing actor state.

In this book, I'll generally pull examples from the open source Knative project (*https://knative.dev*) for examples of serverless principles, but I'll occasionally reach out and talk about other serverless platforms where it makes sense. I'm going to focus on Knative for three reasons:

- As an open source project, it's available on a broad variety of platforms, from cloud providers to single-board computers like the Raspberry Pi.

- As an open source project, the source code is available for experimentation. You can add debugging lines or integrate it into a larger existing project or platform. Many serverless platforms are commercial cloud offerings that are tied to a particular provider, and they don't tend to allow you to modify or replace their platform.

- It's in the title of the book, and I expect some of you would be disappointed if I didn't mention it. I also have five years of experience working with the Knative community, building software and community, and answering questions. My expertise in Knative is at least as deep as my experience with other platforms.

Why Is It Called Serverless?

Armchair critics of serverless like to point out a "gotcha" in the name—while the name is "serverless," it's still really a way to run your application code on servers, somewhere. So how did this name come to be, and how does serverless fit into the arc of computing systems over the last 50 years?

Back in the 1960s and 1970s, mainframe computers were rare, expensive, and completely central to computing. The '70s and '80s brought ever-smaller and cheaper computers to the point that by the mid-'90s, it was often cheaper to network together multiple smaller computers to tackle a task than to purchase a single more expensive computer. Coordinating these computers efficiently is the foundation of distributed computing. (For a more complete history of serverless, see Chapter 11. For a history of how the serverless name has evolved, see "Cloud-Hosted Serverless" on page xiv.)

While there are many ways to connect computers to solve problems via distributed computing, serverless focuses on making it easy to solve problems that fall into well-known patterns for distributing work. Much of this aligns with the microservices movement that began around 2010, which aimed to divide existing monolithic applications into independent components capable of being written and managed by smaller teams. Serverless complements (but does not require) a microservices architecture by simplifying the implementation of individual microservices.

 The goal of serverless is to make developers no longer need to think in terms of server units when building and scaling applications,[2] but instead to use scaling units that makes sense for the application.

By embracing well-known patterns, serverless platforms can automate difficult-but-common processes like failover, replication, or request routing—the "undifferentiated heavy lifting" of distributed computing (coined by Jeff Bezos in 2006 when describing the benefits of Amazon's cloud computing platform). One popular serverless model from 2011 is the twelve-factor application model (*https://12factor.net*),

---

2 "Server units" could either represent virtual/physical machines or server processes running on a single instance. In both cases, serverless aims to enable developers to avoid having to think about either!

which spells out several patterns that most serverless platforms embrace, including stateless applications with storage handled by external services or the platform and clear separation of configuration and application code.

By this time, it should be clear that adopting a serverless development mindset does not mean throwing a whole bunch of expensive hardware out the window—indeed, serverless platforms often need to work alongside and integrate with existing software systems, including mainframe systems with lineage from the 1960s.

Knative in particular is a good choice for integrating serverless capabilities into an existing computing platform because it builds on and natively incorporates the capabilities of Kubernetes. In this way, Knative bridges the "serverless versus containers" question that has been a popular source of argument since the introduction of AWS Lambda and Kubernetes in 2014.

A Bit of Terminology

While describing serverless systems and comparing them with traditional computing systems, I'll use a few specific terms throughout the book. I'll try to use these words consistently, as there are many ways to implement a serverless system, and it's worth having some precise language that's distinct from specific products that we can use to describe how our mental models map to a particular implementation:

Process
> I use the term *process* in the Unix sense of the word: an executing program with one or more threads that share a common memory space and interface with a kernel. Most serverless systems are based on the Linux kernel, as it is both popular and free, but other serverless systems are built on the Windows kernel or the JavaScript runtime exposed via WebAssembly (Wasm). The most common serverless process mechanism as of this book's writing is the Linux kernel via the container subsystem, used by both Lambda via the Firecracker VM library and various open source projects such as Knative using the Kubernetes scheduler and Container Runtime Interface (CRI).

Instance
> An *instance* is a serverless execution environment along with whatever external system infrastructure is needed for managing the root process in that environment. The instance is the smallest unit of scheduling and compute available in a serverless system and is often used as a key in systems like logging, monitoring, and tracing to enable correlations. Serverless systems treat instances as ephemeral and handle creating and destroying them automatically in response to load on the system. Depending on the serverless environment, it may be possible to execute multiple processes within a single instance, but the outer serverless system sees the instance as the unit of scaling and execution.

Artifact

An *artifact* (or *code artifact*) is a set of computer code that is ready to be executed by an instance. This might be a ZIP file of source code, a compiled JAR, a container image, or a Wasm snippet. Typically, each instance will run code using a particular artifact, and when a new artifact is ready, new instances will be spun up and the old instances deleted. This method of rolling out code is different from traditional systems that provision VMs and then reuse that VM to run many different artifacts or versions of an artifact, and it has beneficial properties we'll talk about later.

Application

An *application* is a designed and coordinated set of processes and storage systems that are assembled to achieve some sort of user value. While simple applications may contain only one type of instance, most serverless applications contain multiple microservices, each running its own types of instances. It's also common for applications to be built with a mix of serverless and nonserverless components—see Chapter 5 for more details on how to integrate serverless and traditional architectures in a single application.

These components, as well as a few others like the scheduler, are illustrated in Figure 1-2.

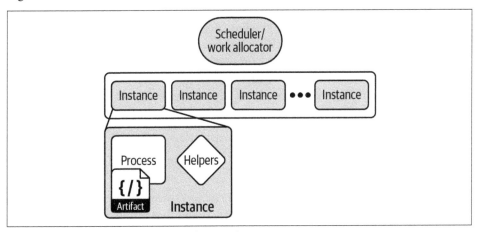

Figure 1-2. Components of a serverless application

What's a "Unit of Work"?

Serverless scales by units of work and can scale to zero instances when there's no work. But, you might ask, what is a unit of work? A *unit of work* is a stateless, independent request that can be satisfied using a certain amount of computation (and further network requests) by a single instance. Let's break that down:

Stateless

Each request contains all the work to be done and does not depend on the instance having handled earlier parts of the request or on other requests also in-flight. This also means that a serverless process can't store data in-memory for future work or assume that processes will be running in between work units to do things like handle in-process timers. This definition actually allows a lot of wiggle room—you can link to the outputs of work units that might be processed earlier, or your work can be a stream of data like "Here's a segment of video that contains motion (until the motion stops)." Roughly, you can think of a unit of work as the input to a function; if you can process the inputs to the function without local state (like a function not associated with a class or global values), then you're stateless enough to be serverless.

Independent

Being able to reference only work that's complete elsewhere allows serverless systems to scale *horizontally* by adding more nodes, since each unit of work doesn't directly depend on another one executing. Additionally, independence means that work can be routed to "an instance that's ready to do the work" (including a newly created instance), and instances can be shut down when there isn't enough work to go around.

Requests

Like reactive systems, serverless systems should do work only when it's asked for. These requests for work can take many forms: they might be events to be handled, HTTP requests, rows to be processed, or even emails arriving at a system. The key point here is that work can be broken into discrete chunks, and the system can measure how many chunks of work there are and use that measurement to determine how many instances to provision.

Here are some examples of units of work that serverless systems might scale on.

Connections

A system could treat each incoming TCP connection request as a unit of work. When a connection arrives, it is attached to an instance, and that instance will speak a (proprietary) protocol until one side or the other hangs up on the connection.

As shown in Figure 1-3, CockroachDB uses a model like this to manage PostgreSQL (Postgres) "heads" onto their database[3]—each customer database connection is routed by a special connection proxy to a SQL processor specific to that customer, which is responsible for speaking the Postgres protocol, interpreting the SQL queries,

---

[3] This is described in Andy Kimball's blog post "How We Built a Serverless SQL Database" (*https://oreil.ly/ UPZRQ*), outlining the architecture of CockroachDB Serverless (which I've summarized).

converting them into query plans against the (shared) backend storage, executing the query plans, and then marshaling the results back to the Postgres protocol and returning them to the client. If no connections are open for a particular customer, the pool of SQL processors is scaled to zero.

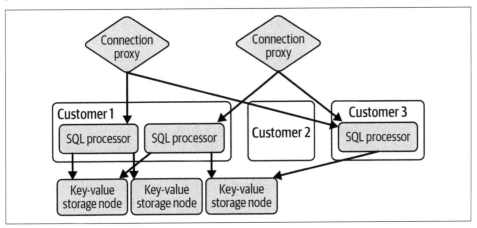

Figure 1-3. CockroachDB serverless architecture

By using the serverless paradigm, CochroachDB can charge customers for usage only when a database connection is actually active and offer a reasonable free tier of service for small customers who are mostly not using the service. Of course, the backend storage service for this is *not* serverless—that data is stored in a shared key-value store, and customers are charged for data storage on a monthly basis separately from the number of connections and queries executed. We'll talk more about this model in "Key-Value Storage" on page 42.

Requests

At a higher level, a serverless system could understand a particular application protocol such as HTTP, SMTP (email), or an RPC mechanism, and interpret each protocol exchange as an individual unit of work. Many protocols support reusing or multiplexing application requests on a single TCP connection; by enabling the serverless system to understand application messages, work can be broken into smaller chunks, which has the following benefits:

- Smaller requests are more likely to be evenly sized and more closely time-bounded. For protocols that allow transmitting more than one request over a TCP stream, presumably most requests finish before the TCP stream, and the work for executing one request is smaller, allowing finer-grained load balancing among instances.

- Interpreting application requests allows decoupling the connection lifespan and instance lifespan. When a TCP connection is the unit of work, deploying a new code artifact requires starting new instances for new connections and then waiting for the existing connections to complete (evocatively called "draining" the instances). If draining takes five minutes instead of one minute, application rollouts and configuration changes take five times as long to complete. Many settings (such as environment variables) can be set only when a process (instance) is started, so this limits the speed that teams can change code or configuration.

- Depending on the protocol, it's possible for a single connection to have zero, one, or many requests in-flight at once. By interpreting application requests when scheduling units of work, serverless systems can achieve higher efficiency and lower latency—fanning out requests to multiple instances when requests are made in parallel or avoiding starting instances for connections that do not have any requests currently in-flight.

- By defining the boundaries of application-level requests, serverless systems can provide higher-quality telemetry and service. When the system can measure the duration of a request, it can measure latency, request sizes, and other metrics, and it can enable and enforce application-level request deadlines and tracing from outside the specific process that is handling a request. This can allow serverless systems to recover and respond to application failures in the same way that API gateways and other HTTP routers can.

Events

At a high level, events and requests are much the same thing. At another level, events are a fundamental building block of reactive and asynchronous architectures. Events declare, "At this time, this thing happened." It would be possible to model an entire serverless system on events; you might have an event for "This HTTP request happened," "This database row was scanned," or "This work queue item was received." This is a very clever way to fit both synchronous and asynchronous communication into a single model. Unfortunately, converting synchronous requests into asynchronous events and "response events" that are correlated with the request event introduces a few problems:

Timeouts

Enforcing timeouts in asynchronous systems can be much more difficult, especially if a message that needs timing out could be on a message queue somewhere, waiting for a process to notice that the timeout is done.

Error reporting

Beyond timeouts and application crashes, synchronous requests may sometimes trigger error conditions in the underlying application. Error conditions could be anything from "You requested a file you don't have permission on" to "You sent a search request without a query" to "This input triggered an exception due to a coding bug." All of these error conditions need to be reflected back to the original caller in a way that enables them to understand what, if anything, they did wrong with their request and to decide on a future course of action.

Cardinality and correlation

While there might be benefits to modeling "A request was received" and "A response was sent" as events, using those events as a message bus to say "Please send this response to this event" misses the point of events as *observations* of an external system. More practically, what's the intended meaning of a second "Please send this response to this event" that correlates with the same request event? Assuming that the application protocol envisages only a single answer, the second event probably ends up being discarded. Discarding the event may in turn need an additional notification to the offending eventer to indicate that their message was ignored—another case of the error-reporting issue previously mentioned.

In my opinion, these costs are not worth the benefits of a "grand unified event model of serverless." Sometimes synchronous calls are the right answer, sometimes asynchronous calls are the right answer, and it's up to application developers to intelligently choose between the two.

It's Not (Just) About the Scale

Automatic scaling is nice, but building a runtime around units of work has more benefits. Once the infrastructure layer understands what causes the application to execute, it's possible to inject additional scaffolding around the application to measure and manage how well it does its work. The finer-grained the units of work, the more assistance the platform is able to provide in terms of understanding, controlling, and even securing the application on top of it.

In the world of desktop and web browser applications, this revolution happened in the late 1990s (desktop) and 2000s (browsers), where application event or message loops were slowly replaced by frameworks that used callback-based systems to automatically route user input to the appropriate widgets and controls within a window. In HTTP servers, a similar single-system framework was developed in the '90s called CGI (Common Gateway Interface). In many ways, this was the ancestor of modern serverless systems—it enabled writing a program that would respond to a single HTTP request and handled much of the network communication details automatically. (For more details on CGI and its influence on serverless systems, see Chapter 11.)

Much like the CGI specification, modern serverless systems can simplify many of the routine programming best practices around handling a unit of work and do so in a programming-agnostic fashion. Cloud computing calls these sorts of assists "undifferentiated heavy lifting"—that is, every program needs them, but each program is fine if they are done the same way.

The following is *not* an exhaustive list of features; it is quite possible that the set of features enabled by understanding units of work will continue to expand as more tools and capabilities are added to runtime environments.

Blue and Green: Rollout, Rollback, and Day-to-Day

Most serverless systems include a notion of updating or changing the code artifact or the instance execution configuration in a coordinated way. The system also understands what a unit of work is and has some (internal) way of routing requests to one or more instances running a specified code artifact. Some systems expose these details to application operators and enable those operators to explicitly control the allocation of incoming work among different versions of a code artifact.

Zooming out, the serverless process of starting new instances with a specified version of a code artifact and allowing old instances to be collected when no longer in use looks a lot like the serverful *blue-green deployment pattern*: a second bank of servers is started with the "green" code while allowing the "blue" servers to keep running until the green servers are up and traffic has been rerouted from the blue servers to the green ones. With serverless request routing and automatic scaling, these transitions can be done very quickly, sometimes in less than a second for small applications and less than five minutes even for very large applications.

Beyond the blue-green rollout pattern, it's also possible to control the allocation of work to different versions of an application on a percentage (proportional) basis. This enables both incremental rollouts (the work is slowly shifted from one version to another—for example, to allow the new version's caches to fill) and canary deployments (a small percentage of work is routed to a new application to see how the application reacts to real user requests).

While incremental rollouts are mostly about managing scale, blue-green and canary rollouts are mostly about managing deployment risk. One of the riskier parts of running a service is deploying new application code or configuration—changing a system that is already working introduces the risk that the new system state does *not* work. By making it easy to quickly start up new instances with a specified version, serverless makes it faster and easier to roll back to an existing (working) version. This results in a lower mean time to recovery (MTTR), a common disaster-recovery metric.

By making individual instances ephemeral and automatically scaling based on incoming work, serverless can reduce the risk of "infrastructure snowflakes"—systems that are specially set up by hand with artisanal configurations that may be difficult to replicate or repair. When instances are automatically replaced and redeployed as part of the regular infrastructure operations, instance recovery and initialization are continually tested, which tends to ensure that any shortcomings are fixed fairly quickly.

Continually replacing or repaving infrastructure instances can also have security benefits: an instance that has been corrupted by an attacker will be reset in the same way that an instance corrupted by a software bug is. Ephemeral instances can improve an application's defensive posture by making it harder for attackers to maintain persistence, forcing them to compromise the same infrastructure repeatedly. Needing to repeatedly execute a compromise increases the odds of detecting the attack and closing the vulnerability.

 Serverless treats individual instances as *fungible*—that is, each instance is equally replaceable with another one. The solution to a broken instance is simply to throw it away and get another one. The answer to "How many instances for *X*?" is always "The number you need," because it's easy to add or remove instances. Leaning into this pattern of replaceable instances simplifies many operational problems.

Creature Comforts: Undifferentiated Heavy Lifting

As described earlier in "Why Is It Called Serverless?" on page 5, one of the benefits of a serverless platform is to provide common capabilities that may be difficult or repetitive to implement in each application.

As mentioned in "It's Not (Just) About the Scale" on page 11, once the incoming work to the system has been broken down and recognized by the infrastructure, it's easy to use that scaffolding to start to assist with the undifferentiated heavy lifting that would otherwise require application code. One example of this is observability: a traditional application needs instrumentation that measures each time a request (unit of work) is made and how long it takes to complete that request. With a serverless infrastructure that manages the units of work for you, it's easy for the infrastructure to start a clock ticking when the work is handed to your application and to record a latency measurement when your application completes the work.

While it may still be necessary to provide more detailed metrics from within your application (for example, the number of records scanned to respond to a work request), automatic monitoring, visualization, and even alerting on throughput and latency of work units can provide application teams with an easy "zero effort" monitoring baseline. This not only can save application development time, but also can provide guardrails on application deployment for teams who do not have the time or inclination to develop expertise in monitoring and observability.

Similarly, serverless infrastructure may need and want to implement application tracing on the work units managed by the infrastructure. This tracing serves two different purposes:

- It provides infrastructure *users* with a way to investigate and determine the source of application latency, including platform-induced latency and latency due to application startup (where applicable).

- It provides infrastructure *operators* with richer information about underlying platform bottlenecks, including in application scaling and overall observed latency.

Other common observability features include log collection and aggregation, performance profiling, and stack tracing. Chapter 10 delves into the specifics of using these tools to debug serverless applications in the live ephemeral environment. By controlling the adjacent environment (and, in some cases, the application build process), serverless environments can easily run observability agents alongside the application process to collect these types of data.

Figure 1-4 provides a visualization of the measurement points that can be implemented in a serverless system.

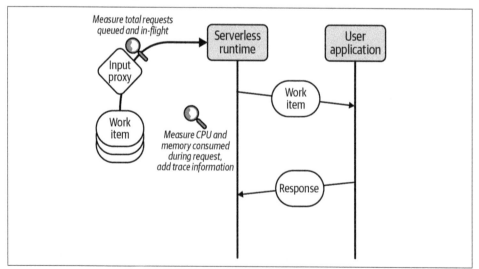

Figure 1-4. Common capabilities

Creature Comforts: Managing Inputs

Because serverless environments provide an infrastructure-controlled ingress point for units of work, the infrastructure itself can be used to implement best practices for exposing services to the rest of the world. One example of this is automatically configuring TLS (including supported ciphers and obtaining and rotating valid certificates if needed) for serverless services that may be called via HTTPS or other server protocols. Moving these responsibilities to the serverless layer allows the infrastructure provider to employ a specialized team that can ensure best practices are followed; the work of this team is then amortized across all the serverless consumers using the platform. Other common capabilities that may extend beyond "undifferentiated heavy lifting" include authorization, policy enforcement, and protocol translation.

For a visual representation of the input transformations performed by Knative, see Figure 1-5.

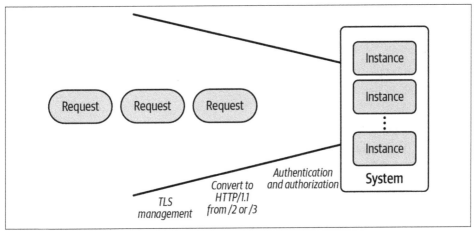

Figure 1-5. Managing inputs

Authorization and policy enforcement is a crucial capability in many application scenarios. In a traditional architecture, this layer might be delegated to an outer application firewall or proxy or language-specific middleware. Middleware works well for single-language ecosystems, but maintaining a common level of capability in middleware for multiple languages is difficult. Firewalls and proxies extract this middleware into a common service layer, but the protected application still needs to validate that requests have been sent by the firewall, rather than some other internal attacker. Because serverless platforms control the request path until the delivery of work to the application, application authors do not have to worry about confirming that the requests were properly handled by the infrastructure—another quality-of-life improvement.

The last application developer quality-of-life improvement is in the opportunity to translate external requests to units of work that may be more easily consumed by the target applications. Many modern protocols are complicated and require substantial libraries to implement correctly and efficiently. By implementing the protocol translation from a complex protocol (like HTTP/3 over UDP) to a simpler one (for example, HTTP/1.1, which is widely understood), application developers can select from a wider range of application libraries and programming languages.

Creature Comforts: Managing Process Lifecycle

As part of scaling and distributing work, serverless instances take an active role in managing the lifecycle of the application process, as well as any helper processes that may be spawned by the platform itself. Depending on the platform and the amount of work in-flight, the platform may need to stall (queue) that work until an instance is available to handle the request. Known as a *cold start*, this can occur even when there are already live application instances (for example, a sudden burst of work could exceed the capacity of the provisioned instances). Some serverless platforms may choose to overprovision instances to act as a buffer for these cases, while others may minimize the number of additional instances to reduce costs.

Typically, an application process within a serverless instance will go through the following lifecycle stages:

1. Placement

Before a process can be started, the instance must be allocated to an actual server node. It's an old joke that there are actually servers in serverless, but serverless platforms will take several of the following conditions into account:

- *Resource availability*: Depending on the model and degree of oversubscription allowed, some nodes may not be a suitable destination for a new instance.

- *Shared artifacts*: Generally, two instances on the same server node can share application code artifacts. Depending on the size of the compiled application, this can result in substantially faster application startup time, as less data needs to be fetched to the node.

- *Adjacency*: If two instances of the same application are present on the same node, it may be possible to share some resources on the node (memory mappings for shared libraries, just-in-time [JIT] compiled code, etc). Depending on the language and implementation, these savings can be sizable or nearly nonexistent.

- *Contention and adversarial effects*: In a multiapplication environment, some applications may compete for limited node resources (for example, L2 cache or memory bandwidth). Sophisticated serverless platforms can detect these applications and schedule them to different nodes. Note that a particularly optimized application may become its own adversary if it uses a large amount of a nonshared resource.

- *Tenancy scheduling*: In some environments, there may be strict rules about which tenants can share physical resources with other tenants. Strong sandbox controls within a physical node still cannot protect against novel attacks like Spectre or Rowhammer that circumvent the security model.

2. Initialization

Once the instance has been placed on a node, the instance needs to prepare the application environment. This may include the following:

- *Fetching code artifacts*: If not already present, code artifacts will need to be fetched before the application process can start.

- *Fetching configuration*: In addition to code, some instances may need specific configuration information (including instance-level or shared secrets) loaded into the local filesystem.

- *Filesystem mounts*: Some serverless systems support mounting shared filesystems (either read-only or read-write) onto instances for managing shared data. Others require the instance to fetch data during startup.

- *Network configuration*: The newly created instances will need to be registered in some way with the incoming load balancer in order to receive traffic. This may be a broadcast problem, depending on the number of load balancers. In some systems, instances also need to register with a network address translation (NAT) provider for outbound traffic.

- *Resource isolation*: The instance may need to configure isolation mechanisms like Linux `cgroups` to ensure that the application uses a fair amount of node resources.

- *Security isolation*: In a multitenant system, it may be necessary to set up sandboxes or lightweight VMs to prevent users from compromising adjacent tenants.

- *Helper processes*: The serverless environment may offer additional services such as log or metrics collection, service proxies, or identity agents. Typically, these processes should be configured and ready before the main application process starts.

- *Security policies*: These may cover both *inbound* and *outbound* network traffic policies that restrict what services the application process can see on the network.

3. Startup

Once the environment is ready, the application process is started. Typically, the application must perform some sort of setup and internal initialization before it is ready to handle work. This is often indicated by a *readiness check*, which may be either a call from the process to the outside environment or a health-check request from the environment to the process.

While the *placement* and *initialization* phases are largely the responsibility of the serverless platform, the startup phase is largely the responsibility of the application programmer. For some language implementations, the application startup phase can be the majority of the delay attributable to cold starts.

4. Serving

Once the application process has indicated that it is ready to receive work, it receives work units based on the platform policies. Some platforms limit in-flight work in a process to a single request at a time, while others allow multiple work items in-flight at once.

Typically, once a process enters the serving state, it will handle multiple work items (either in parallel or sequentially) before terminating. Reusing an active serving process in this way helps amortize the cost of placement, initialization, and startup and helps reduce the number of cold starts experienced by the application.

5. Shutdown

Once the application process is no longer needed, the platform will signal that the process should exit. A platform may provide some of these guarantees:

- *Draining*: Before signaling termination, the instance will ensure that no units of work are in-flight. This simplifies application shutdown, as it does not need to block on any active work in-flight.

- *Graceful shutdown*: Some serverless platforms may provide a running process an opportunity to perform actions before shutting down, such as flushing caches, updating snapshots, or recording final application metrics. Not all serverless platforms offer a graceful shutdown period, so it's important to understand whether these types of activities are guaranteed on your chosen platform.

6. Termination

Once the shutdown signal has been sent and any graceful shutdown period has elapsed, the process will be terminated, and all the helper processes, security policies, and other resources allocated during initialization will be cleaned up (possibly going through their own graceful shutdown phases). On platforms that bill by resources used, this is often when billing stops. Until termination is complete, the instance's resources are generally considered "claimed" by the scheduler, so rapid turnover in instances may affect the serverless scheduler's decisions.

Summary

Serverless computing and serverless platforms assume certain application behaviors, and will not completely replace existing systems and may not be a good fit for all applications. For a variety of common application patterns, serverless platforms offer substantial technical benefits, and I expect that the fraction of organizations and applications that incorporate serverless will continue to increase. With a helping of theory under our belts, the next chapter focuses on building a small serverless application so you can get a feel for how this theory applies in practice.

## CHAPTER 2

Designing from Scratch

To really get a feel for serverless application development, we're going to start with a *greenfield* application—one where we haven't written any code yet, and we can design it to take advantage of serverless. For this exercise, we're going to build a *status dashboard* application. While this is a pretty simple application without a lot of complicated read/write and transactional semantics, one of the benefits of serverless is that it makes it really easy to build and deploy these types of applications. When the cost for launching and running an application is near zero, you tend to build a lot more little "helpful" apps, because it's easy and fun.[1]

We're also going to make a few other choices, motivated by the technology available in 2023, to make the examples in this book as broadly accessible and repeatable as possible. We're also avoiding the use of a database in these examples to simplify setup; if you decide to elaborate on the examples, adding in storage with either a SQL database or the key-value stores suggested in "Key-Value Storage" on page 42 is a good exercise. In particular, we're going to start with the following stack:

- Serverless runtime: Knative Serving, installed locally
- UI provider: web browser (HTML + JavaScript)
- UI framework: React
- Backend language: Python

---

[1] When I was at Google, the presence of Google App Engine as a supported platform led to the development of thousands of internal apps. Some were widely used (like build status dashboards and the menu application), while others were mostly idle. In all cases, they consumed resources only when they were being useful.

We're using Knative Serving installed locally because it's possible to run Knative on a local Kubernetes cluster without needing to set up any billing or contracts. If you prefer to run the examples on a hosted Kubernetes cluster, most of the steps after the initial setup should remain the same.

Similarly, you could choose to build a mobile or desktop application that calls serverless APIs; in that case, you'll probably want to follow the setup steps and then skip ahead to "Adding an API" on page 33 to start building the APIs that your apps will call.

Setup for This Chapter

All the files and directions for this chapter can be found on GitHub (*https://oreil.ly/BSAK-supp*). Each section corresponds to a different branch of the repository; if you aren't familiar with `git`, instructions will be provided in each section about how to check out the appropriate branch.

To quickly get started with a local (*nonproduction!*) Knative cluster, the Knative project has built the `kn quickstart` command. It can automatically set up a local Kubernetes cluster using the `kind` tool and then install Knative automatically. More detailed instructions on installing all of these tools are available in the GitHub repository in the *SETUP.md* file. The tools we will install are listed here:

Docker (https://oreil.ly/W-8mm)
> Docker provides a container runtime; a container is a bundle of software containing all the dependencies needed to run an application. Containers are the basic deployment tool for Knative and Kubernetes; other serverless solutions generally build a similar type of artifact internally even if they don't use containers as a public format. You can use other container runtimes, but Docker tends to have a fairly good UX and is a good place to start if you aren't familiar with containers and Kubernetes. In addition to being a container runtime, Docker provides tools for *building* containers. While other good tools for building containers are out there, we'll be using Docker's built-in tools because they are widely adopted and very flexible.

`kind` *(https://oreil.ly/quM65)*
> `kind` is a tool for running Kubernetes locally. Its name stands for "Kubernetes in Docker," and it can set up and manage a Kubernetes cluster running on a local Docker instance. This is a handy setup for testing and also for trying things out when you don't need persistent data.

kubectl *(https://oreil.ly/HTugo)*

> kubectl is the official Kubernetes command-line tool. `kn quickstart` uses kubectl to install Knative once the `kind` cluster is created. You probably won't need to use `kubectl` directly, but it's possible to manage Knative resources using `kubectl` if you want. Kubectl also makes it easier to manage Kubernetes resources by declaring them based on a resource manifest—a YAML file that contains the definition of the resource. By putting resource definitions into a file, it becomes easier to manage them over time—you can check the resources into source control, compare them with what's running on the cluster, and reapply the resources to a different cluster to move an application from development to production.

kn *and* `kn quickstart` *(https://oreil.ly/6b6mG)*

> kn is the official Knative CLI. We'll be using the CLI for most of the examples because Kubernetes resource definitions can get unwieldy, but it's important to note that there's no magic here—you can mix kn and `kubectl` freely. kn even supports writing Kubernetes resource definitions to file for use with `kubectl` later if needed.

Node.js (https://nodejs.org)

> If you want to follow along with the commands for building and testing the frontend, you'll need a copy of Node.js to build and run React. (We'll use the Node.js command to download and run React and any other dependencies, so you don't need to install anything React-specific.)

Downloading and installing these tools should take 15 to 30 minutes if you dash through the process. Once you have the tools installed, you can run the command in Example 2-1 to create a cluster and install Knative.

Example 2-1. Knative installation

```
kn quickstart kind --registry
```

The command should give you output as it makes progress:

- Fetching the Kubernetes images
- Starting Kubernetes
- Install Knative
- Wait for Knative to be ready

At the end, you should have a Knative cluster with both Serving (autoscaling HTTP processes) and Eventing (event-driven architecture) installed. You can verify this with the kn command in Examples 2-2 and 2-3.

Example 2-2. Knative verification

```
kn service create hello --image gcr.io/knative-samples/helloworld-go
```

Example 2-3. Knative verification output

```
Service hello created to latest revision `hello-00001` is available at URL:
http://hello.default.10.96.0.1.sslip.io
```

You should be able to access the URL from your web browser or using the curl command, but the end result isn't very pretty—just a "Hello World" text page. In the next section, we'll get something much more attractive running.

A Single-Page App

Since we want to build a dashboard application, we're going to kick things off with a JavaScript framework. React is a popular and powerful tool for building web applications with JavaScript. Among other benefits, it comes with a handy create-react-app script that helps you get an application up and running in a minute or so, and tools to help you iterate quickly on the application.

While this book isn't titled *Creating Single-Page Applications to Understand Serverless*, I think it's useful to walk through the actual steps for getting started from scratch. I'm not a JavaScript expert (my last professional engagement with JavaScript and web UIs was in 2007 and was written from scratch), but getting a useful app running was both quick and enlightening. While I find the frontend space bewilderingly fast-paced and confusing with the range of frameworks and technologies, the React team seems to have done a good job of making it easy to get something up and running. If you really don't want to run these commands yourself, you can download the final result from the GitHub repository (*https://oreil.ly/BSAK-supp*).

Bootstrapping a React App

Once we have Node.js installed, we'll get started with the commands in Example 2-4, which will create a new React application in the current directory and then install the mui library to use the "material components" UI design framework. These examples were tested with Node.js version 16 and React version 18, but should generally be forward-compatible. If you'd rather simply have the result of this bootstrapping, git checkout bootstrap will give you the same files. We'll be using the TypeScript version of React, which adds a typing system to JavaScript and helps us notice and fix certain types of errors early on.

Example 2-4. Bootstrapping a React app

```
npx create-react-app . --template typescript

...

npm install @mui/material @emotion/react @emotion/styled
```

Once we have these tools installed, we can start the React local development server and watch our changes update live with the `npm start` command. While this gives us a good place to start, I did a little bit of cleanup and moved the testing library dependencies to `devDependencies` in the *package.json* file. Marking these dependencies as development-only has two benefits: it reduces the size of the final application that we're going to build and deploy, and it reduces the set of libraries we have to worry about vulnerabilities in. `react-scripts` and anything with `testing` in the name can be safely moved to the `devDependencies` section.

A Basic Web UI

Next, we'll get started on converting the simple animated "Welcome to React" page with our own UI. We'll start with some static content, and then evolve things toward being API-driven with a simple datafile standing in for our API, as depicted in Figure 2-1.

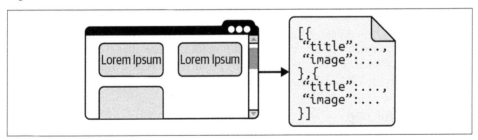

Figure 2-1. Building a data-driven UI

Our first step is to replace the code in *src/App.tsx* with that in Example 2-5; this is pretty much a complete rewrite of the application to build a single dashboard card showing some static information.

Example 2-5. src/App.tsx: a basic dashboard

```
import React from 'react';
import './App.css';
import { Button, Card, CardActionArea, CardActions, CardContent, CardMedia,
  Container, CssBaseline, Grid, ThemeProvider, createTheme } from '@mui/material';

function App() {
  const imgUrl = 'https://knative.dev/docs/images/logo/rgb/knative-logo-rgb.png';
  return (
    <ThemeProvider theme={createTheme({})}>
      <CssBaseline enableColorScheme />
      <Container maxWidth={false}>
        <Grid container justifyContent='center' alignItems='center' spacing={2}>
          <Grid item xs={6}><Card>
            <CardActionArea>
              <CardMedia component='img' alt='Knative logo' image={imgUrl}>
              </CardMedia>
              <CardContent><h2>First item</h2>
                Some info
              </CardContent>
            </CardActionArea>
            <CardActions><Button size='small'>Get Info</Button></CardActions>
          </Card></Grid>
        </Grid>
      </Container>
    </ThemeProvider>
  );
}

export default App;
```

This should produce a page with a single data card that displays some basic content along with an image. Since we've got something locally now that we can see and iterate on, let's see what it's like to deploy this application before we invest too much more work into the UI (we'll come back to that after this brief excursion).

Packaging Our App

To run this application on Knative, we'll need to build it into a container image that we can then ask Knative to run. This bundling will include the following:

- The application source code—in this case, our JavaScript dependencies, our styles and images, and our *App.tsx* file

- The Node.js runtime needed to execute our application

- An underlying set of Linux tools and libraries needed to support Node.js

We use a Dockerfile to describe how to build these layers together into a single container image. Once all these components are bundled into a container image, you can take that image to any computer running Linux,[2] and it should run the same. This is actually a pretty amazing step forward—prior to Docker, getting all your application dependencies working the same on two computers could be a tall order, particularly if they were running different flavors of Linux with different versions of libraries and programming languages available.

Again, since we're just getting started, we're going to err on the side of simple. We'll revisit the Dockerfile in Example 2-6 in the future to make it smaller and more performant. This simply runs npm start to start the React development server, which can dynamically reload the application code when it changes. Of course, since we're packaging this code to run it in a container, we won't be taking advantage of that ability.

Example 2-6. Simple React Dockerfile

```
# Docker Image that is used as foundation to create
# a custom Docker Image with this Dockerfile
FROM node:18

# Application is installed here
WORKDIR /app

# Copies package.json and package-lock.json to Docker environment
COPY package*.json ./

# Installs all node packages
RUN npm install

# Copies everything over to Docker environment
COPY . .

# Uses port that is used by the actual application
EXPOSE 3000

# Finally runs the application
CMD [ "npm", "start" ]
```

Once we have a Dockerfile, we can build a container image by using docker build --tag localhost:5001/dashboard .. in the base directory containing the Dockerfile. This produces a local container image that can be used on our local machine with a remote registry name of localhost:5001/dashboard, which corresponds to the registry for our kind cluster. Our next step is to make sure that the image we've built

---

2 And the correct processor type—building images for multiple processors is possible but outside the scope of this book. The Mac and Windows versions of Docker include a Linux VM to run the containers.

works locally; then we will push the image to a container registry and load it onto our Knative cluster to see the application in action.

If you're using a remote Knative cluster rather than a local `kind` cluster, you'll need to change the `--tag` option to `docker build` to point to your cloud provider's image registry. You'll probably also need to set up authorization for both pushing and pulling images to allow your laptop to push images and your Knative cluster to pull images (for a demo like this, you can make the images public to simplify the pull process). This is all a bit more complicated and cloud-provider specific, but you're the one who decided to head off the rails into something more realistic.[3]

Locally testing our image

This step is optional, but it's a good idea to understand how to test your image on your local Docker installation. Remember, container images should run the same everywhere, so ensuring that your image runs locally is a good first step when debugging "Why doesn't this application work?" in a cloud environment, where things like log files or system processes may be harder to access.[4] Given our container image, we can run it with `docker run --publish 127.0.0.1:8080:3000 localhost:5001/dashboard`. This should start the application and map port 3000 in the container to port 8080 on your local machine; you should be able to use a web browser on your local machine to view the dashboard. If you can't, you'll need to debug further:

- The `docker run` command will connect the output of the container to your terminal. You can look at the command output to see if there are any errors in the application itself.

- You can use `docker ps` to list the running containers. This will also list any exposed ports, which may help if you forgot the `--publish` flag or your container is not running.

- You can use the `docker exec` command to run programs inside an existing container. This can be handy, for example, to open a `bash` shell inside your container image to try out commands in the container environment. Using a shell inside your container can help debug issues with missing or relocated files and programs, for example. Once you've debugged the issues with `docker exec`, the next step is usually to change your Dockerfile to add the missing files.

---

3 Good for you!

4 Generally, we're using these cloud services because we *want* someone else to be in charge of managing our computers and making sure they're up. But handing over that control means that some things become harder than when we can hold the entire application in our hands on a laptop.

Notice that you can change your local files like *App.tsx*, and they don't affect the server running in Docker. This is because your container image has bundled all the application files into the container image, so that they can be run reproducibly anywhere. In general, you'll need to perform this bundling step whenever you want to publish a changed version of your application.

Into the Cloud on Your Laptop!

Once you have a locally working image (or if you're feeling bold), you can push your container image to an image registry. The `kn-quickstart` setup we documented in "Setup for This Chapter" on page 22 includes a local registry running on `localhost:5001`, so we can use `docker push localhost:5001/dashboard` to copy our image from our local machine to that registry. Knative can then fetch that image when needed to run our application.

Now that we've pushed our image to a remote registry that Knative can access, we'll use the same command we used to verify our `kn-quickstart` cluster: `kn service create dashboard --image localhost:5001/dashboard --port 3000`. Note that we added a `--port` argument to tell Knative what port the application is running on. By default, Knative expects applications to listen on the port defined in the `$PORT` environment variable, which defaults to 8080 (a popular server port). In this case, React's default web server listens on port 3000, so we simply direct Knative to use that port instead. Inside the container, the `$PORT` environment variable will be set to 3000, though React won't actually do anything with it.

The `kn service create` command shouldn't take longer than about five seconds to execute, and at the end, it should print out a URL you can use to access your dashboard, running on Knative inside your Kubernetes cluster. You can verify this by listing the pods (running containers) in the Kubernetes cluster with `kubectl get pods`; it should produce output like that in Example 2-7.

Example 2-7. Pod listing

```
NAME                                      READY  STATUS   RESTARTS  AGE
dashboard-00037-deployment-68fbc56fd-c2qnc  2/2    Running  0         15s
```

If you keep running `kubectl get pods` after you close your browser, you'll note that the `dashboard` pod terminates and disappears a minute or two after you close your browser. This is serverless in action, shutting down unused resources. If you reopen the URL in your browser, you'll see a new container start up, and then the page will load once the container is ready. As noted in "Creature Comforts: Managing Process Lifecycle" on page 16, this is called a *cold start*, which takes a few seconds as the image is fetched, React is started, and then the data is sent back to your browser.

Under the Covers: How Requests Are Handled

We'll cover Knative Serving in more detail in "Life of a Request" on page 56, but it's worth a quick summary of what's going on when Knative starts and stops the pods in response to HTTP requests. Many of the behavior thresholds are configurable—for example, Knative will begin scaling down to zero pods in approximately 30 seconds, but that timer could be extended if desired. The following discussion will assume the default Knative behavior—the current set of configurable options is documented on the Knative website (*https://oreil.ly/l6-c2*).

Figure 2-2 illustrates the handling of an HTTP request that causes a new pod to be created; if a pod already exists, Knative will usually choose to reuse the existing pod unless it is at request capacity or is currently shutting down.

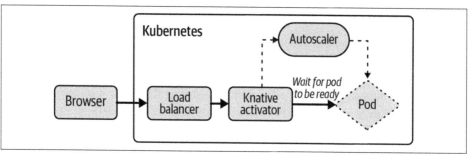

Figure 2-2. Flow of a Knative serving request

All Knative requests first pass through an HTTP load balancer. This is responsible for determining the target Knative Service based on the request hostname, as well as converting different flavors of HTTP (e.g., HTTP/1.1, HTTP/2, HTTPS) to a common format. The next destination after the load balancer is a component called the *activator*: its job is to determine whether there is a currently available pod that can handle the request. If there are no pods, or all pods are currently busy, it reports the need for a new pod to the autoscaler and stalls the request waiting for a pod to become available. The *autoscaler* is responsible for adjusting the requested number of pods for a given Revision of the Knative Service and will increase the desired number of pods from zero to one (or higher, for a large number of stalled requests). Once the pod has come online, the activator will forward the request to the pod, acting as a pass-through proxy for the request.

It's important to note that the pod has no particular insight or interest in this request lifecycle: its only concern is to handle the HTTP request, no matter how it was routed to the pod. In turn, Knative Serving is interested in delivering requests to pods (and measuring the requests in-flight and reporting observability metrics), but has no particular interest in *how* the software in the pod chooses to compute a reply.

Continuing to Build

Now that we've got our application running on Knative, let's extend our simple site to fetch some data from a static file and render it dynamically. The static file is a first step toward rendering dynamic dashboard content through an API—our current API is simply a very static API with a single fixed answer. You can find these files in the GitHub repository (*https://oreil.ly/BSAK-supp*) under the `static-api` branch, but I've reproduced them here so it's easier to follow along. If you want to check out this state of the application, `git checkout static-api` should update your repository to include these files. As shown in Example 2-8, we'll start by adding a simple datafile with two items to the static data directory *public*.

Example 2-8. public/my/dashboard

```
{
  "items": [
      {
          "title": "First Item",
          "content": "Some Info",
          "image": {
            "url": "https://knative.dev/docs/images/logo/rgb/knative-logo-rgb.png",
            "alt": "Knative logo"
          }
      },
      {
          "title": "Another item",
          "content": "Put some words here"
      }
  ]
}
```

By putting the file in the *public* directory, we've told React to serve this content directly. We'll then need to refactor our app to load this file dynamically; in this case, with a simple loop. I've also refactored the presentation of an individual data card into its own React component. The component doesn't do anything particularly interesting; it's just a way to encapsulate all the <Card> formatting into a separate file. The interesting file is the Dashboard component, shown in Example 2-9.

Example 2-9. src/components/Dashboard.tsx

```
import React from 'react';
import { Grid } from '@mui/material';
import DataCard, { CardData } from './DataCard';


interface Params {
    source?: string
```

```
    url?: string
}
interface State {
    items: CardData[]
}

class Dashboard extends React.Component<Params, State> {
    state: State = {
        items: []
    }
    timer?: NodeJS.Timeout

    componentDidMount(): void {
        if (this.props.source !== undefined) {
            this.setState(() => (
              { items: JSON.parse(this.props.source ?? '[]') }))
        }
        if (this.props.url !== undefined) {
            this.Poll()
        }
    }

    componentWillUnmount(): void {
        clearTimeout(this.timer)
    }

    async Poll(): Promise<void> {
        clearTimeout(this.timer)
        if (this.props.url === undefined) {
            console.log('No URL set')
            return
        }
        const response = await window.fetch(this.props.url);
        const { items } = await response.json();
        if (response.ok) {
            this.setState(() => ({ items: items }));
        } else {
            console.log('Failed to fetch from %s', this.props.url)
        }

        this.timer = setTimeout(() => this.Poll(), 2000)
    }

    render() {
        return <Grid container justifyContent='center' alignItems='center'
          spacing={2}>
            {this.state.items.map((value, index) => {
                return <Grid item xs={6} key={index}>
                    <DataCard {...value}></DataCard>
                </Grid>
            })}
        </Grid>
```

```
    }
};
```

```
export default Dashboard;
```

Once we've defined this Dashboard component, we can use it to replace the
`<Grid>...</Grid>` portion of *App.tsx* with a call to invoke the Dashboard, shown in
Example 2-10.

Example 2-10. src/App.tsx with Dashboard

```
function App() {
  return (
    <ThemeProvider theme={createTheme({})}>
      <CssBaseline enableColorScheme />
      <Container maxWidth={false}>
        <Dashboard url='/my/dashboard'></Dashboard>
      </Container>
    </ThemeProvider>
  );
}
```

If you rebuild the container and rerun it, you should see two cards show up. But this
is still a static site, so you'll always get the same two cards. What we need is to
make */my/dashboard* do something more interesting.

Adding an API

Our current application looks reasonably professional for the time we've put into it,
but it's very static. We really want a dashboard that can update and show new information as it arrives. We're going to start by extending our application container to
include both our current React application and a Python server that will serve both
the ReactJS (as static files) and a dynamic */my/dashboard* path, replacing our static
file. We'll need to update our container image packaging to add this Python application. Finally, we'll poke around a little bit and see some of the advantages of building
on a serverless stack like Knative with application health checks and rollbacks.

If you're following along on the GitHub repo (*https://oreil.ly/BSAK-supp*), this code is
available from the `python-api` branch. You can check out the code at this point by
using `git checkout python-api` without needing to type out the code.

If you're typing along rather than jumping directly to the finished product, the first
step is to create an *api* subdirectory to build our application in. Since our first goal
should be to replicate the functionality we had prior to the change, we end up with a
very simple application, shown in Example 2-11.

Example 2-11. main.py for static site

```python
from flask import Flask, send_file, send_from_directory

app = Flask(__name__)

@app.route("/")
def serve_root():
  return send_file("static/index.html")

@app.route("/<path:path>")
def serve_static(path):
  return send_from_directory("static", path)
```

You'll also need to create a *requirements.txt* file with the single line Flask>=2.3.2 to record the version of the Flask library that should be used. Don't worry, this will get a little bigger as we implement our backend API! For now, we're just looking to verify that switching from the Node.js development server to the Python static server hasn't disrupted our application.

Packaging our application with both a Python web server and a compiled React app gets a little more complicated (as shown in Example 2-12), but is relatively straightforward using a two-stage Docker build. In a two-stage build, we start with a Node.js container image to build the JavaScript, and then start a second container to build the Python application. Once the Python application is built, we *copy* the compiled JavaScript from the Node.js container to the Python container.

Example 2-12. Dockerfile for combined Python/Node.js application

```dockerfile
# Docker Image, which is used as foundation to create
# a custom Docker Image with this Dockerfile
FROM node:18 AS package

# App is built here
WORKDIR /app

# Install dependencies first, so code changes build fast
COPY package*.json ./
RUN npm install

# Copy needed files
COPY src ./src/
COPY public ./public/
COPY tsconfig.json ./

RUN npm run-script build

# At this point, we have all the files needed to serve our UI
```

```
# Start building Python application
FROM python:3.10-slim AS run

# Load libraries
COPY api/requirements.txt .
RUN pip install -r requirements.txt

# Copy API application and static JavaScript contents
COPY api .
COPY public ./static/
COPY --from=package /app/build/* ./static/

# Use the same port as express
EXPOSE 3000

# Finally runs the application
CMD [ "python", "-m", "flask", "--app", "main.py", "run", "--host", "0.0.0.0",
  "--port", "3000" ]
```

You should be able to build and run this container in Docker and on Knative without needing to have Python or other software installed locally. Our next step is to add some dynamic content, as shown in Example 2-13. For the purposes of this example, we're going to look up the weather in Honolulu, Hawaii (putting weather information of your family and friends up on a dashboard where it's easy to see can help remind you what's going on elsewhere in the world).

Example 2-13. main.py additions for a dynamic API

```
# Initialize a static noaa object once
noaa = noaa_sdk.NOAA()

def get_weather(zip):
  observations = noaa.get_observations(str(zip), "US")
  current_weather = next(observations)  # Just take the first for now

  content = current_weather["textDescription"]
  image = {'url': current_weather["icon"], 'alt': content}
  if current_weather.get("temperature", {}).get("value", 0):
    unit = current_weather["temperature"]["unitCode"][-1]
    content += f': {current_weather["temperature"]["value"]} {unit}'
  return dict(title=f"Weather at {zip}", content=content, image=image)

@app.route("/my/dashboard")
def serve_dashboard():
  # Flask will convert dicts and arrays to JSON automatically.
  return {"items": [get_weather(96813)]}
```

We've added the first data integration for our application. I'm not going to show more sample code here, but it's easy to imagine integrations with other APIs:

- GitHub or Jira to show number of open issues
- Calendar data for next/upcoming events
- RSS feeds for latest news
- Video feeds with some additional frontend code

Our example used a public API service that doesn't require authentication tokens, but Knative works with the standard Kubernetes ConfigMap and Secret objects to inject configuration at runtime if needed. You can either load the values into environment variables or mount them into the filesystem—the latter is generally preferred if you want your application to receive configuration changes on the fly.[5]

I've also limited the API to fetching data for a single, hard-coded user (/my/). If you have a user-account system, it's easy to use Flask's URL templating to provide different per-user URLs that fetch different dashboards (the user's desired dashboards could be stored in a database like MySQL or a key-value store like Redis). We won't further explore these application-level features because our goal is to have a simple example we can use to explore serverless architectural choices. Feel free to play with the example and try adding your own data source—the sample code on GitHub has a few more data sources already integrated.

While it can be fun to extend this toy example with a lot more integrations, you'll quickly notice that adding all of these integrations into a single application and endpoint can cause a variety of difficulties. In the next sections, we'll talk about complementary serverless services that can augment and empower serverless applications.

API Gateways and Composing an App

One problem with building the entire integration into a single container image is that anytime *any* component changes, the entire application needs to be rebuilt. Additionally, when the dynamic dashboard part of the application is slow or crashes, it can cause the static Node.js application to fail to load, because the static server and the dynamic content are mixed.

---

5 While Knative Revisions attempts to be hermetic, Knative does not detect and restart containers that depend on a ConfigMap or Secret that has been changed at runtime. One solution for making sure that servers are restarted periodically is to set an upper time limit on container lifetime–for example, with the descheduler project (*https://oreil.ly/JOiZx*).

The traditional solution to this problem is to use an API gateway or HTTP reverse proxy to route different URL paths to different backend components. In a production Kubernetes deployment, you would use an ingress implementation like Istio, nginx, or Contour to split traffic. Because we're working with a small Kubernetes installation from kn quickstart, we can write our own ingress. Our setup will look like that in Figure 2-3, where each shape is its own Knative Service.

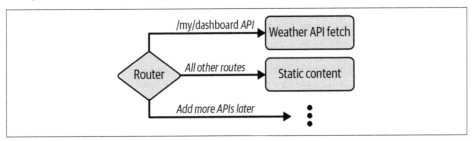

Figure 2-3. Request routing with an API gateway

The easiest way to get started is to simply deploy the same container twice, but separate the traffic so that one container gets the root and static URLs, and the other, the "API" service, gets everything under */my/*. Continuing with Python, we can use the program in Example 2-14 to act as an API gateway.

Example 2-14. main.py of gateway container

```python
from flask import Flask
from urllib import request

app = Flask(__name__, static_folder=None)

@app.route("/", defaults={"path":""})
@app.route("/<path:path>")
def route_to_static(path):
  resp = request.urlopen(f"http://static-app.default.svc/{path}")
  return (resp.read(), resp.status, resp.getheaders())

@app.route("/my/dashboard")
def route_to_api():
  resp = request.urlopen("http://api-app.default.svc/my/dashboard")
  return (resp.read(), resp.status, resp.getheaders())
```

A Note on Routing

Because Knative Services are routed using ingress infrastructure that is shared across the cluster, you need to set the `Host` header in your routing layer so that Knative knows which Service to route the request to. Since we're using Python, `urllib.request.urlopen` will set the `Host` header automatically. You can use the full cluster-local service URL, but Knative also registers the shorter *<SERVICE>.<NAME SPACE>* and *<SERVICE>.<NAMESPACE>*.svc hostnames.

For Istio, you can set the hostname with the `rewrite.authority` argument. For nginx, use the `nginx.ingress.kubernetes.io/upstream-vhost` annotation. For Contour, use a `requestHeadersPolicy` to set the `Host` header. For the Gateway API, the `filters.requestHeaderModifier` provides a `set` mapping of header names and values.

While our sample router supports simple routing with a code push, we could also read the URL route configuration from a file. Our router is also less efficient than a dedicated HTTP router—our implementation reads the entire request or response before forwarding it to the next destination. A dedicated router like Envoy (which is used by Istio and Contour) will pipeline all of this work; it will also be implemented in a high-performance language like C++ with multiple threads and careful data structure management. It will *not* scale to zero like our Knative example router, and it is much more complicated to understand.

While we've taken the first step of splitting our application into smaller independent pieces, API gateways provide many other capabilities beyond routing URLs into a single hostname, including these:

- Authorization policies
- API keys and client rate limiting
- Format transformations (JSON to RPC, or rewriting request formats for older clients)
- Publishing OpenAPI or other API descriptions
- Monitoring, tracing, and observability
- Timeout and retry management
- Caching

Additionally, many API gateways provide custom hooks for extending the API processing for special cases. We'll cover these in more detail after providing some examples and guidance on dividing up an API to take the best advantage of serverless scaling and management.

Splitting an API into Components

We currently have a single API endpoint in our application, so there's not much to separate. Furthermore, if we continue with the current API design, we'll end up with a single API endpoint that collects dashboard tiles from a variety of systems and aggregates them into a single response object. This might look a bit like the Python code in Example 2-15.

Example 2-15. Aggregating many data sources into a single response

```python
@app.route("/my/dashboard")
def serve_content():
  response = []
  for function in dashboard_functions:
    response.append(function())
  return {"items": response}
```

You can probably already see some problems with this design:

Reliability

If any one component fails or throws an exception, it can break the entire application. We could add some exception handling to reduce this risk, but what if one of the functions enters an infinite loop or tries to load 1 GB of data? Separating each of these calls into a separate API makes it easier to implement failure management, since we already expect network calls to be unreliable.

Performance

In addition to the reliability concerns, bundling all the backend calls together means that all the backend data is limited to the speed of the slowest backend data. If one backend has performance problems, all the dashboard tiles will load slowly, even if most are perfectly fine.

The solution to both problems is to split the API into different endpoints and have client-side logic stitch them together. The simplest way to do this is to change the */my/dashboard* URL to return a list of "extension URLs" that the client can call to get a single dashboard entry each. This separates the work into several pieces that we can now apply API gateways and serverless design principles to. We'll end up with a URL structure like that in Table 2-1.

Table 2-1. URL routes for the decomposed API

URL	Backing service
/my/dashboard	Account
/weather/<zipcode>	Weather
/openissues/<repo>	GitHub issues
/news/<source>	News feed
/ai-art/<prompt>	AI-generated art

In addition to the reliability and latency benefits, when we split a large service into multiple microservices in this way, it becomes possible to tune their operational settings much more easily. Maybe the GitHub issues service needs a longer deadline to respond because of API rate limits, while the weather service has much lower limits, and the news feed service doesn't need any rate limits at all—we can adjust the `timeoutSeconds` value in the Knative Service specification based on these needs and possibly use the `autoscaling.knative.dev/max-scale` annotation to limit the GitHub component to three replicas, because more replicas will simply hit the rate limit.

We can also tune other parts of the execution parameters by component—for example, if generating AI art is an intensive process, we can set `containerConcurrency` to a low value to limit the number of simultaneous art pieces being generated, and possibly add a GPU to the resource requests. Because it's easy to build, deploy, scale, and manage these services, it's easy to decide to break out each service into its own deployment, whether or not they are built from the same codebase. I've seen several customers of serverless platforms who effectively deploy the same monolith multiple times in different resource configurations to achieve this result without needing to complexify their build and local development process.

API gateways can improve the value of serverless runtimes by using API routing to create well-fitted microservices and optimizing resources. But serverless runtimes can also improve the value of API gateways by providing a natural and low-friction destination for API extension endpoints.

Augmenting a Proxy

API gateways usually support a variety of built-in functions for things like API key rate limiting, validating authentication tokens, and translating payloads from one format to another. However, sometimes applications have unique needs that don't fit the general-purpose API gateway functionality—translating to an obscure format, or validating authorization tokens against a backend device database, for example. Many API gateways provide extension mechanisms at well-defined request processing points that allow the gateway to either call an external service via a webhook-type request or enable running a small amount of specialized code within the gateway process itself.

Both of these modes of operation are a good match for serverless technologies—running a small bit of code alongside the request is an obvious example of a serverless technology at work, but this custom code can also be used to call a webhook. For simplicity, I'm going to primarily discuss the webhook model because it is more general, but many of the same techniques apply to extension code running within an API gateway sandbox. The request flow in such a scenario looks like Figure 2-4.

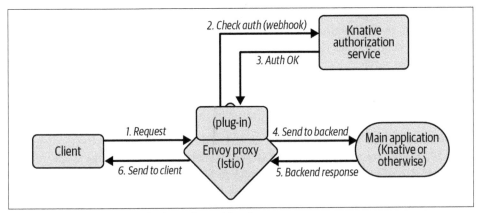

Figure 2-4. Knative as a platform for webhooks

Serverless platforms like Knative are a natural destination for webhook implementations like this because they specialize in answering stateless HTTP requests, which is exactly what these webhooks expect. Using a FaaS model, it is easy to build, iterate on, and deploy API extension hooks for authentication, authorization, or payload transformations. For example, if we were using the Istio gateway and network plug-in, we could build an external authorization service to limit access to certain dashboard functionality to only users in a particular group or even run an Open Policy Agent (OPA) server to provide a deeply programmable authorization interface. Because OPA runs as a stateless gRPC service reading a configuration file, it is easy to deploy and run the application serverlessly, even if the original application was not purpose-built for serverless use.

Existing services like API gateways are sometimes already designed to provide abstractions that focus on units of work rather than processes and instances. In addition to stateless network processing tools, numerous other storage and execution service types complement serverless applications. In the next section, we'll highlight a few of these services; we'll also dive into event-driven complementary systems in Chapter 6.

Complementary Services

Most serverless runtime platforms are designed for stateless applications—that is, applications that store any meaningful between-request state in an external data store. Even for these applications, it's not entirely correct to say that they don't store *any* state—there is a current request context, call stack, set of loaded libraries, etc. that are used during the handling of a request. However, stateless applications *avoid relying on internal state between requests*. Generally, they do this by instead storing the state in an external storage system such as a database or message queue.

There are many types of application state, and different types of systems work best for each one. In this section, I'll give a brief overview of some of the most common and popular service types that complement stateless serverless applications. Note that many of these services fit nicely into our general definition of serverless: they break the work (storage) into independent units that can be scheduled and executed (accessed) independently. It should be no surprise that serverless applications love serverless storage, but it's worth calling out *why* these interfaces are so popular.

While these storage interfaces are the largest and most popular serverless categories, as of 2023 there are a large variety of serverless offerings in the storage space, including those that use traditional interfaces such as SQL databases (Cockroach, Yugabyte, Fly) or POSIX filesystems (Amazon's Elastic File System [EFS] or Google Filestore).[6] While these interfaces are interesting, our first serverless storage system is a much simpler but popular pattern for application caches and a basic storage building block: key-value stores.

 While most serverless runtimes are *stateless*, most useful applications do manage state on behalf of their users (logins, work items, stored images, etc.). Serverless applications do this by externalizing the state into explicit storage systems. Serverless storage systems that distribute work scalably across multiple computers work particularly well for storing serverless application state.

Key-Value Storage

Key-value storage systems have a relatively simple interface compared with traditional database systems: all data is accessed via an application-defined *key*, which provides access to one or more *values* associated with the key (some key-value stores provide only a single value, while others provide multiple values, sometimes defined as "columns"). By requiring all access to data to work through a single key, application access can be spread across many storage servers by assigning each key to a specific server. This allows distributed key-value stores to scale to high levels of concurrent access, which supports the horizontal scaling enabled by serverless applications.

Traditional database systems have finite scaling limits, often on the order of 500 allowed client connections. While these limits may work fine for conventional applications with narrow scaling ranges, these limits can cause problems for serverless applications that are designed to scale by increasing the number of instances, particularly when used at scale or in combination with connection pooling libraries that

---

6 Amazon's Aurora Serverless database has "serverless" in the name and can scale up dynamically, but always has at least one instance running. Is that serverless? It depends on how you define it.

open multiple connections from a single instance. While the frontend system may be able to scale dynamically under load, spawning 200 or 500 instances may cause many to fail as they attempt to initialize their backing database connections. "Inelastic Scaling" on page 165 has a few suggestions about how to work around supporting services with fixed scalability limits, but these limits can impose architectural challenges for serverless systems.

In contrast, distributed storage systems from 2000 onward are explicitly designed to scale horizontally in the same way as application servers, using a technique called *sharding*. Sharding assigns keys in the storage system to different servers: as long as the application access pattern is evenly distributed across different keys, both the application and storage can scale horizontally as traffic increases, as seen in Figure 2-5.

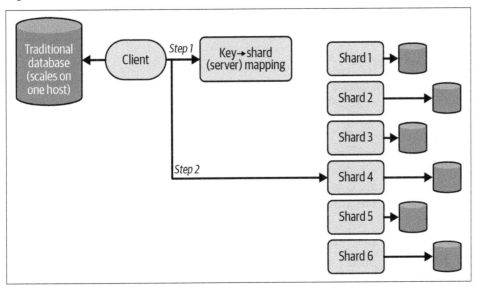

Figure 2-5. Traditional database architecture versus distributed key-value storage

Popular key-value stores include both fast in-memory caches (Redis, memcached) and persistent, replicated data stores (Cassandra, MongoDB). Depending on the durability and access requirements for the data, serverless applications may use one or both types of store, sometimes alongside practices such as external joins (linking two data rows by having the application layer implement linked data lookups outside the database layer). In the case of our sample application, we could address some of the challenges described in "Splitting an API into Components" on page 39 by prefetching the requested data and caching it in a system like Redis along with an expiration time.

Our dashboard application could also use a more persistent key-value store to record per-user dashboard settings or other information such as features or user credentials needed to fetch data from access-controlled APIs like calendars. In both of these cases, the key used for data storage is relatively obvious—in the case of cached dashboard data, the key to the cache is the serialized dashboard query string, while the user settings are most likely keyed by the user (possibly with a prefix or suffix to allow storing other user-related information in the same database).

A wide variety of key-value stores are available as both open source and closed source offerings, each with its own API and storage semantics. One common feature of key-value stores is eventual consistency—while not all key-value stores are eventually consistent, the distributed nature of these solutions makes eventual consistency an attractive way to squeeze out additional performance from some architectures. Key-value storage in many forms is extremely popular with serverless applications because distributing the key space across many servers allows the backend storage to scale in the same way as the application. One popular special case of key-value storage is *object storage*, popularized by Amazon S3.

Object Storage

As already mentioned, object storage (such as Amazon S3, MinIO, Google Cloud Storage, or Azure Blob Storage) is a specialized version of key-value storage that is particularly focused on storing binary blob values along with a small amount of metadata. Conceptually, it is generally organized into *buckets*, and each bucket contains a number of *objects* that are described by string paths. Unlike a traditional filesystem, there is no notion of directories, and object paths are not hierarchical—each object is an independent entry in the bucket, though buckets may support listing only objects whose paths match specific prefixes. Some implementations may also be eventually consistent—a read or list of a recently written object may return an older copy than what was most recently written.

Object storage provides a scalable network abstraction for storing files and object data that is written to with a small number of operations, typically "create," "read," "replace," and "delete." In particular, object storage differs from POSIX filesystem storage by *not* allowing writes or appends to objects after creation. Limiting the set of operations and requiring objects to be uploaded completely before they can be used simplifies the storage API and avoids a number of difficult edge cases.[7] In many ways, object stores are the original serverless service—each object is an independent chunk of work, and can be managed, provisioned, and consumed independently from a client point of view.

---

7 These systems may support incremental upload of content using some sort of chunked encoding for reliability and efficiency, but generally don't allow read access to objects until they have been finalized and can no longer be appended to.

Object storage systems often provide additional support for serverless applications in the form of event notifications for create and delete operations. We will talk more about how to leverage these events to trigger serverless logic in "The Active Storage Pattern" on page 139, but this linkage between object storage and triggering serverless workloads is an extremely popular pattern for building simple workflows.

Another common service for triggering serverless workflows is a simple timer that tracks the passage of time and can generate units of work on either a fixed time interval or at an application-selected relative time in the future.

Timers (Cron)

Traditional applications may often use background in-process timers to periodically execute an action—checking for certain database records, refreshing or clearing stale cache data, or batching transactional data, for example. This approach works well when a small, fixed number of processes are constantly running but does not translate well to a serverless environment when processes run only in response to a direct work request, and then may be shut down at any moment afterward. For small applications, this may mean zero processes available to run a background task, while large applications may end up with hundreds of identical processes competing to execute the same task.

One solution is to move this background work into a small set of traditional application servers, but a much more robust and serverless solution is to export the job of tracking time and scheduling work execution to an external process. When the time comes, the external system can submit the periodic work-to-be-done to the serverless runtime, which can scale as needed to handle the additional scheduled work. The implementation of this external process may be one or more continuously executing tasks, but clients of the timer service can treat it as executing independently scheduled work units at the appropriate time—yet another serverless complement from the perspective of stateless application runtimes.

Timer services can either manifest as relatively static cron-like scheduling services or can be more fine-grained services for scheduling notifications in the future. In the latter case, they start to bleed into the larger area of task queuing, which we will discuss in more detail in "Task Queues" on page 134. In fact, you can implement a cron-type service using a future-scheduled task that does two things: first it schedules the next execution (e.g., one hour or one week later), and then it calls the expected target.

Task Queues

A *task queue* is a service that accepts work orders for execution at some point in the future, as managed by the queue. While most serverless code-execution environments aim to accomplish work as quickly as possible by *horizontally* scaling the number of compute instances, task queues instead scale work in the *time* dimension by deferring work to the future to maintain a certain instance or work-in-flight budget. Task queues can also enable latency-sensitive applications to return results quickly by deferring nontransactional work to execute after the latency-sensitive request has completed.

When used in combination with cached results stored in key-value storage (see "Key-Value Storage" on page 42), we could use task queues to refresh dashboard results in the background, as shown in Example 2-16.

Example 2-16. Using task queues and key-value storage to accelerate our dashboard

```
@app.route("/weather/<zip:zip>")
def get_weather(zip):
  weather = json.loads(redis.get(f"weather-{zip}"))
  # JSON object contains expires and forecast
  if weather.expires < time.now() + time.duration(5, "minutes"):
    # Refresh the weather before expiration
    queue.enqueue(f"/fetchweather/{zip}")
  return weather.forecast

@app.route("/fetchweather/<zip:zip>")
def fetch_weather(zip):
  # ... fetch weather from noaa and store in redis
```

In addition to allowing work to be deferred for future execution, many task queues have additional features that can simplify the design of serverless applications. These are covered in more depth in "Task Queues" on page 134.

Task queues provide a clear mechanism for scheduling work to be executed in the future, as long as the work to be done is independent and self-describing. For more complex, interdependent tasks within a larger series of work items, workflows may be a more appropriate tool. While it is possible to use task queues to build a workflow system, most application authors will find the additional support and structure provided by a workflow system to be a useful addition to their design arsenal.

Workflows

Workflows define a series of dependent work items; the content of later work items depends on the results of work items earlier in the flow. In some systems, users are able to define logical steps to take based on the results of earlier work items, or are able to copy the results of one work item to later flow stages. Often these flows are defined using state machines or flowcharts, rather than in application code; this makes workflow services accessible to applications written in many different languages and can help enforce constraints (such as "a workload must terminate") that may be easier to enforce in a simpler language.

While workflows orchestrate a series of smaller work items within a larger framework of a logical set of steps, workflow engines are also a serverless construct. Each workflow execution represents a single logical piece of work ("Orchestrate this series of steps") that executes independently of other workflow executions and scales horizontally based on the work available. In fact, it is relatively straightforward to combine key-value stores, timers, and task queues to implement much of the flowchart or state-machine functionality of a typical workflow system, as shown in Figure 2-6.

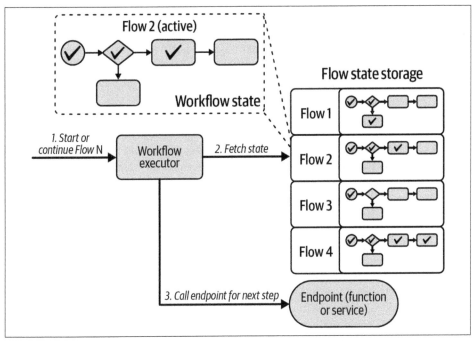

Figure 2-6. Sample workflow execution

While the state machine pattern is the most common form of workflow system, some systems like Azure Durable Functions take a different, more code-based approach to defining the application state machine. In Durable Functions, applications use specially defined libraries to help store and manage application state and use special functions to define the next workflow step during code execution. This approach is much more dynamic—the set of application states may not be defined ahead of time, but it also presents other workflow implementation challenges, such as ensuring that a workflow always reaches a terminating condition.

We'll cover workflow systems and implementing workflow orchestration further in "Workflow Orchestration" on page 129. A prebuilt workflow system has the advantage of testing, deployment experience, and a well-defined and unified set of capabilities, but can be limiting for workflows that have specific needs. Many teams end up building their own workflow systems by accident as their systems slowly evolve from simple task queues to more complex patterns; using an intentionally architected system can help avoid later maintenance pain around inconsistent semantics and special cases that are now depended upon by customers.

While the preceding selection of five systems certainly will not cover all architecture patterns found in serverless applications, it should provide a good flavor and basis for understanding additional patterns you may encounter. As we explored in workflow orchestration, many serverless patterns can also be built out of the other primitives in much the same way that we can build higher-level modules out of low-level library functions. While our dashboard application may not need all of the services mentioned to be successful, understanding the landscape of common services can help trigger pattern-recognition when encountering a problem in the wild.

Summary

In this chapter, we've built a small serverless application from scratch and explored the many supporting services and design patterns that allow stateless applications to handle stateful user requirements. A somewhat-popular refrain in the serverless design community is that the patterns should be called "serviceful, rather than serverless." Using serverless to stitch together stateful storage and scheduling elements with just enough application code helps minimize the amount of maintenance work and the number of systems to administer when building an application.

Now that you have some understanding of how to build serverless software, the next chapter will provide an in-depth look at how Knative provides these abstractions on clusters of physical servers. Although our examples in this chapter all worked on your local laptop, they could easily be moved to cloud-provided Knative services or run on enterprise datacenters with hundreds or thousands of servers. If getting your hands into the underlying guts of serverless isn't interesting, Chapter 4 will provide some more business-focused articulation of how serverless can transform writing software before Part II covers real-world ways to integrate serverless into existing software systems.

## CHAPTER 3

Under the Hood: Knative

In Chapter 2, we kicked the tires with Knative by using the kn quickstart command, but our focus was on getting a running Knative cluster, not on how the tool works. While the goal of serverless infrastructure is to insulate you from managing the day-to-day details of the underlying systems, it's helpful to understand the general request flows and patterns to assess whether a particular pattern works well or badly.

While different infrastructure providers implement specific serverless details differently, many of the main platforms implement fairly similar functionality for serverless compute and event distribution. In this chapter, we'll focus on Knative Serving as an example of the former and Knative Eventing as an example of the latter. Knative is a popular open source serverless platform implemented on Kubernetes; it's fairly easy to install and can scale horizontally for both throughput and reliability.

Many of the principles in the open source software apply directly to hosted services offered by service providers; I'll also call out particular distinctions with popular hosted platforms where appropriate. One pattern that is somewhat unique to Knative is that the Serving and Eventing projects are *independent*: you can use just Knative Serving to implement a REST API (for example), or use only Knative Eventing to deliver events to traditional infrastructure components without Serving installed.

Focusing on the open source software also allows you to actually download and rebuild the source code if needed to explore different implementation choices. Many of these implementation choices are also documented in the issue, document, and pull request (PR) history of the project, all of which are available for free on GitHub.

Knative also serves as the basis for a few commercial serverless offerings (as of 2023), including IBM Cloud Code Engine, Google's Cloud Run for Anthos,[1] VMware's Tanzu Application Platform, the TriggerMesh platform, and the Direktiv platform. The authors of Knative have also previously worked on and been inspired by several earlier commercial and open source systems, so it's fair to say that Knative is a reasonably representative sample.

Before we get into the details of *how* serverless compute and event distribution is implemented in Knative, we'll first need to talk a bit about the underlying capabilities that Knative depends on. It's fair to say that 2017 was the earliest that Knative could have been considered; the rise of Kubernetes, Envoy, and the cloud native ecosystem enabled Knative to be built atop existing components, rather than needing to define its own infrastructure and API layers. Indeed, as we'll see in Chapter 11, earlier open source platforms such as Cloud Foundry generally had to "carry the world on their backs" in terms of scheduling, routing, and API management.

Kubernetes and Envoy provide several abstractions that allowed Knative to avoid reinventing the wheel. Envoy is a high-performance HTTP load balancer driven by several configuration APIs. These APIs allow other projects to focus on exposing and integrating load balancer features without needing to *implement* those features.[2] Similarly, Kubernetes provides an extensible, programmable platform for running clusters of computers. Kubernetes is highly pluggable and is built on the idea of generic API resources that can be managed by external components rather than predefined built-in workflows. The introduction of Kubernetes API extensions in the form of custom resource definitions (CRDs) allowed Knative to leverage Kubernetes infrastructure for much of the API definition and management infrastructure, as well as for provisioning and managing the actual container execution environment.[3]

Infrastructure Assumptions

Diving headfirst into how Knative works is tempting, but it's important to set a bit of background on the infrastructure that runs Knative (and other serverless systems). While it's possible to build an entirely bespoke serverless runtime from start to finish, it's generally helpful to build complex systems in *layers*. For a serverless platform, these layers likely consist of some form of abstraction of the underlying hardware, OS, and process execution layers such that components like scheduling and autoscaling can operate abstractly with directives like "Run this process on this node" without

---

[1] Google has *two* Cloud Run implementations. One is Knative-based, and the other is based on Google's internal serverless platform. I worked on conformance and compatibility between the two from 2017 to 2019.

[2] For more details on Envoy proxy, see *Cloud Native Architectures* by Tom Laszewski et al. (Packt).

[3] For more details on Kubernetes, see *Kubernetes Up and Running* by Brendan Burns et al. (O'Reilly).

intertwining kernel upgrades, hardware repairs, or other minutiae in the higher-level logic. Much of this functionality could be shared with other scheduling systems.[4]

While Knative takes advantage of the API facilities provided by the Kubernetes `apiserver` to expose an interface that is generally compatible with other Kubernetes-based tools, many other serverless platforms (including systems that may use a Kubernetes substrate, like OpenFaaS or OpenWhisk) expose their own API. Each approach has advantages, but the main point here is that existing API infrastructure is not as critical to serverless platforms as the ability to abstract away individual underlying machines into a semi-homogeneous pool of compute (and storage) resources.

Hardware and Operating System Management

At a basic layer, computer hardware requires software to make it useful. The basic underlying layers of hardware management are generally referred to as "the operating system," though in a modern datacenter server (referred to as a "node" henceforth), there are probably dozens of interoperating processors with their own software that needs to be kept up-to-date: device firmware for network, storage, and accelerators, BIOS and kernel patches, and an OS like Linux to coordinate all of these resources and expose them to user-space programs. In a well-run installation, all of these components need to be managed and patched on a regular basis, which may require shutting down all the user-space programs on the node and rebooting the system. Given these requirements, there is also a meta requirement to *coordinate* these upgrades such that releasing a new kernel version does not simultaneously reboot every node in the fleet.

These basic capabilities have been the focus of much of IT automation for the last 30 years (since people realized that for some tasks they could buy many small computers and network them together more cheaply than buying one very large computer). I'm not going to go into too much detail on the specifics of these systems.[5] But I'll highlight that the ability to take a fleet of physical machines and manage them uniformly is a critical first step in enabling every layer above this baseline to treat nodes as a fundamental unit of capacity without getting mired in the details of how nodes are added, removed, and upgraded within the fleet.

---

4 Knative uses Kubernetes as the underlying scheduling system, but it's possible to use other cluster scheduling systems like Apache Mesos or Google's Borg. It's also possible to use a data execution system like Apache's Hadoop or Flink as a scheduler, though real-time performance may suffer.

5 Generally, these systems fall into two categories: vendor-provided cradle-to-grave systems and "We built it ourselves" systems. In my experience, the latter are far more common, and often vendor systems get customized to the point where they are effectively "We built it ourselves."

So far, we've talked about computer hardware and nodes as if they are perfect, immutable collections of resources to be used by higher-level systems. Unfortunately, actual computer hardware tends to be hot, power-hungry, and filled with moving and nonmoving pieces that wear out over time. Some hardware may also be upgraded to increase capacity in a more cost-effective way, meaning that the resources available on a node may actually change over time. A well-implemented hardware and OS management layer will take these requirements into account to enable the addition, removal, repair, and upgrade of nodes in the system. In some environments, virtualization management software may be part of the node management story; in other cases, the "bare metal" hardware will be exposed to the next layer of management. In either case, the upper layers of the platform should not need to know about the tools used to manage, create, and delete nodes; this interface is hidden behind the node-management API.

Scheduling and the Datacenter as a Computer

With the ability to uniformly manage individual nodes, we have the first layer of our infrastructure management stack in place. The next layer is a scheduling and process-management API to describe what applications should run on the hardware fleet. The goal of this layer is to expose all the node-level resources as a single, uniform pool of compute resources—a pattern that's been called "the datacenter as a computer."[6] While individual processes will still be scheduled to a specific node (and are limited by the available resources on the node), this scheduler provides the ability to restart a process on a new node if the first node fails or needs to be taken out of service.

Of course, applications written for a cluster-level scheduling scheme like this must rely on different assumptions than applications written for a single computer: applications must standardize on network communication, be prepared for the failure of one or more processes at any time, and handle the recovery and repair of application state when a process is detected as failed. Today, these capabilities are generally a well-understood cost of building distributed systems, but they can be quite a learning curve for developers who have previously worked on client-side or mainframe applications for which the failure domain is "all or nothing."

Implementing cluster scheduling generally requires two components working together: a node-level agent (such as the kubelet in Kubernetes) and a cluster-level scheduler (which may itself be a distributed application as previously described). Node-level agents, as the name suggests, run on an individual node and are generally spawned as part of the "operating system" layer managed in the hardware and OS abstraction layer. The node-level agents are responsible for monitoring the health of

---

6 For more background, see *The Datacenter as a Computer* by Luiz André Barroso et al. (Springer).

the node, starting processes that are scheduled to that node and reporting status to the cluster-level scheduler. The cluster-level scheduler exposes an API for starting and stopping processes on the cluster (which may be "run this process, restarting it as needed," or may be a more sophisticated "run N copies" API) and then communicates with the node-level agents to start the process on the given node. The cluster-level scheduler is generally also responsible for assigning network addresses and storage resources to processes; in Kubernetes, this is handled by a coordination between the OS-layer Container Network Interface (CNI) and Container Storage Interface (CSI) agents and the cluster control plane. This is illustrated in Figure 3-1.

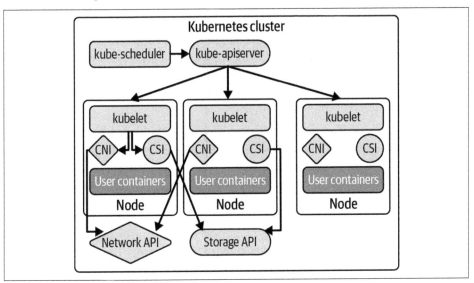

Figure 3-1. The Kubernetes node and cluster schedulers

By leveraging the Kubernetes scheduler when scheduling serverless instances, Knative can natively take advantage of advances in the Kubernetes scheduler, such as preferring to schedule instances on nodes that have already fetched the container image. With a cluster-level scheduling API built on a lower-level hardware and OS management API, we have the baseline capabilities needed to implement a serverless platform. Knative also leverages additional infrastructure-level capabilities to implement HTTP load balancing and message routing, but neither of these are fundamental serverless dependencies on the order of uniform cluster scheduling and execution APIs.

While Knative Serving and Eventing are independent components that work well together,[7] books are written in sequence, so we're going to talk about Serving before

---

7 Joe Beda dubbed this the "Voltron effect," and I like it.

Eventing. This is somewhat fitting, as the Serving APIs were the first developed and the first to reach a "v1" status.

Serving

Knative Serving implements a serverless code execution runtime based on the idea that many applications can be implemented as stateless, HTTP-serving containers. This builds on the twelve-factor application manifesto (*https://12factor.net*) and earlier work on platforms such as Google App Engine and Cloud Foundry, which provided a platform-as-a-service (PaaS) focused primarily on handling web-based applications. While not a fit for all applications, the prevalence of REST-based APIs and web-based interfaces along with the ability to treat each HTTP request as a unit of work makes stateless HTTP-based work a good fit for serverless. With the rise and standardization of OCI containers as a packaging and execution format (boosted by Docker and Kubernetes), containers were a natural way to encapsulate applications portably across different implementations.[8]

With the skeleton of a runtime execution contract laid out, it becomes easy to see how our applications in Chapter 2 worked well on Knative Serving. What's not yet clear is how to describe the application to the serverless platform as a whole—while serverless makes it *easier* to run your application, important information often isn't captured in the compiled artifacts, such as "what name do you want to use to access the app" or "how much memory does a process need."[9] This information about your application, sometimes called *metadata*, is part of the control plane.[10] The control plane encompasses all the higher-level systems that manage the intent to run the application, but that don't need to be involved for each HTTP request. Being based on Kubernetes, Knative uses Kubernetes custom resources to define the *intent* around your application container.

---

8 Many earlier serverless systems, such as AWS Lambda and Google App Engine used "source code bundle" or "JAR" as the public packaging format and then converted these to internal storage formats through confidential build systems. This generally worked, but occasionally introduced "works on my machine but not in the cloud." OCI containers have largely solved this.

9 Some serverless platforms have attempted to minimize these requirements by (for example) automatically assigning a generated name to your application. This generally introduces another layer somewhere else where you map a "nice" name to the computer-generated name. It turns out that humans really like meaningful names.

10 The "control plane" and "data plane" terms derive from network switching, where specialized hardware is used to route packets in the data plane. The control plane is then responsible for programming the data plane to perform the correct routing. This allows using fast, dumb hardware for the data plane and slower, smarter hardware for the control plane.

Control-Plane Concepts

Much as the scheduler and hardware-management layer build on each other by managing different layers of the infrastructure stack, the Knative control plane defines several levels of objects to allow different levels of management of the serverless stack:

Services

Services provide a high-level definition of a serverless application.[11] They provide an easy on-ramp and simple management experience for common use cases. A Service manages two different lower-level resources in a 1:1 relationship: a Route defines the mapping of a hostname to particular versions of an application, and a Configuration defines the current desired state of an application.

Routes

A Route manages the configuration of inbound request routing to compute resources. A Route is responsible for provisioning and configuring the routing of a hostname on the shared Knative HTTP load balancer to a set of active Revisions based on traffic percentages specified in the Route.[12] A Route can also map a Revision to an (unweighted) tag to enable accessing just that Revision. Revisions that are not referenced by at least one Route cannot receive requests and will remain scaled to zero.

Configurations

Configurations describe the current desired application state as a template for Revisions. Each time a Configuration is updated, it creates a new Revision capturing the current desired state of the application. Configurations can be thought of as the HEAD of a version control configuration—the latest state to which updates should be applied.

Revisions

Revisions are an immutable checkpoint of the application's configuration as requested by the Configuration. They act as the unit of scaling and as traffic targets: Knative automates the management of Revisions (creation and garbage collection), so users shouldn't need to actively manage Revisions. At the same time, Revisions are extremely handy when the latest changes introduce an error—it's trivial to update Routes to point to an earlier Revision to restore service.

The relationships among the Knative Serving resources can be visualized as Figure 3-2.

---

11 The name Service is overloaded; in Kubernetes, it means a cluster TCP load balancer; in other systems, it has other meanings. Naming is hard.

12 The actual load balancer implementation in Knative uses a pluggable interface called *Ingress* in the `networking.internal.knative.dev` API group.

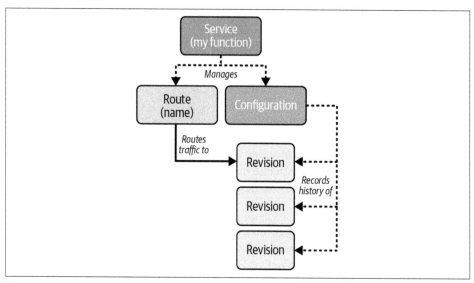

Figure 3-2. Knative serving resources

Most Knative users are happy to manage their applications with Services and occasionally update the traffic routing of the Service to redirect traffic to an older or newer Revision (for incremental rollouts or to roll back a failed change). Some users with more sophisticated needs (for example, having "beta" and "GA" interfaces using the same Revision pool) will end up managing Routes and Configurations directly, bypassing the Service layer altogether. By composing Services from the fields in Route and Configuration, it's easy to switch between the two layers if you discover your needs are more sophisticated than you first expected.

Now that we understand how to express our application's desired configuration in Knative, let's dive into *how* Knative takes these intents and delivers a serverless platform.

Life of a Request

Earlier, we described the difference between control planes and data planes in a footnote; in particular, we described the data plane as components that need to directly handle each request. In this section, we'll give a tour of the Knative Serving data plane, tracing the different components that handle an incoming request from the point that the TCP connection from a user reaches the edge of a Kubernetes cluster until the last response byte is sent back to the user. Note that Knative Serving supports multiple HTTP protocols, so some of these descriptions may gloss over details like HTTP/2 multiplexing of request streams over the same TCP connection.

Because Knative aims to be Kubernetes-native and take advantage of the existing Kubernetes ecosystem of infrastructure components, Knative Serving implements a plug-in load-balancing API that supports multiple HTTP router implementations, including Istio, Contour, and the Gateway API. There is also a bespoke implementation of this API called Kourier for clusters that do not need a general-purpose HTTP proxy implementation.

 The plugability and integration with other Kubernetes components is a core tenet of Knative—the goal is to enable developers and system administrators to leverage their existing investments in both proxy setup and advanced policies such as authentication or rate-limiting that the proxy might support.

Because Knative uses an HTTP load balancer to route traffic between Revisions, the recommended Knative configuration is to use a wildcard (match-any) DNS record like *.mycluster.mydomain.com to point requests to the Knative load balancer. Knative can then be configured to provision Service hostnames of the form <myservice>.<mynamespace>.mycluster.mydomain.com, which allows new Services to be created and configured by simply adding new accepted hostnames to the existing HTTP load balancer without needing to make further changes to DNS (which often requires tickets in most organizations).

Once requests have arrived in the cluster, Knative handles routing the requests either directly to an application pod (if one is ready) or to a component called the activator if there are no pods with available capacity. The activator's job is to stall (buffer) the request until a pod is available, sending a signal to the autoscaler that there is additional demand for the requested Revision (this could be a scale-from-zero event or scaling additional pods to handle a traffic burst). Each pod in the system consists of an application instance as well as a queue-proxy container that communicates load to the autoscaler and handles undifferentiated heavy lifting. The diagram in Figure 3-3 illustrates the components of the Knative data plane.

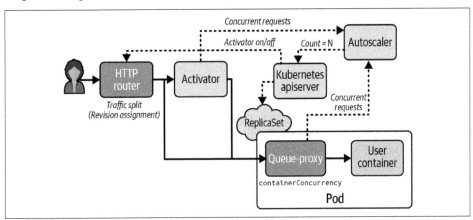

Figure 3-3. Knative serving request flow

In the following subsections, we'll explore the components starting from the application client on the left through the various request-routing layers. After completing our tour of the request-processing components, we'll discuss how the metrics reported from the data path are utilized by the Knative autoscaler to provision new instances when needed.

Load balancer and cluster ingress

The cluster ingress may be shared with other nonserverless applications on the cluster; Knative Serving will leverage the ingress for both general-purpose and Knative-specific functionality. Most Kubernetes clusters that provide HTTP services will find it useful to install an ingress provider. Some of the reasons for this are as follows:

- Provide HTTP protocol version translation from the client's application to the server's supported version. Newer versions of HTTP, such as HTTP/2 or HTTP/3, implement more complex traffic and flow-control mechanisms to achieve higher performance over congested and high-latency internet links. Within a datacenter, latency is much lower and bandwidth is more readily available, making it attractive for application authors to use simpler libraries that may not support the latest HTTP versions.

- Implement best practices and protect applications from protocol-level attacks by normalizing request headers and URLs and implementing defenses against protocol-level attacks. Proper request handling is an ongoing cat-and-mouse game, and it's much more efficient for a platform team to implement these defenses once at the ingress router than to ensure that each application has patches available and that the patches have been applied. This can also include implementing request-level timeouts to provide error messages to clients when backends are unavailable.

- Terminate and manage TLS connections and certificates in a consistent manner, so that individual applications do not need to implement TLS. Similarly to HTTP protocol translation, implementing and managing the various TLS-level configuration options for high performance is a task best performed once, as requests enter the Kubernetes cluster.

- Using a single ingress can be advantageous in preserving IPv4 address space; by using a single router with multiple certificates and routing requests based on the Host header, hundreds or thousands of applications can be hosted behind a single IP address. Most Kubernetes ingresses support using a TCP-level load balancer to distribute the requests across a pool of ingress proxies; Envoy is a common proxy option that implements a high-performance reverse proxy with a gRPC configuration interface.

- Relatedly, sharing ingress components helps reduce the incremental cost of adding a new low-traffic serverless application to the cluster. With a shared load balancer, DNS record, and IP address, a serverless application with no traffic consumes practically zero resources when not in use.

In addition to the general best practices supporting the use of an ingress proxy or router, Knative also leverages the advanced capabilities of several routers to implement traffic splitting between Revisions. Knative implements traffic splitting by defining multiple backend destinations with weights corresponding to the desired traffic split, and encoding the traffic split decision in a custom header that can be used by the `activator` downstream component to ensure that the split decision is made exactly once. Once a given Revision is selected, it is routed to a Kubernetes Service named for the Revision.

Depending on load and Revision capacity, the Kubernetes Service corresponding to the Revision will contain *either* endpoints corresponding to the Revision pods or endpoints of shared Knative `activator` processes. When the service does not have sufficient capacity to handle a burst of traffic, the `activator` is configured as the destination for Knative Revisions to act as a capacity buffer and enable scaling from zero instances if needed. As Revision capacity crosses the burst threshold, the `activator` endpoints are replaced with the Revision endpoints directly, avoiding an extra proxy hop and reducing the overhead per request.

Activator

The Knative Serving `activator` is a shared pool of proxies that serve as a capacity buffer for Revisions. When the `activator` receives a request, it attempts to route the request to an active Revision instance. If no Revision instance is currently available, it enqueues the request (reads the HTTP headers but does not forward the request), and signals the autoscaler that there are queued requests for the given Revision. The `activator` also reports ongoing metrics about requests in-flight and total requests for aggregation by the autoscaler scaling algorithm. While the `activator` has requests queued, it tracks the pool of available Revision instances and attempts to find an instance that has capacity—either an existing instance that has finished processing a request or a newly started backend created by the actions of the autoscaler.

The `activator` maintains the request in its queue until either a backend is available or the request times out. If sufficient requests arrive in a burst, the `activator` can end up with many queued requests, but in normal operation, few, if any, requests are waiting in the queue. Because the `activator` is actively forwarding the request to an instance, the `activator` must process both requests and responses; this allows it to report to the autoscaler on metrics like throughput as well as requests in-flight for a given Revision.

While it would be possible to extract the `activator` from the data plane as soon as a single backend is ready, keeping it in the request path when a Revision is lightly loaded has these advantages:

- When the activator is in the request path, the Kubernetes Service points at a *subset* of the `activators` on the cluster. Using subsetting means that the connections are aggregated to a small number of proxies, which enables the use of load-balancing algorithms like least-loaded without coordination overhead. This has been validated by benchmarking to reduce the latency variability when using a small pool of application servers.[13]

- Reprogramming the ingress control plane can be expensive. By deferring the change in backends until it's clear that the application is under sustained load, the autoscaler can reduce the amount of churn in the ingress control plane.

If scaling to zero is not important, it's possible to disable the `activator` completely by zeroing out the burst threshold and setting a minimum number of instances on each Revision. This might be appropriate, for example, in a system that needs to be highly available even if the Kubernetes control plane is down or if the application has a long startup time.

Once the `activator` has found a Revision instance with available capacity, it will forward the request to the `queue-proxy`, which is colocated with the application container and performs the final level of processing before routing the request to the application.

Queue-proxy

The `queue-proxy` process is added automatically by the Knative Serving control plane and runs as a sidecar alongside the application container.[14] The `queue-proxy` implements per-instance request-handling functionality including lifecycle management, request metrics, and concurrency enforcement. Unlike the `activator`, the `queue-proxy` is *always* in the request path, even under high application load. Because it is running in the same pod as the application container, it communicates with the application container over `localhost`, which has much lower overhead than off-machine network communication.

---

13 See this Knative design document—"Better Load Balancing in Activator" by Victor Agababov (*https://oreil.ly/LhBHJ*)—for some of the background on these changes; these changes evolved over the course of about six months across more than fifty pull requests.

14 In Kubernetes parlance, *sidecars* are helper containers that run alongside the main application. These containers might provide debugging, networking, or security services, for example.

The main responsibilities of the `queue-proxy` are as follows:

- Report request metrics to both the autoscaler and to any configured monitoring system. Being adjacent to the application container, the `queue-proxy` can measure application latency separate from the network queuing delays that might happen through either the ingress or the `activator`.

- Implement hard request-concurrency limits, if requested. Because the `queue-proxy` is 1:1 with the application container, it can easily keep track of the number of concurrent requests in-flight. If a request is made beyond the application's concurrency limit, the `queue-proxy` can queue the request until the application has finished another in-flight request. Many FaaS platforms enforce a concurrency of one in-flight request per instance; this feature enables running those types of functions safely while also enabling threaded applications to implement request-per-thread or other threading models with higher concurrency limits.

- Quickly detect readiness at startup. The default Kubernetes behavior is to check for application readiness at most once per second. This can add up to a second of additional cold-start delay when starting a new instance; the `queue-proxy` implements more aggressive subsecond probing until the readiness probe returns success, then reduces the probe frequency to the requested rate. Combined with rapid probing from the `activator` for newly created pods, these optimizations can reduce cold-start time by approximately one second.[15]

- Implement graceful shutdown using the "lame duck" technique: continue handling existing requests until all have completed, but refuse new requests. While some application frameworks implement graceful shutdown on their own, implementing graceful shutdown on Kubernetes requires coordinating between the `terminationGracePeriodSeconds` parameter and the application shutdown code. Knative does this automatically, so application containers can simply exit when they receive a termination signal.

Unlike other components like the autoscaler, the `queue-proxy` runs alongside each application container. Many hosted serverless runtimes combine the `queue-proxy` type component with the component that creates containers; because Knative is built on Kubernetes, which already has a container management component, the `queue-proxy` can be much smaller. In hosted platforms, the equivalent component that does the job of `queue-proxy` and `kubelet` may also be a multitenant component; in Knative, each `queue-proxy` instance is associated with exactly one instance (and therefore, one customer or Kubernetes namespace).

---

15 One second may not sound like a lot, until you're the user staring at your web browser wondering, "Will this page load anything?"

Now that we have a fairly complete understanding of the data-plane components of Knative serving, we'll dig into the component that bridges the gap between the control plane and data plane: the autoscaler.

Autoscaling Control Loop

As we saw in the "Life of a Request" on page 56, Knative components handle incoming requests at several points in the request path. This provides substantial additional visibility into application behavior and performance compared with the typical Kubernetes Horizontal Pod Autoscaler (HPA), which typically operates on high-level CPU and memory metrics at an interval of one minute. While it's possible to request that a Knative Revision is managed by the HPA, Knative also provides its own autoscaler (called the *Knative Pod Autoscaler*, or *KPA*), which operates on higher-fidelity request metrics collected from the request path.

The KPA can collect metrics from both the `activator` (if in the path) and the `queue-proxy` component, and implements request-based autoscaling based on either concurrency (the number of requests in-flight) or request rate (requests per second, closer to a traditional HPA design). This is illustrated in Figure 3-4.

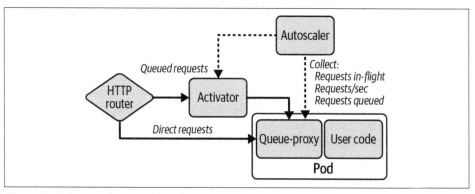

Figure 3-4. Autoscaler metrics collection

In either case, the autoscaler collects data on a much higher granularity and can also scale from zero because it can read "delayed request" counts from the `activator` when there are no `queue-proxy` pods. The autoscaler implements a few tricks to make this data collection rate more scalable than the Kubernetes metrics API; in particular, it implements an efficient gRPC protocol and uses sampling for large backend sets to limit the amount of work per cycle. The autoscaler then implements a number of control loop calculations[16] to compute a desired replica count for the current load,

---

16 I'm not describing most of the tuning knobs here because they are likely to change over time, and the website information will be most up-to-date.

---

and then updates the desired number of instances of the underlying deployment to trigger the standard Kubernetes pod provisioning or removal processes.

One special autoscaling algorithm that is worth mentioning is *panic mode*: if the autoscaler detects that pending traffic awaiting assignment to an instance is greater than some multiple of the current capacity, it immediately attempts to increase capacity in a doubling manner until capacity exceeds the requests in-flight. This mode may produce some overshoot but ensures that a sudden burst of requests does not cause requests to be timed out while waiting for an instance to become ready. This pattern of sudden bursts of traffic is common for clock-driven fan-out scenarios in serverless, such as a cron job that enqueues an update message for each item in a database table.

Most other serverless compute platforms follow a similar model to Knative on the data plane, with requests being routed from client to server with one or more components that can "pause" a request until an instance is ready to handle it. The one major exception that I'm aware of is AWS Lambda, which uses a slightly different data path, which we'll cover next.

Comparison with AWS Lambda

Much of the detail in this section comes from a great re:Invent talk in 2018 by Holly Mesrobian and Marc Brooker titled "AWS Lambda Under the Hood" (*https://oreil.ly/ Mdh8X*). In it, they dive into the details of how AWS Lambda handles requests. Unlike Knative and many other serverless platforms, AWS Lambda functions operate on a *pull* model of fetching work to be done. As components within the AWS ecosystem request Lambda invocations, the invocation record is put onto a per-function queue in shared infrastructure, as shown in Figure 3-5. Lambda workers then fetch work from this queue, with a worker manager process scaling the number of workers as needed.

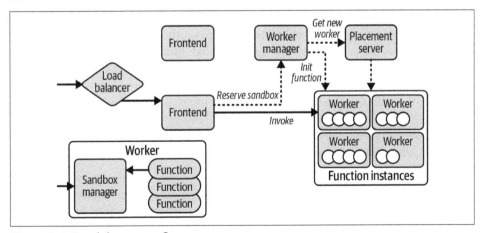

Figure 3-5. Lambda request flow

This mechanism needs a high-performance queue and careful coordination between the workers and the top-level scheduler. Each node-level AWS worker process spawns and manages multiple application containers on the host, each of which processes a single request at a time by long-polling the worker for invocation records. While an application is polling the worker, the worker can throttle the application CPU until it is ready to return from the API call with a new invocation request.

Similarly to the Knative autoscaler, a central coordinator process monitors the active workers and directs additional workers to monitor the function queue when a backlog occurs; this is similar to the queues that can occur in the `activator` when a burst of traffic occurs. Unlike the `activator`, AWS Lambda invocation requests are *always* stored and read from a queue. By storing the request in a queue, if a request fails because of timeouts or application crashes, it is possible to retry the invocations. In Knative Serving, these failed requests will be returned to the caller; in exchange, Knative Serving supports a wider range of HTTP behaviors, including WebSocket and streaming HTTP/2 requests. These protocols would be difficult for Lambda's queue-based architecture to support.

The Lambda design is well suited for asynchronous invocation and event processing; synchronous events require the requester to await the completion of an invocation. Given the origins of AWS as an event-processing mechanism and the integration of event registration and delivery into Lambda, the use of a pull-based mechanism makes sense. As Knative components aim to be separable and independently useful, Knative chose instead to build an HTTP-based serverless mechanism and separate event-distribution tools in Knative Eventing.

Eventing

Knative Eventing aims to provide a platform for asynchronously routing events from event producers (components that can observe the events taking place) to event consumers (components that want to be notified that the event occurred). "Events" is a fancy way of describing stored messages that indicate that a certain change was observed. Because the messages are stored and delivered asynchronously, producers publish events without knowing how many components are consuming the message—the message can be copied to each interested consumer (or there may be no interested consumers, and the message would be discarded). In this context, asynchronous delivery means that producers can durably send events without needing to wait for acknowledgment or delivery to consumers and without needing to worry about managing retries and delivery failures.

In particular, an early goal of Knative Eventing was to enable *late binding* of producers and consumers—it should be possible to connect consumers to producers without either component needing to know the configuration of the other. For example, an order-processing system might publish an event to Knative Eventing indicating that a customer has placed an order. The order-processing system doesn't need to keep track of all the other systems that react to the order being created, and it's easy to add a new system to the set of listeners for the order creation—for example, a fraud-detection system or a loyalty rewards system can be added without needing to change the configuration of the order-processing component.

 When building loosely coupled applications, the event itself acts as an API between the source system and further event processors. Knative Eventing provides the glue between the components using the attributes of the event to route the event to the correct location.

Some serverless platforms (like AWS Lambda, mentioned earlier) make the subscription part of the serverless resource definition. Knative Eventing goes in the opposite direction to describe event delivery infrastructure that is independent of the infrastructure used to process the events. It's entirely feasible to use a Kubernetes deployment or even a VM as a destination for event delivery; Knative Eventing is *serverless* in the sense that each event delivery is a unit of work, and the underlying components can scale dynamically without needing developer intervention.[17]

While Knative Eventing is independent of Serving, the two are designed to work well together. Knative Eventing uses a standard called CloudEvents (*https://oreil.ly/ GOLXP*) to store and process event messages—in particular, CloudEvents defines a mechanism for delivering events using the HTTP protocol. By standardizing event delivery on CloudEvents-over-HTTP, it is easy to connect Knative Serving as a consumer of events routed by Knative Eventing. Additionally, since the CloudEvents format is intentionally simple (a CloudEvent contains multiple header-like `attributes` and an arbitrary opaque payload), it is easy for applications to act as event publishers with a simple HTTP POST. Finally, the event-distribution components of Eventing support transactionally enqueueing a reply message in response to an event delivery by leveraging the HTTP response to return an event to the message sender.

We'll start our overview of Knative Eventing in the same way as Serving, by describing the major control-plane concepts and the mental model for interacting with Eventing.

---

17 Since Knative Eventing is pluggable into different underlying message transports in the same way that Knative Serving plugs into different ingresses, how serverless the eventing experience is depends on the underlying message transport.

Control-Plane Concepts

While Serving has a single top-level object to manage a single application, Knative Eventing has two core objects, illustrated in Figure 3-6, which represent the two sides of the producer/consumer relationship:

Brokers

Brokers represent a single event-routing domain. Within a Broker, CloudEvents are dispatched by matching patterns of attributes on the CloudEvent, which can either be well-known attributes like `type` (a reverse-DNS string) or custom attributes defined by the sender (similar to HTTP headers). Producers can send an event to the Broker for delivery using an HTTP POST of the event contents in CloudEvents format. Because the Broker represents an abstract interface, each Broker resource can request a specific implementation (such as Apache Kafka, RabbitMQ, or in-memory storage for testing) when it is created.

Triggers

A Trigger represents a subscription or expression of interest from an event consumer in a specific set of event messages routed by the Broker. Consumers use an attribute-matching pattern to indicate the events of interest. A single Broker may host zero or many Triggers; a Trigger that points to a nonexistent Broker will not receive any messages until the Broker exists.

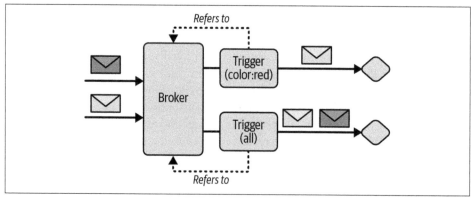

Figure 3-6. Broker and Trigger

In addition to the core Broker and Trigger concepts, Knative Eventing has an ecosystem of additional, optional resources that simplify producing events and building certain messaging patterns:

Sources

    While applications can submit events to a Broker by POSTing events that they observe, event sources provide precanned resources for observing changes in common external systems. Examples include Amazon S3 uploads, Kubernetes `apiserver` changes, and GitHub comments. Sources provide a prebuilt resource and implementation that exposes the common configuration options without requiring the user to understand how the underlying event listener is built and configured.

Channels, Subscriptions, Sequence, and Parallel

    These resources provide low-level event-routing capabilities for building event-processing pipelines; unlike Brokers and Triggers, these resources do not provide built-in filtering capabilities, though Sequence and Parallel may use functions that do not return an event to shortcut further processing of an event, as illustrated in Figure 3-7.

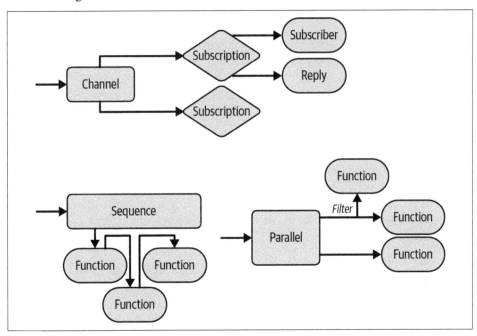

Figure 3-7. Knative message-processing constructs

For the purposes of our exploration in this chapter, we'll focus primarily on the Broker and Trigger abstractions. As mentioned in the description of Brokers, Knative Eventing supports pluggable message transports with substantially broader semantic variations than the Serving ingresses. I'll attempt to describe the major differences in the text, but a variety of smaller differences will be glossed over. As always, all the details of the implementations can be found in the Knative documentation or source code.

Delivery Guarantees

Before going into the life of an event, it's worth defining the semantics of what it means to "deliver an event." Unlike an HTTP request in Serving, Eventing clients don't receive feedback on whether the destination was able to handle an event successfully (that's the drawback of asynchronous delivery). Messaging systems generally attempt to fall into one of two categories in terms of delivery semantics: "at least once" and "at most once."

As the name describes, *at-least-once* message delivery systems attempt to make sure that any message accepted into the system reaches each recipient at least once. Users of the system can be sure that messages will be delivered to their desired destination, but they may need to cope with *duplicate event delivery*. Consider the case that a message is sent to a consumer, the consumer processes it, and then the consumer crashes before it can acknowledge the event. The event-delivery system must now decide: should it attempt to deliver the message again? In an at-least-once regime, the answer is yes.

The complement[18] of at-least-once message delivery is *at most once*. In this delivery system, users will never need to worry about duplicated messages, but some messages may be dropped. At-most-once messaging is helpful when building low-latency data streams, but requires careful thought and design to handle the possibility of missed messages.

As Knative Eventing aims to simplify common use cases and provide tools that can be used safely by nonexperts, Knative Eventing aims to implement *at-least-once* delivery. "Exactly Once Is Hard" on page 186 describes how to handle duplicate event delivery in some detail, but a good rule of thumb is to try to make event delivery idempotent (repeatable) where possible, and use a transactional database to track events otherwise. Now that we've set the stage, let's talk about how event delivery actually happens.

 Knative Eventing (particularly the Broker component) is specifically targeted at simplifying the process of building event-driven applications for new practitioners. Of course, part of providing a tool that fits the needs of new practitioners is baking in the most common patterns used by experts, so Eventing is also a good tool for more complex scenarios.

---

18 In the mathematical sense.

Life of an Event

As described briefly earlier, events are observed and published by application code when something of possible interest happens. From the point of view of the event distribution system, there's no systematic difference between events published from a packaged "Source" resource type and events published by an application whose main purpose is something else.[19] In either case, once the event is received and acknowledged by the Broker with a 200 response, it's the responsibility of the Broker to deliver the event to all registered Triggers that match the event.

Because Knative Eventing supports multiple transports with different implementations of storing and routing events, the descriptions here will be somewhat less precise than the request flow in "Life of a Request" on page 56. At the time of this writing, the three main implementations for Knative Eventing are Kafka, RabbitMQ, and an in-memory implementation for testing. I'll call out the differences when these implementations vary—for example, RabbitMQ Topic Exchanges natively support filtering, while Kafka supports delivering messages in order. Native broker implementations can take advantage of and expose these features to applications using Broker configuration references or annotations on the resources in question.

Figure 3-8 illustrates the general data-plane components of a Knative Source, Broker, and Trigger implementation, along with a generic underlying storage system for the Broker. Note that the Broker and Trigger combination is the only component that interacts with the underlying message persistence system; other components leverage the Broker's high availability to avoid needing to implement their own message persistence.

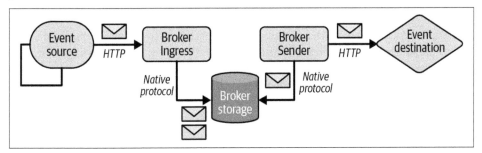

Figure 3-8. Knative Broker event flow

---

19 We'll talk about this "inner monologue" more in Chapter 7.

In the following subsections, we'll explore the components starting from the event source and then covering the capabilities and responsibilities of each process that interacts directly with the event. After completing our tour of the event-processing data flow, we'll talk a bit about the larger Knative ecosystem of event sources and how applications can leverage the same data-plane capabilities as event sources.

Event source

Event sources may be implemented in several ways. In general, event sources either participate in or observe occurrences of events in an outside system. This system might be a third-party API (such as GitHub) or an internal component like an application login service.

Event sources break down along two major axes, which roughly align with the control plane and the data plane for event sources. The two main control-plane categories are declarative components represented as Kubernetes objects and integral events implemented as a side effect of a running application. On the data plane, event sources may collect the events to be sent either via polling the system state (pull based) or via immediate reactions to occurrences (push based). Most integral event producers are push based because it is often easiest to implement the event-publishing observation alongside the code that implements the state change. Declarative event sources may use a mix of these two techniques, depending on the APIs available to observe the system.

In all cases, it is the responsibility of the event source to transform observations of state changes to CloudEvents that are published to the Broker using HTTP POST (the push model). While it is possible for event sources to implement durable storage for events that have not yet been published, it is often simpler in the push model to add some synchronous retries to the delivery, particularly for event publishers that are implemented in the integral pattern. Generally, event sources will rely on the event ingress to be highly available—the goal for Eventing is to make simple common cases easy (such as publishing events from an existing application) while making hard things possible with some elbow grease.

Broker Ingress

The job of the *Broker Ingress* is to receive CloudEvents from senders (event sources) and persist the events in the backend storage service *before* responding to the sender with a 2xx HTTP response code (success). Sending an HTTP response only after the message has been successfully stored enables at-least-once delivery: if the sender does not receive a successful response, it should retry the event delivery. If the Broker already successfully received the event, resending the event might cause a duplicate message; the eventual recipient should be prepared to handle duplicate events either by implementing idempotent delivery or by ignoring events with duplicate source and id attributes.

A successful event delivery to the ingress (the normal case) looks like Figure 3-9. If there are errors validating or persisting the event, the ingress will report a 500 error code, indicating that the sender should try again.

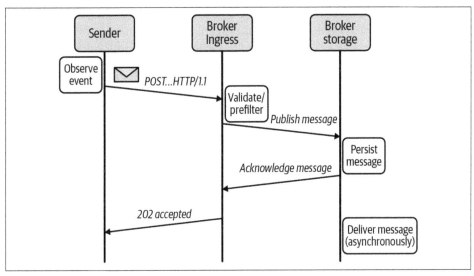

Figure 3-9. Event acceptance process

While not required, most of the Broker data-plane implementations are multitenant; that is, the same underlying ingress instances can provide the ingress for multiple Brokers, including Brokers in different namespaces within the same cluster. They typically do this by advertising either different hostnames or different URL paths for the different Broker addresses; using a single pool of data-plane components reduces the cost of allocating a Broker that may handle only a few events per day.

This type of multitenant service, where many low-capacity resources are mapped to a single service instance, is another example of a serverless design pattern—since the developer is not exposed to the number of servers backing their resources, they may be assigned a fraction of a larger pool of autoscaled instances. At the same time, running a single pool of ingress instances makes it easier for platform providers to manage the instances compared with provisioning and managing hundreds of small, underutilized service instances.

Running a multitenant Broker implementation introduces additional security requirements depending on your environment. While each Broker has a unique ingress URL, sharing the underlying infrastructure may lead to sharing more resources than desired: network IPs and ports (for TCP-level NetworkPolicy), network bandwidth, and CPU time may all be shared among components. For many organizations running a private serverless infrastructure, these problems can be handled with a pinch of overprovisioning and a handful of "my boss knows your boss."[20] For environments that need stronger isolation guarantees, it's worth investigating the implementation strategies of different Brokers when choosing your infrastructure.

Some Brokers may implement additional functionality in the ingress. If the underlying storage layer supports it, the ingress may automatically deduplicate redelivered events—either by keeping an in-memory map of recently seen events or by mapping the source and id attributes to fields that can be deduplicated in the underlying messaging system. Another optimization (at the cost of complexity) is to perform early filtering of messages in the ingress—events that do not match any Trigger filter when the event is received can be immediately dropped without writing them to storage. This can help in implementing the inner monologue pattern in Chapter 7 by reducing the cost of publishing events with no current listeners. The trade-off for this optimization is that the Trigger configuration needs to be propagated to more components, increasing the complexity of the Broker implementation.

Typically, the ingress component will be implemented to take advantage of horizontal pod autoscaling (adding more instances as load increases), within the bounds of instances supported by the underlying message storage. This storage may be a single storage instance or a clustered solution—the latter solutions are ideal for large numbers of clients or high-volume processing.

Broker storage

The underlying message storage and transport used by the Broker will tend to be an existing messaging system, such as RabbitMQ or Kafka. These systems generally have dozens to hundreds of years of engineering experience applied to the problem of message durability and performance, taking into account various distributed failure scenarios and management concerns. Rather than attempt to match and reimplement all of these features, Knative Eventing implements a stateless translation layer that presents the most important transport options from the messaging system (for example, partition count for Kafka or delivery parallelism in RabbitMQ) while abstracting away implementation details (like message prefetching in RabbitMQ).

---

20 I think of this as the traditional IT solution matrix.

Why Wrap Message Systems?

You might be wondering: why wrap an already perfectly capable messaging system with all this additional pomp and infrastructure? It's a good question, and there are two main motivations for this extra layer.

First, each messaging system has its own language-specific libraries, configuration, and behavior. Knative Eventing defines a unifying abstraction across several messaging systems, allowing applications to be built and deployed with different transport mechanisms for development and testing environments (where a cheap in-memory transport may suffice) and staging and production environments (where a more expensive durable message queue may need to be provisioned). Abstracting the delivery mechanism also simplifies the process of building polyglot (multiprogramming language) systems; it's no longer a concern if library X for language A implements a different set of message-processing features than library Y for language B. For example, the Kafka Broker data plane is implemented in Java because of that language's superior Kafka support, while the RabbitMQ data plane is implemented in the Go language.

Second, many existing libraries and messaging systems are implemented based on polling the message server. This works well for applications that are running all the time but works poorly for serverless applications that scale to zero in the absence of work. The Kubernetes-based Event Driven Autoscaler (KEDA) project takes a different approach and uses queue depth metrics exported by the message server to drive autoscaling of traditional polling libraries. This is a good piecemeal approach but doesn't mesh well with Knative Serving or other HTTP-actuated applications.

While it's helpful that the Broker abstracts away some of the details of the underlying messaging system, it's important to note that Broker specification allows considerable leeway for different message-delivery behaviors based on the underlying messaging system. This is by design—attempting to force all implementations to implement the same inter-message ordering semantics (for example) would add expensive and hard-to-get-correct wrappers around the underlying battle-tested delivery mechanisms. Furthermore, users who wanted different delivery semantics would then be dependent on Knative to add support for their desired delivery mode.[21] Instead, Knative Eventing offers users a choice of message-delivery semantics by allowing users to choose the underlying Broker implementation—Kafka users get partition-ordered delivery, while RabbitMQ, NATS, or in-memory implementations get unordered delivery.

---

21 The main example is ordered delivery, which implies that a message that is slow to process blocks delivery of later messages. This is called *head-of-line-blocking*; this property is desirable for stream-processing systems that like to handle messages in order, but undesirable for systems that attempt to minimize overall message-processing latency.

Some implementations (such as RabbitMQ) natively support filtering mechanisms *within* the messaging system. In RabbitMQ, this is called a *Headers Exchange*, and supports exact-match semantics on an arbitrary list of message attributes. The Broker can configure the underlying RabbitMQ exchange with the exact-match filters from the Trigger, reducing both the amount of code and the number of messages that need to be read and handled by the Broker Sender (see the next section for the responsibilities of the Broker Sender).

The main underlying Broker requirement on a messaging system is that it supports publish-subscribe semantics: a message published by a sender can be delivered and acknowledged *independently* for each subscriber, as shown in Figure 3-10. Some messaging systems implement a single point-to-point delivery channel where enqueued messages can be read by only a single subscriber. A Broker implementation based on a point-to-point channel would need to attempt delivery to *all* Trigger endpoints before acknowledging the message—if any Trigger endpoint failed, the message would need to be requeued and delivery to *all* Trigger endpoints reattempted. While this would technically be a valid implementation, it would generate an undesirably high number of duplicate deliveries if a single endpoint malfunctioned.

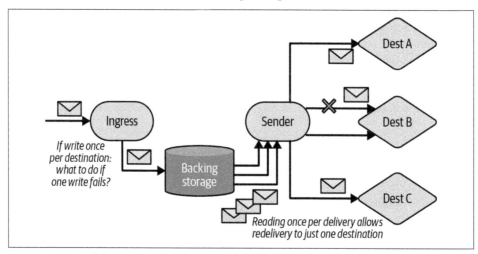

Figure 3-10. Redelivery to a failing destination

Most messaging systems are implemented as storage systems with a "watch" or "long poll" behavior for subscribers; others simply implement a polling loop in the subscriber library. The storage system semantic means that both the Broker Ingress and the Broker Sender will initiate connections to the messaging system. Since Knative Eventing implements a consistent "push" semantic for work in the system, the sender component of the Broker needs to run continuously to convert the messaging system pull semantics to Eventing's push semantics.

Broker Sender

The *Broker Sender* is the complement of the Broker Ingress; for each Trigger destination, the sender consumes messages from the messaging system and then delivers them to the event destination if appropriate. Each Trigger typically corresponds to a separate fan-out subscriber; a single Broker Sender may manage many messaging system subscribers (one per Trigger), or the Broker implementation may spawn a separate process for each Trigger subscription. This is an implementation trade-off between simplicity, efficiency, and isolation: a Broker that implements a multitenant sender may need to implement some form of fairness among different Triggers or among Triggers in different namespaces, while a Broker that implements separate processes for each Trigger may end up with a high per-Trigger overhead that eliminates any resource savings associated with serverless scale-to-zero.

Regardless of the tenancy model, the message processing for a single Trigger subscription is consistent; multitenant senders simply pack many subscription handlers into a single container process. In most implementations,[22] Trigger filtering patterns are evaluated in the Broker Sender process; messages that don't match the Trigger's filters are acknowledged in the messaging system but not delivered. This filtering takes places in the Broker Sender rather than the ingress because a particular event might match some Triggers and not others. This architecture is illustrated in Figure 3-11.

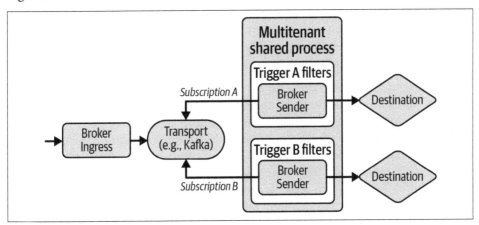

Figure 3-11. Broker sending implementation

An alternative architecture would be to create separate messaging topics for each set of Trigger matches; e.g., "matches A and C but not B," "matches A but not B and C,"

---

22 Some transport implementations, like RabbitMQ with Topic Exchanges or Google PubSub, support defining filters within the transport. This simplifies the implementation of senders.

etc. As you can probably see, this would create 2^n message topics for a single Broker. For most messaging systems, message topics introduce a high overhead in the system, so it's more efficient to perform the filtering at the Broker Sender than to manage many topics and classify messages at the ingress.[23]

Once a message has been selected by the Trigger filter, delivery uses a similar (reversed) pattern from ingress: the sender attempts a delivery to the destination, and ensures a successful destination response before marking the message as completed in the messaging system. Again, this pattern preserves the at-least-once delivery guarantee of Knative Eventing, at the possible cost of duplicate event deliveries in the case of a partial delivery failure. Depending on the Broker settings and the underlying messaging system, it's possible for the event sender to have many outstanding delivery attempts to the destination at the same time.[24]

In addition to delivering the filtered message stream to the event destination, the event sender is responsible for handling any response events returned by the event destination in the response to the HTTP event delivery. This response event contract provides a simple way for applications to implement transactional "process event X and produce event Y" transformations and implement simple workflows. For Event Brokers, the reply events are implicitly delivered to the same Broker that originated the event and can be filtered to other Triggers on the same Broker. While the Broker can detect and break simple loops, it is possible (and occasionally useful) to construct reply routing loops within a set of Triggers on a Broker. Because the lower-level Channel and Subscription primitives do not support filtered delivery, Subscriptions have an explicit reply parameter to allow delivery of responses to a different Channel. The processing of reply events is depicted in Figure 3-12.

The event sender is responsible for much of the "heavy lifting" around at-least-once delivery semantics to the event destination defined in the Trigger. In the common successful case, most events will be delivered directly to the destination once; in the case of failure, the event sender is responsible for implementing timeouts, retries, and, in the case of persistent failures, storage of messages on a dead-letter queue if configured. Handling all of these semantics along with delivery parallelism allows the destination to focus on the logic of handling the event in an HTTP transaction without worrying about the remaining messaging administrivia.

---

23 It would be an interesting experiment to optimize between early- and late-filtering automatically based on the message topology. I'm not aware of any systems that do this today; early discussions in Eventing included the idea of separating high-volume message flows into a separate topic, but this has so far not been necessary.

24 Networking-inclined readers may note that the message-delivery pattern looks a bit like guaranteed delivery protocols like TCP, and may wonder about flow-control semantics like TCP's slow start. As of 2023, I'm not aware of any Broker Senders that implement this type of flow control.

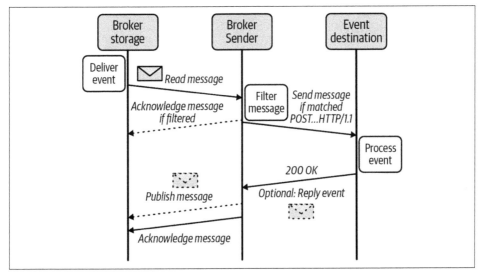

Figure 3-12. Trigger delivery sequence

Event destination

The event destination could be a Knative Service or any other endpoint that supports HTTP. A Knative subscription follows a pattern known as *deliverable* (shown in Example 3-1), which supports delivering events to both Kubernetes objects by name, other resources by URL, or combining object references and relative URLs if needed. The deliverable shape is used consistently for event destinations across Knative Eventing resources; in addition to the subscription of a Trigger, it is used for dead-letter destinations, within Channel subscriptions, and in packaged event sources.

Example 3-1. Knative deliverable shape

```
subscription:
  ref:  # A Kubernetes object reference
    apiVersion: serving.knative.dev/v1
    kind: Service
    name: myapp
  uri: /eventhandler  # URI, relative to ref if present
```

The deliverable shape supports objects that have a `status.address.url` field or a list of `status.addresses` objects listing preferred URLs for the object in order (this pattern is called *Addressable*, and Knative Services as well as eventing objects implement it). Additionally, the deliverable supports Kubernetes Services using the standard service DNS names. The `uri` field on the deliverable can be used to further customize the base URL provided by the Addressable, or it can specify an absolute URL with a hostname when appropriate. Because resources like Brokers and Knative Services support Addressable, this makes it easy to chain Eventing components into larger pipelines as appropriate.

Ecosystem

The broader Knative Eventing ecosystem includes not only Brokers and Triggers, but a variety of additional tools for extracting events from external systems and building processing pipelines. It is also extensible through the Addressable contract described in Example 3-1; it's entirely possible to send and receive events through Knative Eventing by using VMs or traditionally scaled services; for example, the Kamelet project wrapping Apache Camel K provides a variety of event-sourcing and management connectors using this approach, as do the Debezium and Apache EventMesh projects.

In addition to the event-routing primitives recommended for common cases, Knative Eventing provides low-level messaging primitives in the Channel and Subscription fan-out primitives and common pipeline patterns building on those primitives in Parallel and Subscription. For more details on event-processing patterns accessible through Knative Eventing, see "What Does Event-Driven Mean?" on page 124.

The important point about Knative Eventing is that event routing is not a closed ecosystem. There are many good reasons to route events from one set of tools to another, and CloudEvents provides the common glue to translate between one messaging system and another. With that said, let's compare the functionality of Knative Brokers with three existing messaging systems: a hosted cloud service that *could* be used to implement a Broker and two existing systems that have Broker implementations.

Comparison with Amazon SNS and Other Cloud Providers

Amazon Simple Notification Service (SNS) is a hosted publish-subscribe system from AWS. Clients publish messages to an SNS topic, and subscribers can filter messages from the topic for delivery to a variety of Amazon services as well as HTTP and SMTP (email) delivery. SNS uses a custom message envelope that contains a set of message attributes and a message payload that is conceptually similar to CloudEvents. Unlike CloudEvents, the exact attribute schema is specific to SNS and is not shared by other systems.

Much like Knative Triggers, SNS subscriptions support filtering messages before delivering them to their destination. SNS supports filtering on both message attributes and message contents for messages in JSON format. The default behavior for SNS is out-of-order delivery, but it also supports a first in, first out (FIFO) ordering in combination with Amazon Simple Queue Service.

Other cloud providers offer similar services under different names with different protocols and message envelopes; these can be a good (serverless) choice if you're interacting mostly with a single cloud provider.

Comparison with RabbitMQ

RabbitMQ is a widely deployed message broker based on the AMQP specification. Written in Erlang, RabbitMQ provides a variety of message-delivery patterns (implemented as exchanges and queues) to support different reliability and event distribution needs. In addition to AMQP, RabbitMQ supports publishing and subscribing via STOMP and MQTT protocols. Configuration is largely performed in-band by application code using the AMQP protocol.

AMQP defines messages that contain a set of attributes and a payload; this maps reasonably well to the CloudEvents model. There are actually two forms of AMQP supported by RabbitMQ: AMQP 0-9-1 (the native model) and AMQP 1.0. The two specs differ substantially in overall semantics, but the message envelope semantics are roughly equivalent. RabbitMQ supports simple fan-out exchanges, prefix- and exact-matched topic exchanges, and a flexible attribute matching ("header") exchange used by the Knative RabbitMQ Broker.

RabbitMQ supports both replicated clusters and federation between clusters to establish larger routing topologies; the default delivery mode uses per-message acknowledgments that can deliver messages out of order; a recent "streams" extension supports in-order delivery.

Comparison with Apache Kafka

Apache Kafka is a distributed event-streaming platform built on a the notion of a partitioned append-only log. It is popular in data processing environments and supports broad message fan-out due to pushing much of the processing to clients. Clients connect to a set of bootstrap servers to get a mapping of topics and partitions to broker instances, and then directly connect to the brokers to read and to write messages to a particular partition. Clients are responsible for mapping messages to partitions and handling mapping updates; the Kafka client library is a thick library (this pattern means that clients manage much of their own state, reducing the state storage requirements on the brokers and bootstrap servers).

Kafka topics represent an append-only set of binary messages (a message log); each message has a payload and a set of headers, and is associated with a particular partition key. The partition key is used to enable parallelism in reading the message log; Kafka maintains a *consumer group* for each reader that records the highest log offset read in each partition by that consumer. The Knative Broker maintains a different consumer group for each Trigger, so that Triggers can retry delivery independently from one another.

Kafka has a broad ecosystem supported by Confluent, Inc.—the core platform is part of the Apache project but a number of additional data-processing tools are commercially licensed. Kafka is also offered as a cloud service by several providers, including Confluent and Amazon.

Eventing Summary

While not all message-storage or message-processing implementations are serverless, serverless systems are an ideal platform for implementing event-driven applications that process independent events. If we look at event-processing systems, we will also notice that receiving and forwarding an event looks a lot like our "independent units of work" definition from Chapter 1. We'll explore more patterns of event-driven architecture in Chapter 6; some of these patterns are supported by Knative, and others are implemented in other systems.

As the summary suggests, many event-routing solutions are available to developers today; a conservative estimate is at least a dozen commercially viable offerings along with a smattering of additional open source offerings that might be related to one or more commercial offerings. Rather than compete with the storage and routing capabilities of these tools, Knative Eventing aims to provide a standard, portable event-distribution layer leveraging existing message-routing systems. Additionally, by orienting around a push model with simple semantics for event destinations, Knative Eventing aims to simplify the process of writing event-handling code, enabling a broad selection of programming languages to participate in event-driven applications.

Functions

A more recent addition to the Knative project, Knative Functions provides a simple way for application developers to write event-processing or HTTP containers. In many FaaS platforms, the input to the runtime is the application source code, and the platform itself compiles the executable from source code as an implementation detail. In contrast, the core abstraction for Knative Serving is a prebuilt container image that can be produced by any number of tools. While Knative Functions introduces an additional tool into the process (as shown in Figure 3-13), it also allows the platform to support new languages and build semantics without changing the core runtime.

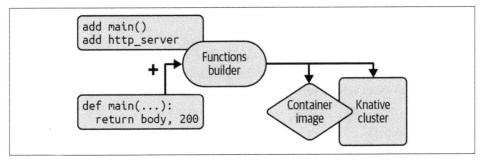

Figure 3-13. Building a function with Knative Functions

Knative Functions leverages the Cloud Native Buildpacks standard (*https://oreil.ly/ _B1q0*) to provide language-specific wrappers and getting-started experiences that simplify the on-ramp to Knative so that developers don't need to understand or manage the process of writing an HTTP server and packaging it into a container to be productive with Knative. While Functions is not "serverless" according to our definition (because it's concerned only with building code and not with running it), FaaS is a popular interaction paradigm for serverless practitioners, and Knative Functions provides a FaaS experience on top of the more flexible underlying Knative Serving primitives.

Because the process of converting source code to a running binary is, by definition, language-specific, Functions provides a language-specific plug-in model for a language-*independent* toolchain that supports a variety of developer use cases:

- *Create* a sample function with the appropriate function signature and documentation on how to use the tool. This provides quick scaffolding for both new and experienced developers.
- *Build* and *publish* a container, either locally or on a remote cluster. This step produces an HTTP-serving container as an independent artifact that could be deployed to any environment.
- *Run* a function locally, using the built container. Running a function locally can be handy for integration testing or for debugging issues.
- *Deploy* a function as a built container on a Knative Serving cluster. This command handles building and publishing the container as well as generation of the Service manifest and applying it to the cluster.

To support these use cases, a language author needs to provide two components:

Function template
This is a source blob with limited templating that should include all the build requirements and a skeleton source file indicating where to add application logic, and any documentation around input/output (I/O) conventions and building the project.

Language buildpack
This is a Cloud Native Buildpack builder that can add the necessary source to produce a functioning application (typically, a main function, an HTTP server, and an HTTP-to-Functions adapter) and then package it into a container. Because Cloud Native Buildpacks are already available for a variety of programming languages, most language buildpacks need only a thin `detect` script and some logic to add source files and appropriate dependencies to the existing user source code.

Knative Functions are an *optional* but convenient way to write small HTTP or event-processing handlers; unlike traditional FaaS platforms, the open ecosystem allows third parties to author language buildpacks supporting less-popular languages, or to experiment with different function signatures and libraries for popular languages (for example, a platform-specific function signature for handling webhooks from a specialized platform).

Summary

Knative provides a capable and full-featured serverless implementation of stateless computation and event routing built on Kubernetes. While the code required to implement Knative itself is not small (a few hundred thousand lines of Go code, including tests), it is much smaller than the full set of code needed to implement a serverless platform. The implementation of Knative in particular is highly dependent on other open source projects such as Kubernetes, Envoy, and Linux, but other serverless platforms have either built comparable abstraction layers or borrowed from existing projects (or a mix of the two). As I'll discuss further in Chapter 11, much of the serverless stack we take for granted is standing on the shoulders of earlier giants.

Before we dive into Part II and the patterns of applying serverless to new and existing applications, we're going to close out the theory with a summary of the business benefits of adding serverless to your technology stack. Adding a new technology to an existing organization has costs—both in training or retraining and in complexity and mental overhead, so even exciting new technologies need to prove that their benefits outweigh the costs. Chapter 4 focuses on why adding serverless to the mix is a net win, even if you can't replace any of your existing tools.

Forces Behind Serverless

This chapter is focused primarily on understanding the ingredients that have come together to make serverless successful now and in the future. (I don't have a crystal ball, but the structural advantages of serverless seem likely to continue until someone figures out an even better way to help developers build scalable applications.)

Three main forces have combined to enable serverless to become a popular paradigm. Today, many organizations still have large, business-critical monoliths—even mainframe applications are a critical part of many industries! Over the next 20 years, I expect to see serverless take a larger role in many of these existing applications, living alongside the existing monoliths and mainframes. This is great—most technologies don't completely replace their predecessors but offer *new* options that are better for new requirements. I expect serverless to become the dominant paradigm for new applications (including low- and no-code applications) *and* for clever technologists to find ways for serverless to integrate with existing technology stacks. The mice and the elephants will be living together, so to speak (Figure 4-1).

Figure 4-1. Serverless and the monolith

The two main drivers of serverless adoption are as follows:

Reduced drag on innovation
All infrastructure has some friction on its use, but serverless reduces the wasted energy in running software.

Microbilling
Focusing on units of work enables a clearer relation between service costs and value delivered.

On first adoption of serverless, these benefits may be small, but each new serverless component increases the payoff for the application as a whole. Once the benefits reach a tipping point, serverless becomes the default for an organization, and tools and infrastructure start to leverage these capabilities in a built-in way. Let's take a look at how each of these drivers works and why the value adds up.

Top Speed: Reducing Drag

Most service projects start out with one or a small number of main server processes—this is called the *monolith* model of development. Over time, the monolith accumulates more and more functionality, until it is the combined work of twenty, fifty, or even hundreds of developers—a total investment of hundreds or thousands of engineering-years (not to mention product-manager years, testing years, etc.). Eventually, monoliths reach the point where they are so large and sophisticated that no one person understands the entire application, and large-scale changes become very difficult. Even small changes may need careful planning and consideration, and working on the monolith becomes more akin to major public works projects than a stroll in the park.

In reaction to this tendency toward slowing velocity in large projects, the *microservice* model was born. This model favors separating each piece of functionality into a separate service and stitching them together with a mix of explicit remote invocations or asynchronous messages. By building smaller services, it becomes harder for one service to entangle another in its implementation details, and it becomes simpler to reason about changing the behavior of a particular service while holding the other services constant. The exact size of each microservice is a matter of taste; what's critical is that the contracts among microservices are expressed by clear APIs that change slowly and carefully.[1]

---

1 If the APIs among these components change rapidly and carelessly such that pushes between components need to be coordinated, you may have a distributed monolith. This is as much a cultural as a technical problem.

In addition to the antientropy properties of separating the implementations of disjoint services, microservices allow application teams to choose the best set of implementation languages and tools for each job. For example, an order database might be represented by a Java frontend and a backing Postgres database, while a product catalog might be implemented in TypeScript with storage in MongoDB. By separating each microservice into a separate process, teams are better able to choose technologies that match the problem space—Python for AI problems, Java for complex domain logic, JavaScript or TypeScript for presentation and UI, and Erlang for parallel highly available messaging.

Continuing this trend, the FaaS model decomposes each microservice into a set of even smaller units: each separate invocation endpoint or event handler is built and deployed as its own separate computational unit. In this model, even two different methods on the same API do not share the same compute process and might not even be implemented in the same language. This separation has a few benefits:

Component changes can be shipped independently
Because each function is a separate service and set of server processes, it's possible to upgrade one function without impacting the rest of the system (assuming that the "upgrade" actually still works). This means that rollouts (and rollbacks) have the smallest possible blast radius when things go wrong—look at what you last changed, and undo that change to get back to working. It's amazing how often a simple "undo" can get a system back to up and running. Functions make that undo as simple as possible.

Resource allocations can be sized per method
When you put a bunch of related but different operations into the same server process, you need to plan for the worst-case combination of those operations. Maybe the List operation needs to allocate 50 MB of RAM to deserialize, format, and assemble a response, but takes only 0.1 seconds of CPU to do the computation. Meanwhile, the Predict operation needs 20 seconds of CPU to compute a response and caches a shared 200 MB model in memory. If you want each server to be able to handle 10 requests, you need to plan on $200 + 10 \times 50 = 700$ MB of RAM to be able to handle 10 Lists, and allocate 10 CPUs to handle 10 Predicts. You'll never have both happening at once, but you need to plan for the worst case of each.

If you allocate separate functions for List and Predict, the List method may need 500 MB of RAM for 10 requests (they don't need to load the prediction model at all), but only 1 CPU. Meanwhile, the Predict method needs 200 MB of RAM and 10 CPUs for each instance. Since you're separating the two types of requests, you can reduce the size of Predict instances by lowering the requests in-flight per instance. Assuming you're using a serverless model and automatically scaling these two methods, then a mix of 34 Lists and 23 Predicts would require 6 servers in the classic model, and 4 List and 5 half-sized Predict servers in the FaaS model. Even though FaaS is running an extra instance, the total resources required are 60% to 70% higher for the traditional microservice model. Monoliths suffer from this even more; capacity planning for monoliths can be a substantial closed box depending on the degree of interaction between components. Table 4-1 can help visualize these two scenarios.

Table 4-1. Instance fitting for 34 List and 23 Predict requests

Component	Methods	Worst-case CPU	Worst-case memory	Instances	Resources
Shared instance	List and Predict, 10 concurrent requests	10 × 1.0 (Predict)	200 MB (model) + 10 × 50 MB (List)	6	10 CPU, 700 MB RAM per instance
Total				6	100 CPUs, 7 GB RAM
List instances	List, 10 concurrent requests	10 × 0.1	10 × 50 MB	4	1 CPU, 500 MB RAM per instance
Predict instances	Predict, 5 concurrent requests	5 × 1.0	200 MB	5	5 CPUs, 200 MB RAM per instance
Total				9	29 CPUs, 3000 MB RAM

Given these obvious benefits, why aren't microservices and FaaS even more popular than they are today? As you might have guessed by the title of this section, an opposing force drives teams toward monoliths: *friction*. For all the benefits of deploying microservices instead of monoliths, one major drawback of microservices is the proliferation of little services, as in Figure 4-2. Each service requires care and feeding—wouldn't it be easier to just feed and care for one large hippo, rather than hundreds of little hamsters that each need separate vet appointments?

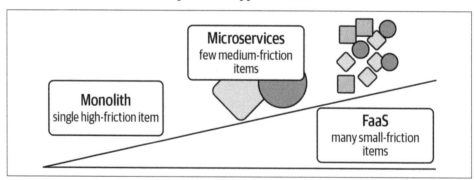

Figure 4-2. Code size and maintenance effort

This friction has many sources; some are intrinsic to live services, and others are imposed by various organizational processes. Intrinsic costs are things like writing application configurations, uptime monitoring, maintaining API compatibility, and artifact builds. External costs from organizational processes are launch reviews, application acceptance testing, or compliance audits. External costs are not necessarily *bad*—they are tools for achieving business goals that aren't required by the underlying technology. Serverless can help reduce the intrinsic costs of running an application by simplifying configuration and automating monitoring. Tools like continuous delivery can help reduce both intrinsic and external costs by simplifying build, test, and even audit processes.

Each team makes these trade-offs every time it looks at adding a new feature or capability—whether this should live inside an existing delivery unit like a microservice, or live in its own unit, adding a new instance of "running a service" cost to the burden paid by the team. (Remember, the team has a number of ongoing burdens, including "keep the unit tests green" and "communicate with stakeholders." Adding "maintain 273 microservices" to that burden contributes to fatigue and burnout.) By reducing the cost of "maintain a service," it becomes easier for a team to shift right along the spectrum of Figure 4-2 into smaller units of delivery.

Continuously Delivering Value

So, microservices can be easier to run and maintain and make it easier to change one component without cascading consequences. In exchange, they require more discipline when making changes that cross microservices. But why are we talking about microservices here? Do I need to adopt serverless to run microservices?

You don't need serverless to run microservices, and you don't need microservices to run serverless. But the two *do* go together like peanut butter and jelly (or whatever your two favorite sandwich fillings are). From here on out, we'll generally assume that you've chosen to run your microservices on serverless to take advantage of the operational benefits described in Chapter 1, as well as the benefits I'll describe next.

In general, microservices make it easier to implement a number of modern deployment practices, including data separation, progressive delivery, and continuous delivery. Microservices make it easier to change the deployment practices for each small piece of the delivery puzzle without needing to coordinate across several handfuls of teams and dozens of individuals. These improvements build on one another, with data separation and progressive delivery each providing capabilities toward the ultimate goal of continuous delivery:

Data separation
Well-architected microservices interact with one another through explicit APIs, either direct RPC or via asynchronous messaging. This allows each microservice to manage its own datastore through the team's chosen abstractions. For example, a team responsible for managing shopping carts in an online store might expose an API in terms of orders and line items. The checkout system might expose a separate API that consumed orders and payment instruments to execute a transaction.

Letting teams choose the abstractions they expose to other teams allows them to define interfaces in terms of business domain concepts, rather than tables and relations. Hiding the implementation of those abstractions behind an API allows the microservice team to *change* the storage and implementation choices behind the microservice without affecting other teams. This could mean adding a cache to an existing query API or migrating from a single-instance relational database to a scale-up NoSQL database to deal with increased storage and I/O demand.

Data separation enables the following practices; without data separation, application changes become coupled across microservices, making it harder to implement progressive or continuous delivery.

Progressive delivery

Once teams are able to deliver changes to their microservice implementation without affecting the APIs they use to coordinate with other services, their next challenge is to make that application delivery safe and repeatable. Progressive delivery is a technique for applying changes in smaller, safer steps. Rather than rolling out the whole microservice at once, a subset of requests is routed to the new version, with the ability to evaluate the performance and stability of the new version before sending most application traffic to the new version. Blue-green and canary deployments are popular examples of progressive delivery, but this can also manifest as traffic mirroring or "dark launch" of new code paths, where both new and old services are invoked.

The goal of progressive delivery is to make delivering software safer by reducing the impact of bad changes and reducing the time to recover when a bad change happens. As a rough rule of thumb, the overall damage of an outage is a product of *blast radius* (the number of users affected) times the duration of the outage. Progressive delivery aims to reduce the damage of a bad rollout, making it safer and quicker to roll out software.

Continuous delivery

With teams able to independently roll out changes and to reduce the impact of bad configuration changes, they can start to implement continuous delivery. Whole books have been written on this topic, but roughly speaking, *continuous delivery* is the practice of automating software delivery such that software can be delivered safely on a frequent basis—daily or even on each code change in a repository. Implementing continuous delivery often means automating all aspects of the software build-and-release cycle and connecting the automated delivery mechanism with application monitoring such that a bad release can be detected and rolled back automatically.

We've already talked about how serverless can simplify application management and continuous operations, but serverless often has benefits in reaching continuous delivery nirvana as well.

Continuous delivery is not about never having an outage or failing to roll out software. The goal is to reduce the risk of rolling out software by reducing the damage potential of an individual rollout. Small, rapid rollouts reduce the pressure of combining must-fix patches with large new features. Splitting up the push scope reduces the risk of all-at-once failure. Automation reduces the risk of failure due to process variations.

While serverless does not require data separation (and a microservice might actually be implemented as several coordinating serverless processes sharing a common database), the API surface provided via direct RPC calls or asynchronous messaging lends itself well to the serverless unit-of-work model. By motivating teams to define APIs that can drive serverless scaling metrics, teams also end up implementing scalable APIs in front of their application data sources, and it becomes easier to define subsets of the application that interact with a given data source and need to be pushed together.

Progressive delivery is often directly supported by the serverless runtime; because the serverless runtime is already aware of the units of work, mechanisms are often built into the framework to enable splitting or routing those units to specific application versions. For example, Knative and many FaaS offerings provide the option to split traffic between application revisions that are tracked by runtime automatically on deployment.

Capping off the acceleration of application deployment, serverless platforms can assist in continuous delivery because they are well placed to track high-level application metrics at the unit-of-work level. Latency, throughput, and error rate should all be accessible to deployment automation based on integration with the platform monitoring stack. Obviously, some deployment metrics (such as the number of successful shopping cart orders) may not be available to the deployment machinery without application-level metrics, but generic unit-of-work monitoring can provide a basic performance envelope suitable for many teams. I'll talk more about the monitoring capabilities of serverless platforms in Chapter 10.

Winning the (Business) Race

It's fun to push code and have it show up live on the production site within 30 or 60 minutes, but the real benefit to continuous delivery is removing the technological limits on organizational reaction time. By providing a supporting scaffold for implementing continuous delivery, organizations that implement a serverless-first development model can react more quickly to changes in customer needs and experiment in more agile ways than organizations that need to tend to a monolith.

Summing up, organizations benefit in two ways from adopting a serverless-first microservices architecture:

Reduced operational toil

Historically, the main benefit of monoliths was that a single operations team could specialize and focus on building an execution platform that managed *all* of the applications on one or a fixed fleet of servers (think cgi-bin or J2EE application servers loading dozens of microapplications onto a single server). Microservices mean maintaining dozens of servers, each with only a single application, leading to increased operational burden as each server is unique to the installed application. By simplifying application operations and automating some of the common day-to-day monitoring tasks, much of the toil of a microservices architecture can be avoided.

Scaffolding for continuous delivery

If reduced toil is the aerodynamic shell for applications, continuous delivery is the turbocharger. Reducing the lead time for change is one of the key metrics used by DevOps Research and Assessment (*https://dora.dev*) in identifying organizations that are elite performers in software execution. With software making its way into more and more aspects of business, continuous delivery allows faster reaction time to uncertain world events. Tightening the observe-decide-act loop helps organizations keep up with whatever the world throws their way.

Hopefully, these arguments explain how serverless can help organizations make better, faster decisions. The next section explains how serverless can help organizations make *smarter* decisions as well.

Microbilling

The previous section talked about splitting up monolithic applications into microservices from the point of view of application delivery and development team comfort. We're about to talk about something that can make development teams distinctly *un*comfortable but that can shine a fascinating light on an organization's economic status—the cost of delivering goods and services (aka cost of goods sold, or COGS for all you business majors out there).

It may surprise some of you to learn that many businesses don't understand their computing costs. The rest of you are nodding along and saying, "Evan, just cut to the punchline." By splitting monoliths into microservices and tracking units of work, it becomes possible to allocate computing costs for individual lines of business, sometimes down to the transaction level!

Even though costs can be measured at a fine-grained level, return on investment (ROI) may be much harder to calculate. For example, customer loyalty programs may have an easily measurable cost but a difficult-to-measure contribution to customer loyalty and repeat sales.

By splitting out costs on a fine-grained level, it becomes easier to understand which services drive profit as well as revenue. If it costs $0.50 to engage a user via a text-chat application, for example, you can compare that cost with the cost of hiring a human operator at $15/hour to answer text questions; if the human can answer more than 30 customers per hour, they are actually cheaper than the application, ignoring training costs and app development costs. Furthermore, you might be able to zero in on a particular AI component that contributes $0.30 of the interaction price and optimize it—either moving it to CPU to GPU or vice versa, or changing the model itself to optimize for costs.

A Deal with the Cloud

Billing down to the individual unit of work is simplest with cloud-provided serverless platforms, which often bill directly for the work performed, sometimes down to the millisecond of CPU or RAM. With cloud-provider serverless offerings, the cloud provider is responsible for provisioning sufficient capacity and managing the extra unused capacity. In turn, the cloud provider captures some of the extra value of having the illusion of infinite capacity. Some studies have suggested that serverless compute is approximately four times the cost of standard IaaS instances like Amazon Elastic Compute Cloud (EC2) (which, in turn, command a premium over on-premises installations). While cloud providers can and do change their pricing, the value provided by serverless is likely to continue to make serverless offerings more expensive per capacity than less flexible infrastructure.

Because cloud providers typically charge on either the basis of units of work performed (i.e., function executions) or on CPU or memory occupancy time while processing requests, it's easy to map costs for a particular microservice to that service's callers and up into the related application stacks. It is possible to take advantage of scaling to zero to deploy multiple copies of a microservice, one for each application, but this is typically unnecessary because it's easy to determine a per-request cost from the cloud-provider pricing.

While mapping per-request charges to application usage works quite well for single-threaded applications with one request in-flight per instance, the billing can get somewhat more complicated with platforms like Google's Cloud Run (or Knative), where multiple requests can be processed by an instance at once. The main benefit of the more complex execution model offered by Cloud Run or Knative is that many serverless applications end up spending a considerable amount of wall time waiting on API or service responses. Since wall time is often used as a billing metric for both memory and CPU occupancy, this can make multithreading and handling multiple requests in a single instance an attractive capability even if it makes billing somewhat harder. The efficiency gains of enabling request multiplexing can be seen in Figure 4-3, where a double-sized instance may be able to handle four times as many work units—this would be a cost savings of 50%!

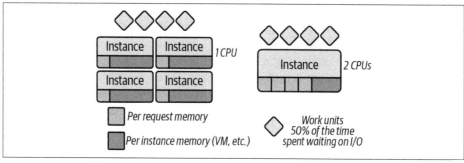

Figure 4-3. Handling multiple requests per instance

Even if you're using a more complex multithreaded model like Knative, averaging costs across all requests will generally work well unless you combine requests with very different execution profiles into one microservice. One common example is Get versus List requests—typically, the former read a single database row, while the latter might read thousands of database rows, possibly filtering out the results or marshaling large amounts of data. Separating Get and List into different functions or microservices can reduce contention between the two, but can also contribute to operational complexity for limited value, so test before you blindly apply this advice.

One final warning: using serverless services may have hidden costs that are harder to account for in determining request costs. Here are a few examples:

Network egress
> Nearly every cloud provider charges separately for network bytes sent. Hopefully, your serverless platform can report the fraction of total sent bytes that are due to your serverless applications, but accounting for all this traffic can sometimes be difficult.

Data systems
> While a few database systems can truly call themselves "serverless," most are still attached to a fairly fixed set of servers or a primary/replica topology. Because serverless systems generally externalize their storage, data services can be a hidden cost of serverless that is difficult to account for in your cost of goods and services.

Multitier services
> When an application is decomposed into multiple software layers, additional work is required to understand how the backend costs should be attributed based on frontend operations. If all the systems are serverless, distributed tracing (see "Tracing" on page 192) can provide the mapping from frontend to backend costs. If the backends are not serverless, costs can become opaque in the same way as data services.

Clouding on Your Own

There are many good reasons why you might choose to build a serverless platform on your own rather than relying on a cloud-provider offering—existing investments or cost sensitivity, missing cloud capabilities (for example, GPU support or specific feature integrations), edge and physical or regulatory computing requirements, or a desire for consistent tools across different clouds are all good reasons. Does this mean that you need to abandon the dream of serverless cost models and understanding your cost of providing services? Obviously not!

If the cloud providers can do it, it's not *magic*. At most, it's a bit complicated, but it's possible to build your own cost model for computation—tools like Kubecost allow Kubernetes platforms to compute costs based on metrics and cloud economics around VMs, networking, and storage. With these platforms, you can use monitoring information to determine the resources used by each pod, sum them up by component (across both serverless and more serverful services), and then allot those costs to individual groups.

It's also possible to have these tools amortize (share) the costs of the underlying platform: load balancers, node agents, monitoring, log collection, etc. all have a cost that is typically run in a multitenant fashion for the benefit of all users. These costs can be split by many policies—equal cost per application, equal cost per used compute-minute, or cost per reserved/provisioned compute-second are all reasonable approaches that have been used in practice.

Accounting for provisioned but unused capacity can be tricky in this world; physical or virtual machines that are on but are not running application code can either be apportioned as supporting platform costs or accepted by the organization as a "loss leader" to attract internal customers to the platform. In some cases, organizations can recoup some or a lot of this cost by overprovisioning (selling the same cores or memory twice, assuming some known inefficiencies) or with opportunistic work described in the next section.

What Happens When You're Not Running

So far, we've talked about how serverless works for running your application, but we haven't talked much about what happens to the servers when there's no application work to be done. One option is simply to allow the processors to enter low-power states; this can save hundreds of watts of power on recent x86 processors. The hardware is still sitting there, and other components like RAM, disk, and add-in cards also consume nontrivial amounts of power, generating heat and load on datacenter systems like cooling, networking, and power distribution. It really feels like we should be able to do something better with that capacity. (And no, I'm not talking about mining Bitcoin!)

As I suggested in the previous section, one use for this baseline capacity is opportunistic computing. Systems like Kubernetes allow work to be scheduled at different priority levels; CPUs that are idle with high-priority tasks can allocate time slices to low-priority work while being ready to pause that work when a new high-priority task comes in.

Depending on your operational comfort, you can capitalize on this idle capacity in several ways:

Batch computation
Many organizations collect large amounts of data for later analysis; this analysis is often needed "next business day" or under similarly loose time constraints. By running this work at lower priority on the same resources consumed by serverless, the batch work can be completed during times when real-time interactive demand for work is less. Batch workloads are often actually serverless as well—"map all these records" or "reduce across these combinations" are both scaled by units of work. This pattern works well for embarrassingly parallel problems, but can end up being very inefficient for batch workloads requiring each worker to directly connect to other workers. If these direct connections stall because of the sender or destination losing resources to a serverless process, it may lead to cascading stalls of hundreds of tasks.

Build services
Software builds are another opportunity to parallelize work and improve development velocity. This can also extend to other compute-intensive processes such as 3D rendering or AI model training. Rather than provisioning expensive laptops and having the fans kick in and videoconferencing stutter, users can offload these tasks from their local machine onto spare capacity temporarily available between spikes of usage. This model works better for large builds or renders that may take tens of minutes to hours of time; it's rarely worth offloading all the state for a one-minute build to the cloud.

Development and research
With sufficient spare capacity and strong isolation of serverless tasks, an organization may decide to allow development teams to use the idle low-priority capacity for development environments or pet research projects. This can serve as both a perk for development teams and an opportunity for innovation within the organization.

The Gravitational Force of Serverless

Hopefully, I've convinced you that serverless is here to stay rather than a flash in the pan. Furthermore, the compelling advantages of serverless development will cause serverless to gain an increasing market share in the same way that minicomputers, desktop applications, web services, APIs, and cell phones have all grown market share alongside the preexisting models of application development.

If you believe that serverless will have an increasing impact on day-to-day computing and application development, then it stands to reason that other technologies will grow and evolve to better support serverless. In the same way that JavaScript became ubiquitous because of the rise of web- and browser-based applications, languages, tools, and computing infrastructure will put new pressures on computing. In turn, tools that address these challenges well will grow and flourish (for example, both Ruby on Rails and PHP were born for the web), while applications that aren't well suited will retain their existing niches (in 40 years, we'll still need COBOL programmers to help banks manage their mainframe applications).

Implications for Languages

Serverless's emphasis on managing units of work connects to and externalizes two existing language patterns: inversion of control and reactive design principles. *Inversion of control*,[2] popularized by the Spring framework, is a model in which the framework controls the flow of the program, calling application-specific code at specified times. In the *reactive programming* model, applications express themselves as a set of reactions to changes to upstream data sources.[3] By externalizing these patterns from specific languages, serverless democratizes access to these capabilities without requiring the use of specific language frameworks or tools. For example, serverless systems are naturally elastic under varying amounts of work, and the units-of-work paradigm maps well to both "don't call me, I'll call you" control flows and a message-driven model of communication.

While serverless may provide scaffolding to support existing language and system design patterns, it introduces new requirements as well:

Fast startup
> Tying application execution to work available means that serverless systems tend to execute scaling up and down operations more frequently than traditional systems. In turn, this means that application startup (and shutdown) should both be fast and generate a low amount of load. Compiled languages and languages that have lightweight JIT processes have an advantage over languages with heavyweight JIT or module import processes that need to be run on each application start.

---

2 Sometimes described by the Hollywood principle, "Don't call us, we'll call you."

3 While reactive programming doesn't have as clear a tagline as inversion of control, it has shown impressive performance improvements compared with a traditional thread-per-request model.

Failure handling

Because serverless systems rely heavily on scaling based on units of work, they often employ external services to store state or as microservice boundaries. This means that applications built in a serverless style are exposed to many remote service calls, each of which may fail or time out because of networking issues.

Network storage over disk storage

Local-disk storage in serverless environments tends to be highly ephemeral. Therefore, the ability to quickly access and manage files on local disk may be less important than in traditional applications, where caches or precomputed results may be stored on disk to avoid later work. At the same time, the ability to easily call network storage services and externalize state outside the serverless instance may be more important than in traditional systems—for example, the ability to easily access systems like Redis or object stores like S3 is more critical when local storage is truly ephemeral.

Serialization

While all applications need to serialize and deserialize data, serverless applications may put additional weight on both the ease (for developers) and the speed and efficiency (for computers) of serializing and deserializing data. Because serverless architectures tend to be composed of microservices and backing data services that each have their own storage or network formats, the ability to efficiently and easily serialize and deserialize data across different endpoints is increasingly important.

Implications for Sandboxing

Traditional applications have used VMs and Linux containers to sandbox applications. These tools are well tested and understood but introduce substantial startup performance challenges as well as overhead for kernels, shared libraries, and network interfaces. Startup times for VMs with a general-purpose OS can be tens of seconds, while Linux containers can introduce hundreds of milliseconds of setup time.

Newer technologies like Wasm and service workers in the JavaScript runtime allow defining much more restrictive sandboxes (only a handful of custom-designed I/O methods exposed) that can spin up in *ten milliseconds* and have per-sandbox overheads of a megabyte or less. Platforms like Cloudflare Workers show some of the promise of this approach, though there are also substantial limitations that probably mean that all levels of sandboxing will live alongside each other for a long time.[4]

---

4 For more details on Cloudflare Workers specifically, see Kenton Varda's talk from QCon London in 2022: "Fine-Grained Sandboxing with V8 Isolates" (*https://oreil.ly/py1Eh*).

Implications for Tooling

The serverless paradigm is a great fit for developer tooling (and general tools for non-developers). Tools and automation generally nicely break down into units of work—building a binary, generating an API, handling a ticket, or responding to a text message. Given the size of a typical function, integration testing can be a feasible approach for much of the application coverage, rather than needing to maintain both unit and integration tests.

For developers, GitHub Actions is a great example of a serverless tooling platform. Developers can write actions that operate on a single commit, pull request, or release and don't need to think about long-running servers, job scheduling and concurrency, or connecting platform components and services. For nondevelopers, services like IFTTT (If This Then That) that provide simple automations between packaged services offer a similar serverless experience without needing to write any code or automation scripts.

With an easy-to-operate platform for applications, tools like low-code and no-code application builders and integration platforms benefit from serverless as an underlying application substrate. As applications become less about large continuously running processes and more about small amounts of glue between existing services, low-code and serverless approaches complement each other by reducing the requirements for users to write and manage applications.

Implications for Security

Serverless processes tend to start up and shut down frequently across a pool of hosts. Instance-level security tools may struggle in a dynamic environment like this, making cluster-level tooling more important and relevant. At the same time, the ephemeral nature of serverless processes can give defenders an advantage as natural turnover of instances can erode attackers' beachheads after the initial success of the attack.

Looking at historical trends, serverless seems likely to improve the ability of defenders to ensure consistent patching at the OS level. Consistent packaging formats such as OCI containers may also help with indexing and visibility of applications built with vulnerable libraries and data. Unfortunately, many of the high-impact security vulnerabilities tend to manifest as application-level defects like insufficient input validation, access control errors, and design errors. Serverless functionality is largely agnostic to these failures; they are equally serious for both ephemeral and persistent instances, and need to be addressed elsewhere in the software-design process.

Implications for Infrastructure

The most obvious challenges for infrastructure supporting serverless applications relate to application startup (particularly cold starts when a request is in-flight) and providing the illusion of infinite scale of capacity and speed. In addition to the language-level cold-start problems mentioned, infrastructure needs to get the application code to the cold-starting instance, and needs to handle this problem for many instances at once. Beyond startup times, serverless platforms also need to consider managing costs and efficiently provisioning and deprovisioning instances, as well as connectivity to and from the platform for all instances.

Beyond the day-to-day challenges of serverless platforms mentioned previously, a few larger challenges with serverless infrastructure have solutions that are not obvious or "do more of the same, but faster."

One of the challenges of data processing is whether to "ship data to code" or "ship code to data." Current serverless architectures mostly ship data to code, though improvements in sandboxing with Wasm may change that balance. While many applications are small enough that the two approaches have mostly similar overheads, most organizations have at least a few data-intensive applications for which the overhead of shipping and converting data between different formats dominates the overall cost. Being able to run these platforms in a serverless manner and derive the velocity, cost, and efficiency benefits thereof is an open problem.

Another related challenge with serverless is how to handle intertwining units of work. As long as each unit of work is independent, it is easy to understand how to scale and subdivide the problem so that different computers can work on different aspects. Unfortunately, some problems consist of a mix of easily divided work and work that synthesizes the easily divided parts into a more coherent whole. Physical simulations, stream processing, and neural network training are all examples where some work is highly independent, while other work requires tight coordination among computing components. While serverless can be used to handle the easily divided parts, having to cross platforms and paradigms to gain the benefits of serverless for only part of the solution is not very helpful. Mechanisms to bridge easily between serverless and more conventional computing patterns will help expand the range of problems that serverless can address.

Summary

Serverless is not just about making it easier to run software services. Simpler software services make new architectures feasible, which in turn allows teams and organizations to change their application development model. New ways of building applications (and new tools supporting these patterns) shift the constraints of delivering and testing software. New ways of running applications enable new business processes like evaluating the cost-per-operation and ROI of software initiatives. In the next part, we'll see how to apply serverless to system architecture and software design to realize these benefits—but the software architecture serves the needs of the organization, not the other way around!

## PART II

Designing with Serverless

So much for introduction! In this next part of the book, we'll be covering patterns for designing (and building) serverless applications to get a feel for how that theory shakes out in practice. After all, the best story in the world is still only a story until you figure out that it's true.

## CHAPTER 5

Extending the Monolith

In Chapter 2, we explored building a serverless application from scratch. Greenfield development is fun, fast, and feels superefficient because there's no legacy and historical decisions to deal with and everything is small and easy to move around. If you want to change your framework, language, or testing strategy, there's not a whole lot you need to do before you can start to reap the rewards of your efforts.

Those of you who read the chapter titles probably know where I'm going with this: what if you don't have a greenfield application? Most existing businesses have at least one application that can generously be described as an "heirloom"—it's large, the architecture was set 20 years ago, and (worst of all) it's absolutely critical to the business, so you can't just shut it down and replace it with the latest fashion.

Fortunately, serverless is still interesting and useful for these large, gnarly applications that weren't designed with serverless in mind. I actually want to embrace serverless as a tool for dealing with these applications. They often suffer from a bad reputation as creaky, subtle morasses with stubbornly low test coverage and achingly long push and qualification processes. My SRE friends would call them *haunted graveyards*:

> It's easy in this line of work to become superstitious:
> "This part of the system is risky—let's not touch it."
>
> —John Reese, Usenix SRECon 2017

This sounds like the opposite of what we want! By focusing on the difficult, we're missing the good and the value in these systems: they weren't built to be cranky and difficult, but have encoded thousands of hours of learning about actual business problems and rules that need to be followed. They are complex and hard to reason about *because that's how our world is*, and we should celebrate the achievement of order over chaos.

Just because these monoliths are marvels of modern engineering, you might *not* want to spend all your time and energy attempting to move around the load-bearing walls supporting your heirloom software. This is particularly true if you aren't sure exactly where you're going, or you're looking to perform a quick experiment to see whether a certain feature would be an improvement. While serverless is unlikely to transform your monolith,[1] it can be fairly straightforward to mix a little serverless into your existing architecture to improve your software delivery agility.

Before moving on to some practical mechanisms for extending monoliths, I'll leave you a bit of praise for software monoliths that I often quote when considering a rewrite:

> There [is] a fence or gate erected across a road. The more modern type of reformer goes gaily up to it and says, "I don't see the use of this; let us clear it away." To which the more intelligent type of reformer will do well to answer: "If you don't see the use of it, I certainly won't let you clear it away. Go away and think. Then, when you can come back and tell me that you do see the use of it, I may allow you to destroy it."
>
> —G.K. Chesterton, *The Thing*

Assuming that you've decided to live with and extend your neighborhood heirloom software stack, let's talk about *how* to make friends and invite them over for tea.

The Monolith Next Door

We've established that monolithic software can be big, complicated, and not a good fit for the small, agile serverless world. Large applications tend to be hard to build, push, and run for some of the following reasons:

Multiple entry points
Unlike a serverless function or application, which takes input in exactly one format (one HTTP request, one event, or some other small unit), monolithic software often has multiple responsibilities and entry points. In addition to an HTTP interface, the monolith may also accept work by pulling it off one or more messaging queues, or handle non-HTTP traffic, or even establish stateful session-oriented communications with other processes. Worse yet, input from different entry points can become connected, leading to...

Intertwined lifecycles
Most monoliths manage a variety of domains, storage, and communication systems. Each of these has its own lifecycle—for example, databases may need a connection pool, caches, and an object-relational mapping (ORM)—a way to convert database rows into richer programming-language objects). A domain

---

1 See "A Serverless Monolith?" on page 115 if you want to give it a try, though!

like computing shipping costs may need to manage item locations, weights, vendor APIs, and configuration related to the same. As more databases and domains become intertwined (for example, the shipping domain wants to interact with warehouses to figure out the smallest number of different shipments for an order), the monolith grows and bakes in value (solutions to business problems) because of…

Shared functionality

There are two worlds of software. In the beautiful world of theory, software libraries fit together and perfectly encapsulate code reuse. In the dirty, gritty world of software delivery, software libraries introduce demands and configuration difficulties that are solved by bundling things together to minimize the new external services that need to be configured. If library A needs a cache and a database, and library B needs a messaging system and a cache, there's a nonzero chance that the same backing cache gets used for both. And then some clever programmer in the future building library C realizes they can reuse library B because it's already there and it's going into the same monolith. All of a sudden, splitting libraries A and C will double the connections to messaging system D, so A and C are coupled in practice, if not in theory. This is further complicated by…

Layering violations

With so many domains and functions all encapsulated in a single binary, it can be hard to maintain a simple, directed depends-on graph between the modules. A classic example comes from the insurance industry. Like most companies, insurance companies need to track their customers' contact information, including things like physical address. Additionally, insurance often uses physical location like neighborhood as part of the input into rate pricing. It would be useful to automatically issue a new insurance quote when a customer moves to a new location, which means that the customer-address system depends on the rate-quoting system. But once a rate is quoted, it needs to be sent to the customer, which means that the rate-quoting system depends on the customer-address system. Untangling these circular dependencies is critical for maintaining a sane microservice architecture where reliability is higher than the product of the worst-case scenarios.[2]

All of these make it hard to modularize and encapsulate the monolith's functionality, and interactions among these entrypoints, domains, and functions can tie a poor application programmer in knots. In turn, this makes shipping new experiments and

---

2 To understand how this works, say you have five microservices. Each has 99.9% internal reliability but depends on the other being up. Therefore, all systems will be up only 99.95% of the time—five times more downtime than any individual team is responsible for. Furthermore, it's not clear where to invest to improve uptime; in a cleanly layered system, the bottom levels should have the highest reliability, but upper levels can choose lower reliability targets.

features slow and hard—who wants to wade through tens of thousands of lines of API and configuration to build a customer-satisfaction experiment comparing shipping smaller packages more frequently versus batching packages for lower shipping costs?

Everyone working on the monolith gazes jealously over at the microservices team experimenting with serverless and new application patterns, while the microservices folk walk around with their noses in the air and mutter about just *how much* the monolith costs to extend. Everyone misses the point that the greenfield microservices are simpler because they haven't baked in all the edge cases from the monolith that disorder it like the building in Figure 5-1. But, at the end of the day, the monolith is critical to the business (it's baked in all that knowledge), so we hold our noses and give them what they need. Surely this isn't healthy, and nobody's really having fun with this rivalry.

What we need is a way to extract small pieces of the monolith and encapsulate them with boundaries that are more difficult to breach than library calls. This is the promise of microservices, and as we discussed in Chapter 4, serverless and microservices go together like peanut butter and jelly. By enforcing a single entrypoint and avoiding state accumulation within the microservice, serverless helps avoid building a second, entwined monolith.

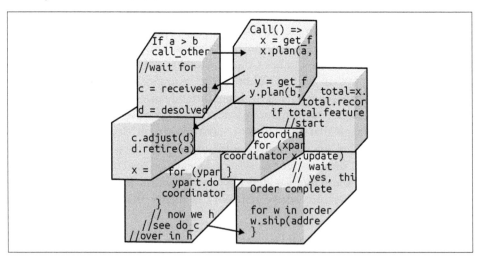

Figure 5-1. Entwined monoliths

For this section, we'll imagine that our monolith is a website that hosts an online store and the backend order management, fulfillment, and shipping functionality. That's a lot of functionality, and we may be feeling a bit like Amazon did in 2004 when it embarked on its transformation to microservices. We'll talk about a few example scenarios:

1. Providing manuals and documentation for purchased items for logged-in users

2. Automatically adding coupons and deals when users make combination purchases

3. Optimizing shipping across multiple orders

4. Adding a customer retention program, to reengage users who haven't ordered in a while

The following sections will provide three techniques for leveraging serverless to build clean extensions on top of existing monolithic applications. By building monolith extensions this way, we can take advantage of common capabilities (see "Creature Comforts: Undifferentiated Heavy Lifting" on page 13) and other infrastructure benefits of serverless to automatically track the success of our extensions. We'll start with the simplest cases and then venture further into the realms of eventual consistency and integration.

Microservice Extension Points

The simplest way to build serverless extensions for an existing monolithic software stack is to treat the new functionality as an external service that the monolith calls to achieve the desired result. By moving the functionality behind a network call interface, the existing chaos and entanglement of the monolith is kept at arms' distance—any attempt to reuse existing components or services of the monolith needs to be handled by either extracting the code into a standalone library with minimal dependencies or by exposing the data from the monolith over a network interface.

If the existing functionality is already nicely factored into a library, it may be tempting to simply link the library into both your monolith and the new, serverless microservice. Before doing that, take a careful look at the library's dependencies—for example, if the library depends on the monolith's ORM layer and underlying database, you may want to find a different way to access the data—for example, through an API exposed by the monolith. We're trying to maintain good microservices practice here, and you probably *don't* want to couple your serverless application to schema changes in the monolith's database.

Instead, you can follow the standard microservice pattern and expose the monolith's data through an internal API that your serverless application can call if needed.[3] If your monolith is like many, it probably already exposes some of these APIs for either external or internal integrations. In some cases, you may need to extend these APIs to present additional information, optimize the query pattern using batching or

---

3 While this introduces a bit of a circular RPC dependency, this will ideally relax into a layered system as more bits of the monolith are split apart.

GraphQL, or expose additional collections. As you build more extensions, these APIs will continue to add value and help you maintain a healthy microservices ecosystem around the existing monolith.

In some cases, you may want to avoid the round trip from the monolith to the microservice and back to the monolith's data API. You may be concerned about the latency impact, the amount of data movement, or the reliability of such a back-and-forth. One alternative to fetching data from the monolith via an API is to have the monolith fetch and serialize the data upfront as part of the request. This works best when the actual data may not be particularly complex or sensitive, but there is a lot of logic or presentation that can be cleanly handled outside of the core.

When the data is complex and prefetching is not a good option, data can be continually exported to a microservice-specific database using an Extract, Transform, Load (ETL) process. Giving each microservice its own independent database that is managed using simple techniques (avoiding stored procedures, etc.) is a common microservice pattern for scalability, so this type of ETL data integration can work well as long as all changes flow in one direction. Change data capture, described in "Is Your Database Your Monologue?" on page 140, is a tool that can help with building these ETL pipelines.

In our previous list of scenarios, "providing manuals and documentation for purchased items for logged-in users" is a good candidate for packaging the data in the request to the microservice. Figure 5-2 illustrates several of these data transfers between an existing software monolith and a serverless microservice.

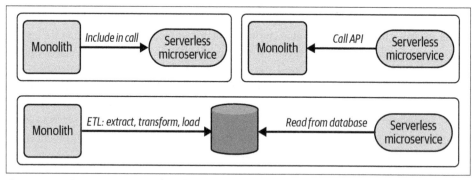

Figure 5-2. Communicating data between a monolith and a serverless microservice

Assuming that we have a table of users, another table of orders, and then each catalog item has a collection of links to assets that contain the manuals and other documentation, we can export the formatting and rendering of the documentation to an external microservice. Moving the formatting and rendering to a separate microservice allows us to push any rendering changes more quickly and to sandbox the potentially computationally expensive steps of converting a page for display to a separate service that can scale up as needed.

If the rendering of a single page is sufficiently heavyweight, we could even have the extension microservice further delegate the page rendering to a worker microservice, where each request to the worker provided the payload of one page to be rendered. Microservices that operate entirely on their input like this are like pure functions in programming—easy to test and straightforward to implement.

The approach of marshaling data for execution by pure functions could also work well for the second and third scenarios, if the data is easily available in the monolith when the work needs to happen. The last scenario with the customer loyalty program may be a little bit more difficult, and we'll cover that more in "Extract, Transform, Load" on page 109.

Now you might be objecting, "Hey, if I'm doing all the work to collect this data in the monolith and then calling a pure function, what's the benefit of pulling all of this out of the monolith and sending it to serverless?" That is a good question from a code and execution efficiency point of view—you've added a bunch of network calls and data marshaling for something that could just be a library. But remember that serverless gives us other benefits:

Independent scaling
> If we have CPU or memory-intensive work to do, we can size and scale it rapidly, even if the main monolith is unable to scale quickly.

Independent interface
> The pure function is not beholden to the particular database schema of monolith. While a database can have only one schema at a time, an API "seam" between components can expose both old and new versions, easing migration.

Independent pushes
> We can potentially push out the extension multiple times per day, while the main monolith may need a month or longer for even small code changes to go live.

Independent experimentation
> Because the serverless microservice is independent of the main monolith, it can be a great place to experiment with new technologies and languages before adopting them more widely. The cost to reimplement two or three microservices is much lower than the cost of qualifying a new language combination in the existing monolith.

Sounds great! Why wouldn't we want to use microservices APIs to extend our monolith? Well, a few more options can decouple our serverless components even further from the monolith, not just in space, but also in time.

Asynchronous Cleanup and Extension

We've talked a few times previously about using messaging- or task-queuing systems with serverless. In many ways, serverless is a natural fit for such systems, because each message or task enqueued is an independent unit of work that can be executed on its own. Better yet, many monoliths already integrate with at least one such system. Because the communication in these systems is one-way (from the message sender or task creator to the recipient), these are called *asynchronous systems*.

The big advantage of asynchronous systems is that the initiator of the work doesn't need to wait around for the work to be done. In many systems, failure of the work units is also managed and retried automatically if needed (up to a maximum retry limit). This means that it's relatively easy to extend the monolith to send a message or enqueue a task without changing the latency or failure modes of a system. As you can see in Table 5-1, asynchronous communication is a great fit when our monolith doesn't need an immediate response.

Table 5-1. Comparing synchronous and asynchronous extension

Synchronous	Asynchronous
Invoked directly by the monolith	Invoked indirectly through a queue
Typically blocks (waits) for completion	Does not block on completion
Caller detects and handles failure	Caller cannot detect failure; system handles failures
Receives a response message directly	Does not receive a response; may build correlations manually

If you're building an extension where the monolith needs to handle or act on the result of your serverless computation, it will often make more sense to use the API call method of microservice integration. If the microservice is optional to the results of the monolith and can update the monolith's results later using the internal API exposed by the monolith, then the asynchronous pattern can be more resilient and lower risk.

Looking at our feature list just before "Microservice Extension Points" on page 105, this means the first extension (providing and formatting manuals) is not a great match for asynchronous execution. The monolith will immediately want the formatted results for presentation to the user, and sending the results back through another path is unlikely to be simpler than an API call. The third feature (optimizing shipping) is almost certainly a good fit for asynchronous execution, because there's usually a delay of minutes to days when the asynchronous service could call the monolith's API and calculate a better shipping plan as the shipping status changes.

The second feature (automatically adding coupons) is an interesting case. If our goal is to optionally update the customer's cart with a discount code, an asynchronous call to a service with the current set of coupons might be compelling. On the other hand, if we want to be able to render a fancy animation when the user completes a purchase combo, then we might decide that we need to make a synchronous call when items are added to the shopping cart in order to render the animation.

The fourth feature (customer retention messages) could be a good match for asynchronous invocation, assuming that an existing process in the monolith scans all customers and determines when they last placed an order. If not, we may need to consider ways to move the data we need outside the monolith, so that we can implement our own logic for recognizing and engaging customers who are not currently active.

Extract, Transform, Load

The ETL pattern of migrating data rows from one location to another is common in data warehousing but is also a great fit for serverless applications. Each row needing transfer can be thought of as a small unit of work, or a particular table can act as a "key" for migrating associated rows in other related tables as well as the original. For example, updates to an "orders" table might cause the order row and all the associated customer and item information to be extracted into a JSON document and written to a transaction log like Apache Kafka.

Numerous tools are available for performing ETL tasks; typically, these tools connect directly to a backing database or cloud service and leverage the database's replication or notification technology to produce the set of rows to be extracted. ETL can also be implemented using a periodic task to scan the rows of a table and emit a work item for each row that meets certain criteria (such as "changed in the last week"). This periodic scan can act as a fallback approach for database systems that already support a native "extract" or "notify" functionality, as well as acting as a primary method for databases without that functionality.

In either case, the ETL pattern can help extend a monolith by replicating the core database information into read-only copies that are better suited for a particular task, such as large-scale analysis, integration with other systems, or training machine-learning models. The process of extracting and transforming the data also offers an opportunity to normalize or "clean" the data as it is extracted—many production systems end up with generations of data stored with slightly different semantics as the application evolved, and scanning the data during the ETL process can provide an opportunity to validate references and standardize field formats that may have drifted over time. Of our four proposed features, the customer retention program would be a good fit for an ETL process to export all the customer activity into a separate data store where we can analyze user behavior and run experiments to see which types of loyalty and retention content drives return visits.

ETL can also be useful when you're attempting to escape the gravitational force of a monolith, such as when the monolith has finally outlived its useful life. In that case, you'll be looking to extract the data from the current monolith, so that you can complete the task of replacing it. Next, we'll talk about one strategy for doing exactly that.

The Strangler Fig Pattern

While "The Monolith Next Door" on page 102 talked about how we can coexist with a monolith, sometimes the time comes that the monolith really is costing more than it's worth. When that happens (and usually before), it becomes time for *the great rewrite*. If we can just rewrite the system in something more modern, we can clean out all the cobwebs and failed experiments that coupled parts B and C that really should have been separate. We'll understand the new system much better, and now that we know what we're doing, we can set some quality bars on the new system that really should have been there from the start.

Sounds great! We've already been through Chapter 2, so time to close up the book and get coding!

Not so fast. Remember how we described the monolith as a business *heirloom* earlier in the chapter? It's *critical* to the business, and minutes or hours of downtime may make the news or at least shake the confidence of critical partners who are depending on its services. Even though serverless may let us move fast, sometimes business requirements may force us to move slowly.

In the next sections, we'll explore ways to break down an heirloom monolith safely. Many of these are based on a facade pattern that Martin Fowler has dubbed the *Strangler Fig pattern* (*https://oreil.ly/5JHeD*). Strangler figs are trees that sprout in the upper branches of existing trees and slowly extend their roots down to the ground, entangling and eventually killing the host tree while producing an amazing lattice-work of roots. I've used the Strangler Fig pattern successfully to entirely replace an existing monolith, but it can add value even if it doesn't completely replace the monolith, by providing a simpler mechanism for implementing the extensions points described in "Microservice Extension Points" on page 105.

The basics of this pattern are fairly easily described: in short, you implement a pass-through interface to the underlying monolith, as shown in Figure 5-3. By capturing all the inputs to the monolith, you can start to control when and how the monolith is executed, and you can use this to slowly extract the monolith's capabilities into the scaffolding, until the scaffolding can stand on its own and the monolith can be retired.

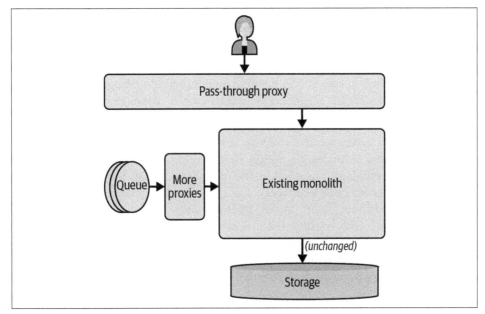

Figure 5-3. The Strangler Fig pattern

Since many existing monoliths have more than one source of input, be thoughtful about how you want to capture existing inputs. In Figure 5-3, we've explicitly introduced a shim on an existing message queue that triggers monolith behavior. Each input to the monolith should be assessed this way—implementing an interposer will be easy for some but more difficult for others.

From easiest to most difficult, here are some of the common input sources to monoliths and some recommendations for handling them when strangling a monolith:

HTTP, REST, and RPC interfaces
    These tend to be very easy in the normal case—typically, the monolith is fronted by an HTTP reverse proxy (aka application load balancer, API gateway, or load balancer) that implements various routing and load-balancing policies. If not, introducing such a reverse proxy will probably have independent benefits, so start there.

    Assuming you have a reverse proxy in place, it should be easy[4] to reroute requests between your facade and the underlying monolith with a simple configuration change. During the early stages of your rewrite, this also provides an important safety valve—you can point the reverse proxy directly at the monolith to rule out the facade as a source of issues when they arise.

---

4 Technically. I can't really fix any of the political challenges you might face.

Message queues

Message queues are a popular way to manage asynchronous interactions between applications. Generally, message queues provide durable at-least-once delivery of messages, which means that (unlike HTTP) we can't rely on senders to retry the messages. This also means that inbound and outbound messages are separate, so we need to handle only the inbound messages for the strangler pattern.

For *inbound* messages, you can implement either a pass-through proxy or a message copier. I recommend a message copier; it's likely to be much simpler to implement and provides an option in the future to translate new messages to existing messages understood by the monolith (or even to translate messages to HTTP calls or other interfaces). The copier reads messages from the public queue and delivers them to an internal queue *before* acknowledging the public message (this ensures the at-least-once property of the messaging systems). The monolith then consumes from the internal queue, unaware of the copier. The drawback of a message copier is that you need to provision a second message queue, possibly doubling the required throughput of your messaging system.

Nonstandard protocols

While the preceding protocols are fairly standard, some monoliths will have other interfaces. Some common examples are SMTP (email), XMPP (chat), and FTP (file transfer), but hundreds of well-known protocols as well as thousands more proprietary protocols exist in a single enterprise. It's hard to make too many general recommendations here, but most protocols will be message-oriented (stateless), while others will be session-oriented (stateful). For stateless protocols, it's generally fairly easy to implement a proxy similar to the HTTP reverse proxy described in the first section. Stateful protocols are likely to be much more difficult to interpose; looking at databases as a data transfer protocol will highlight some of these challenges.

Databases

While less popular than message queues, many systems exchange data by storing work items or other state in well-known database tables, which are then scanned by a second system. While this may work a bit like message queues (and you can build a "row copier" like the message copier), the patterns for handling and updating an external database are much less clear-cut, and copying updates between two tables may need to use the ETL patterns described in "Extract, Transform, Load" on page 109.

Alternatively, it may be worth refactoring the monolith to convert direct database reads into either a message queue or HTTP or RPC patterns. This type of rework may also have benefits in terms of improving observability and debuggability.

Now that we've scoped out the work involved in implementing the Strangler Fig pattern, I'll outline several techniques to help make your microservice sprout successful at replacing your existing monolith.

Experiments

The first goal of any Strangler Fig project should follow the Hippocratic oath: "First do no harm."[5] In the case of the Strangler Fig, this means that we should design and plan our interception layer to faithfully pass through the original inputs to the monolith, collect metrics and instrumentation to compare original and reimplementation behavior, and provide a quick mechanism to reroute requests from the rewrite to the original in the case of problems.

In many ways, this looks a lot like an experiment framework, a common modern software toolkit for performing controlled comparisons of new features to see how they affect user behavior. In fact, our Strangler Fig application *is* a kind of experiment, but in a different style than the normal usage of an experiment framework. In our "experiment," the goal is to measure *no difference* between the clean rewrite and the original application, rather than a change in customer behavior. Note that our experiment framework doesn't say anything about what protocol we're intercepting—the same patterns work for both HTTP-style synchronous requests and message queue-based requests (where they might be called a *content-based router*).

We'll also need a fair amount of flexibility in our request routing—for example, we might want to start out by intercepting only GET requests that don't request extra attributes or intercepting create requests only for specific customers or "simple" resource types. Once the facade and experiment framework is in place, the goal is to get *some* part of the rewrite into customer-facing usage as quickly as possible to start learning from the system. It may take five or ten experiments to fully replace a complicated endpoint: with a safety net that makes it easy to detect and roll back on failures, the risk of pushing out a "we think this works, but there might be an edge case" can be mitigated, and the team can test and experiment with higher velocity until the feature is stable.

Looking at the requirements for this system, we can see that the interception-and-experiment layer is actually a good fit for a serverless implementation: forwarding a single request is the unit of work, each request should be independent of other requests, and the complexity of work for each request is high enough that it may be hard to meet your needs with an off-the-shelf proxy.

---

5 There's some other stuff in there about doctor-patient confidentiality that might not apply.

If you're implementing the facade yourself, you may want to apply several other patterns, drawn from the world of experiment frameworks. We'll talk about two in the next section.

Dark Launch and Throwaway Work

In the last section, we talked a little bit about making incremental progress using a content-based router and experiment configuration to incrementally roll out partial implementations of the monolith's functionality. This section introduces two patterns based on the ability of the router to manage requests and retries that go beyond the typical blue-green or percentage-based software rollout. Both are based on the idea of a *dark launch*—a mechanism for testing a software change that calls the new code for measurement purposes but doesn't take action on the results of the code:

Request mirroring

Rather than choosing to send a request to either the new implementation or the monolith, the router can send the request to both systems and compare the results between the two before returning the *canonical* result. Typically, the router configuration will indicate which system is canonical for a given request; the other system will still do the work of answering the query so the results can be compared (and possibly logged, if the results differ). Typically, administrators will monitor for differing results and may need to tweak the differencing algorithm if (for example) the response includes timestamps that differ in unimportant ways. In some systems, the router may indicate to the backend systems which one is canonical and which is a backup; this can be used (for example) to short-circuit storage operations when the request would write or modify state.

Note that while the previous section talks about measuring responses, the request mirroring pattern can also apply to asynchronous messaging; in this case, the message router would simply copy the incoming message to both application queues for processing. This might be appropriate if each system has partial data about a user or backend system, for example.

Fallback to monolith

In this pattern, the content-based router sends requests first to the rewritten application. If the application is able to handle the request, it operates as normal. If the application is *unable* to handle the request (too complicated, or the request is for data that hasn't been migrated out of the monolith yet), the application returns a special error code that tells the content-based router to retry the request against the monolith. This pattern mostly applies to synchronous request-response protocols like HTTP, but has a few benefits over the standard experiment configuration:

- Rather than configuring the router with specific rules about which types of requests the rewritten application can manage, the application itself is able to encapsulate that data. This can make it easier to manage the rerouting configuration from a single location, rather than needing to two-step the work in the rewritten component and then in the router.
- The fallback to the monolith can be implemented to cover several application exit codes, limiting the fallout if the new application becomes unavailable or unreasonably slow.
- The fallback-to-monolith pattern can be combined with the request mirroring pattern to prefer results from the rewrite but to proceed with results from the monolith in the case of problems.

Both of these patterns make some assumptions about the nature of the requests to the monolith and may not be useful in all cases. Table 5-2 may help you compare the three patterns (normal request forwarding, request mirroring, and fallback requests) and help choose which is appropriate for which scenarios.

Table 5-2. Comparing request-routing strategies

Request forwarding	Request mirroring	Fallback requests
Requests go to exactly one service.	Requests go to all services.	Requests are tried at one service but may fall back to another.
Works for both read and write requests.	Works well for read requests; write requests may cause data inconsistency.	Works for both read and write requests.
Works for synchronous and asynchronous requests.	Works best with synchronous requests, but can handle asynchronous requests as well.	Works only for synchronous requests where an error can be detected.

Now that we're armed with the knowledge of how to live with the monolith in our neighborhood and how to slay a monolith if necessary, let's talk about when we might invite one in for tea.

A Serverless Monolith?

At the beginning of this chapter, I talked about many of the properties that can make monoliths challenging: multiple entrypoints, intertwined lifecycles, shared functionality, and layering violations. While many monoliths may suffer from one or more of these faults, some large software projects have mostly managed to architect around these problems. If so, there's nothing magical about serverless that says that it can be used with only *small* software projects. If you have a well-architected monolith that cleanly separates the processing of each request, you may find that you can leverage serverless for some of the advantages described in Chapters 1 and 4.

Serverless platforms that support a generic Linux container environment, like Knative, are a good match for this sort of serverless monolith. Containers are a good fit for serverless monoliths because they provide a generic interface that supports a range of existing applications and integrates with many different build tools. Some serverless environments are more restrictive than others when it comes to what applications are allowed to do; a platform (like Knative) that is built on an extensible substrate can more easily be extended if your application needs to support specific hardware or network protocols.

To set expectations: migrating your monolith to a serverless runtime won't magically change your application from a grueling monthly push process to a sprightly multiple pushes per day, but you may still find that life gets a little bit better in a lot of different ways:

Undifferentiated heavy lifting
You've probably already done the monitoring and observability work provided by the serverless runtime; you can choose to keep this work or retire it in favor of consistent platform-level metrics.

Process lifecycle
You've likely already implemented substantial bespoke process management. Rather than maintaining this tooling, you can replace it with the serverless runtime and save the ongoing maintenance of process rollout and restart tooling.

Resource allocations
Since you're already running multiple copies of the monolith, you may be able to take advantage of the resource-sizing tricks described in Table 4-1. I've seen this used quite effectively to save money by splitting "cheap" and "expensive" request paths in an intentional monolith onto different hardware classes, giving expensive requests additional CPU and memory capacity.

Progressive delivery
Similarly to process lifecycle management, the tools provided by serverless systems to manage progressive delivery and canary rollouts can help replace bespoke tooling with off-the-shelf versions at much lower costs.

Common process
If you've already introduced serverless tooling elsewhere in your application stack, migrating your monolith onto the serverless toolchain may reduce the number of *different* systems you need to keep track of.

In the following section, I'll give a few examples of (open source) monoliths that are amenable to serverless runtimes. For counterexamples and warnings that things may be tougher than expected, see Chapter 8.

WordPress (PHP), Discourse (Ruby), and Mastodon (Ruby) are three examples of open source monoliths that can be amenable to serverless runtimes. Perhaps unsurprisingly, they are built with programming languages that focus on web application development and ease of use. In this section, I'll highlight a few places where a serverless platform may change the standard usage of these large monoliths; many of these changes may apply to closed-source monoliths as well:

Local file storage

WordPress, Discourse, and Mastodon all offer file hosting and storage. The default storage for these items is on local disk, which works fine when running a single instance in something like a VM, but fails when running in a serverless environment where instances come and go. Container-based serverless runtimes like Knative can provide Network File System (NFS)-based shared file storage across instances, but using the POSIX filesystem interface has limitations and drawbacks. While it's possible to use a system like NFS to store these files, all three systems also offer extensions to store these files using an object store API like S3.[6] Object stores are a great choice for serverless applications, as they provide a scalable infrastructure experience where the "unit of work" is "store a file."

Configuration

Many of these open source monoliths provide some form of guided setup tutorial. Fortunately, once they have been set up, they tend to persist the setup data into a database or filesystem in a way that can be replicated to each serverless instance. When first migrating a monolith onto a serverless runtime, you'll probably need to pay attention to how these environment variables and files are stored; once you have an effective management strategy, you'll probably find that storing the configuration in something like source control gives you extra confidence in your change management process.

Upgrades and version management

The mentioned open source monoliths provide self-upgrade capabilities to help users run on the latest version of the platform. When running on a serverless runtime with nonpersistent disk, these upgrade options tend to fail in somewhat perplexing ways: the upgrade will run and succeed, and (at least one copy of) the site will be upgraded, but if you walk away and allow the service to scale down, the next time you visit the site, it will have downgraded itself. Unlike the standard VM experience, upgrading one of these monoliths will require updating the serverless runtime to point to a new release artifact. Again, over time you may appreciate this more explicit roll forward and roll back, but it's a change in pattern.

---

6 If you're replacing a shared filesystem with object storage, check the consistency guarantees of your storage provider. S3 is *eventually consistent*, which means it may take a short time for written objects to be available for read. Many other object stores such as MinIO or Google Cloud Storage offer "read after write" consistency, which can be closer to filesystem semantics.

Multiple instances

> Some applications, such as Ruby on Rails–based applications with background queuing and processing with Sidekiq, may end up needing to run two serverless services—one handling HTTP and the other scaling based on the size of the Redis queue that is managed by Sidekiq. Each of these containers is handling individual units of work, but (like the monolith pictured in Figure 5-3) some of the work is coming from a queue, while other work is handled via HTTP.

While these can be additional work over simply installing the monolith in a single-instance container, the discipline of making the monolith start repeatably and portably gives you confidence that the server will work in a failover or disaster-recovery scenario.[7]

Summary

While much of the excitement about serverless is about enabling new architectures and capabilities, serverless patterns and architectures also deserve a place when considering how to extend existing heirloom applications that run critical business processes. While many monoliths won't be suitable to or benefit from a direct lift-and-shift to serverless, you can choose from many serverless patterns to keep that monolith running for a bit longer or to replace it when the time comes.

You may have noticed that this chapter talked a little bit about asynchronous as well as synchronous invocation methods for serverless applications. This domain is called *event-driven applications*, and we'll spend the next chapter diving deep into the ways that independent asynchronous events fit together with serverless applications.

---

7 Assuming that you properly backed up your databases. You did, didn't you?!

## CHAPTER 6

More on Integration: Event-Driven Architecture

In the last chapter, we touched a bit on one-way messaging architectures and their utility in integrating existing monoliths. In this chapter, we're going to dive in and explore the patterns of event-driven architecture (sometimes called *EDA*) and how serverless can be a compelling fit for these applications. Event-driven applications produce and consume events as their primary I/O interfaces, usually interacting with some sort of message bus or event router.

Serverless is a great fit for event-driven architectures because each message acts an individual independent unit of work that can be processed serverlessly.[1] Many serverless systems have built-in event-handling architectures, and some (AWS Lambda in particular) are built specifically around an event-processing lens such that even synchronous requests are treated as events and corresponding responses.

If you've done much UI programming in the last 20 years, you're probably familiar with events from a desktop application perspective—rather than poll for the current mouse position, keys pressed, etc., you can register *event handlers* for certain events of interest, and specify a function that should be called when that event happens. Internally, your computer fires hundreds of events every minute—keys pressed, keys released, time passing, mouse moving, windows updating—every behavior you might be interested in reacting to is presented as an event.

---

1 Some types of systems accumulate events to process them as a group, where the previous state is carried over to the new messages. If you're interested in that, *Streaming Systems* by Tyler Akidau et al. (O'Reilly) is probably one of the best summaries of that area. We'll talk a bit later about how serverless and streaming might overlap.

Similarly, an enterprise may want to design a system for managing internal processes: adding an item to the sales catalog, updating product availability, adding an item to a cart, user publishes a review, supplier submits an invoice—all of these are interesting to some part of the business, and all of them can be treated as a one-way announcement of a thing that happened.

You'll notice that so far I've talked a bunch about "event driven" and "messaging," but I haven't defined these terms. Let's do that now, and then go into depth on the differences between the two.

Events and Messages

While event-driven architectures and messaging systems overlap in some respects, the two systems have key philosophical differences that are worth understanding.

Messages are encodings of specific data that is to be handed off to another process for execution. The core concerns of messages and messaging systems are, roughly, as follows:

- Defining message sender and receiver interfaces
- Defining the format (envelope) for the message
- Ensuring that messages are delivered from the sender to the receiver without loss

Generally, message-passing systems define mechanisms for encapsulating the data in the message and transmitting it to a destination, but don't particularly care about what's in the message—it could be a log message, a command, a database record, or even an *event*. Eventing systems are typically built *on top* of a messaging layer, but eventing uses messaging as an implementation detail for a larger idea of making systems reflectable and observable.

Events are statements or observations about things that have happened in the world.[2] "Erik applied for a loan," "I stubbed my toe," and "This computer is on fire" can all be recorded with events and exchanged and acted upon in an event-driven system.[3] Typically, events are concerned with not only making observations but also making those observations systematized and useful. To that end, events often leverage messaging systems to define the following:

---

2 In his talk "Towards a Serverless Event-Sourced Nordstrom" (*https://oreil.ly/dUJDr*), Rob Gruhl describes high-quality events as "written in the past tense at this date and time this thing occurred," where that thing could be an observation or a decision.

3 Though I'm not sure what system would be interested in all three of those events!

- Metadata about an event: when, who, how much, and so on may all be recorded in standardized ways

- Schemas and catalogs of event types, so that observers can request certain types of events

- Subscription interfaces, to allow one system to request to receive events of interest

One of the key differences between traditional messaging systems and event-driven systems is the inversion of responsibility for managing event flow and architecture: in a traditional messaging system, the architect defines the event flow, and senders and receivers are connected to specific named queues that contain a particular type of messages (the CQRS pattern, for example, separates "command" messages and "query" APIs to different channels[4]). In an event-focused or event-driven system, each component is responsible for describing the type of information it is interested in and then subscribing to that information, possibly via a central event broker. In some cases, the event system is incomplete and applications may need to specify particular messaging channels to subscribe to certain types of events, but other systems like Knative Eventing Brokers allow subscribers to simply subscribe to event patterns of interest.

While I said in the previous section that eventing systems are often implemented on specific messaging systems, event systems *conceptually* do not rely on a particular messaging system—any mechanism for subscribing to events of interest and sending one-way messages should be adequate for implementing the event system.[5]

Why CloudEvents

The CNCF project called *CloudEvents* is a good example of system independence—it defines a mapping from an abstract set of eventing properties (metadata, payloads, etc.) to multiple underlying messaging systems (called *bindings* in CloudEvents parlance). This chapter focuses mostly on the CloudEvents view of the world; the project aims to make it easier to share libraries and tools across messaging platforms by defining a flexible and broadly supported messaging envelope that is content agnostic—the "HTTP of Eventing."

---

4 CQRS stands for *command query responsibility segregation*. For a longer discussion of CQRS, see *Event Centric: Finding Simplicity in Complex Systems* by Greg Young (Addison-Wesley).

5 If you have a two-way messaging system, it's easy to use it to produce a one-way system by sending empty responses.

This might seem boring and not much of a big deal, but a look back across the last 50 years of messaging systems suggests that each system has defined its own envelope, properties, and capabilities. In some cases, language-specific libraries like Spring Messaging provide a language-specific abstraction across multiple messaging protocols, but there is no cross-language and cross-protocol mechanism for automatically translating a message on a Kafka topic to a RabbitMQ exchange or a NATS topic.

Why Does a Universal Envelope Matter?

Unlike synchronous application interfaces, through which a client can get immediate feedback if they submit an invalid request, asynchronous messaging makes it harder for message recipients (called *consumers*) to provide feedback to senders (called *producers*). Some libraries and protocols (such as Confluent's schema registry) provide specific support for enforcing that messages on a particular channel match a particular schema, but these are generally language-specific and value-add capabilities.

Without standard ways to understand a message on a topic, message consumers need to rely on out-of-band information, such as documentation pages or application-specific infrastructure. CloudEvents provides a standard way to find information such as "what type of data is in this message" and "what kind of message is this" on at least eight common messaging platforms. The CloudEvents working group also defines the process to extend and document the mapping for messaging protocols, whether they are open source or proprietary.

Similar to HTTP, CloudEvents provides a simple baseline of functionality, onto which additional standards and mechanisms can be layered. At the base layer, CloudEvents defines a message envelope with a flat map of named and typed envelope fields called `attributes` and an arbitrary payload. CloudEvents reserves a small number of attributes for core functionality—`specversion`, `type`, `source`, and `id` are required attributes for the 1.0 spec, and a number of well-known optional fields are defined, including extensions for data format, event time, tracing, sampling, data protection, and ordering. Additionally, the spec reserves the names `data` and `data_base64` for encoding the event payload.

The separation of attributes and data payload is an important abstraction—it is expected that attribute fields will contain metadata about the event that is useful for tracking, routing, and handling events in a content-agnostic way, while the payload will be most useful to event consumers who need to process the details of the message. For example, an event about an object upload might include metadata about the filename, bucket, and size. These attributes could be used to apply a function to uploaded videos only above a certain size ("filename ends in `.mov` and size greater than `5MB`").

When mapping CloudEvents onto a particular protocol such as RabbitMQ, Kafka, or HTTP, CloudEvent attributes will typically be stored as extended attributes on the message, while the payload will be stored as the message body. Mapping attributes this way allows systems like Knative Eventing to use message attributes as selection criteria for event triggers and to easily record message-tracing information for debugging and observability purposes.

Events as an API

We've already covered how CloudEvents provides a standard mechanism for translating events across messaging and storage systems. One specific benefit of this standard format is that it simplifies the process of defining event-based APIs.[6] The standard CloudEvents fields include payload metadata like `datacontenttype`, which is a MIME type, and `dataschema`, which can reference schema documents such as JSON or XML schemas. By publishing these schemas in standard formats, it becomes easier for teams to look up and exchange information. In particular, because each CloudEvent includes a plain-text URL for the data schema used, CloudEvents can be considered self-describing—no additional context information is needed to understand an event outside of the attributes and payload.

As of this writing, the CloudEvents group is also in the process of defining machine-readable standardized schema registry, subscription, and discovery mechanisms. Even without these mechanisms, a message can be automatically translated from a JSON envelope to Avro and stored in a log system for several months, then converted to protocol buffers and sent to a recipient who can interpret the message without needing any context on the original sender. This property is very important in an event-driven system in which event messages may be handled several systems away from the producer and possibly offset in time by significant amounts—as anyone who's written a large system knows, code that you wrote six months ago might as well have been written by another person.

Automatic format translation particularly shines when building aggregated event records across an entire system: no matter what format is "native" to a particular component, it can be translated to a common language and stored in the same stream of events as other components for later analysis.

---

6 Other efforts such as AsyncAPI focus on defining schemas for specific message topics, but CloudEvents provides a *context-agnostic* mechanism for defining these APIs—no matter where you happen to find a `Microsoft.Storage.BlobCreated` event, it will have the same format.

What Does Event-Driven Mean?

I've referred a lot to event-driven designs and systems in this chapter, but while we're setting out definitions, let's define the criteria for considering a system event-driven:

> A system is *event-driven* if the majority of the system behavior is executed as the consequence of receiving and handling events.[7]

Note that event-driven has been a common paradigm in desktop and GUI applications for the last 20 years. Most UI frameworks explicitly describe a set of UI interaction events and a mechanism for registering callbacks, listeners, or other code to react to those events. Even the cancellation mechanism of browser events can be mapped to deciding whether to propagate a received event or acknowledge it without further processing. Backend systems have adopted some of these same principles in the Reactive Manifesto (*https://www.reactivemanifesto.org*).

Combining event-driven architecture with serverless runtimes helps achieve high levels of efficiency, as applications run only when there is work to process. An event-driven architecture has several potential patterns for message- or event-based communication between systems; the following are the most common, but you may encounter other patterns in the wild:

Event distribution
> This pattern is concerned with routing requests from event producers to interested receivers. Generally, producers and consumers are systems rather than individual instances, and neither producers nor consumers may know all the details of the other involved parties. Maintaining these systems at arm's length with an event distribution system can help teams maintain a decoupled architecture.

Task queues
> Unlike event distribution, task queues are more of a messaging (command) construct. The task queue receives messages or events to process, and schedules work execution to meet various goals of the system, which can include capacity or efficiency goals, acceptable latency, and failure handling. Many task-queueing systems also include the ability to schedule work for future execution.

---

7 If the majority of the work is executed as a result of received messages, this implies that at least some system flows consist of events that were triggered by processing other events. These event chains are a common sign of event-driven architecture.

Workflows

Unlike event distribution and task queues, workflows focus on handling a series of events or actions correlated with a particular resource. Workflows are akin to the plan for assembling an engine from parts on the factory floor. They lay out the order that parts need to be assembled, as well as the procedures to follow if an error is detected (for example, set the part aside for later examination for defects[8]). Workflows are often used to manage more complex request-reply or Scatter-Gather messaging patterns.

Event streaming

Stream processing is a complex topic worthy of its own book. For the purposes of this book, it's worth pointing out that stream processing typically involves building up long-lived state across multiple correlated events (for example, different readings over time from the same meter). As such, event streaming is not an obvious fit for serverless, though projects like Flink's StateFun mechanism (*https://oreil.ly/z46pc*) allow using serverless functions for some parts of the processing pipeline.

Broadcast

While distribution, task queues, and streaming all involve routing events or messages *between* systems, broadcast is more often used *within* a system to share information between instances in the same system. One common use case is for cache invalidation—when one instance writes a new value to a shared cache, it needs to broadcast the value update to other instances that might have cached a previous value. Broadcast is primarily different from the event distribution problem because it involves the dynamic registration of many application instances.

Now that we have some idea of the patterns we may encounter in our event-driven adventure, let's see how these patterns play out in actual serverless applications.

Event Distribution

Event-driven applications are composed of multiple event-processing components; typically, these applications can be connected by configuration after they are written. This is called *late binding*, and it contributes to the flexibility of event-driven architectures. Event distribution platforms enable this late binding by providing a configurable mechanism to collect events from one component and distribute the event to other nodes. Event distribution also provides a solution to the layering violations

---

8 In messaging systems, an undeliverable message is often put into a *dead-letter queue* for similar later analysis. This keeps the workflow or "factory floor" moving, even as one part is set aside. When you set up dead-letter queues, it's important to monitor how many messages are being diverted to that queue, or you may miss event processing failures!

introduced in "The Monolith Next Door" on page 102: rather than two systems each taking a dependency on the other to react to changes, each can publish a well-known event and subscribe to events of interest. This transforms the system from a cross-layer dependency to two shared dependencies on the event-distribution system. This typically means that the event-delivery mechanism needs to run as a reliable low-dependency infrastructure component in any system that uses it. Figure 6-1 provides a simplified picture of the role of an event-distribution system; note that a single software component can act as both an event sender and an event receiver.

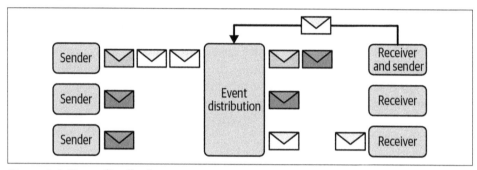

Figure 6-1. Event distribution

The Knative Eventing Broker model supports this use case by providing a central endpoint that can receive and store events from event senders. Receivers can then register their interest in specific types of events by using a Trigger that specifies the desired event attributes. In the case of Knative, these events are transmitted using the CloudEvents over HTTP API, and the Broker may store the received events in an underlying messaging system like Kafka or RabbitMQ before routing the events to the appropriate Triggers. The Knative Broker implements a pattern called a *content-based router*, which allows clients to receive events by indicating the expected event attributes.

An alternative model for event distribution is to curate a set of event topics or channels and require each receiver to subscribe to specific topics that contain the messages that they are interested in. Knative eventing also supports this model by using the Channel and Subscription constructs.

Content-Based Routing Versus Channels

It's great that Knative offers two event distribution models, but it can be confusing to determine which model to use. I recommend starting with the Broker model, as it generally creates fewer objects and requires less coordination about resource names and types compared with the Channel model. Table 6-1 summarizes the differences between the two models.

Table 6-1. Knative brokers and channels compared

Broker	Channel
Single entrypoint for all events.	One entry point per category or topic.
Need a registry of event types and attribute values.	Need a registry of topics and event contents.
Filtering code executes for each Trigger and event.	Every event on Channel X is sent to all Subscriptions.
Reply events are routed through the Broker again.	Reply events are routed to a new destination based on the Subscription.

Here are three main use cases for using Channels instead of Brokers:

- For high-throughput applications (several thousand events per second), there may be throughput advantages to separating messages by channel and avoiding Broker filtering.
- Existing use cases may translate more naturally to Channels and Subscriptions.
- Channels and Subscriptions can be helpful when building other eventing components like a task queue or workflow system. For example, the Sequence construct (see Figure 3-7 for an illustration of sequences) is built on a series of Channels and Subscriptions.

Internal and External Events

Event distribution makes it easy to route events from one component to another in an event-driven architecture. Sometimes, however, we need to ask ourselves not "Can we do this?" but instead "Should we do this?" For many applications, some events or commands may effectively be implementation details, while other events form a strong public contract that other systems can rely on.

In general, public or external events are key or critical moments in the business process flow that may be of interest to other participants in the larger software system. Typically, these will be state changes in the domain model of the application that correspond to high-level human-language outcomes in the system.

As an example, a retail store system may have events for "order placed" and "store picker scanned item." The former event would be a good candidate for a public event, because refactors of the software involved in managing the store are unlikely to remove the idea of ordering items because that's a core part of the model. In contrast, the "item was scanned" event, while critical for ensuring that the right items were added to the correct order, is a detail that could be changed as technology progresses.

In general, it's useful to document the external or public event interfaces (generated and consumed) in the same manner as you would synchronous APIs. Internal events may be less formal and documented primarily in code or on internal collaboration systems. Depending on the degree of desired separation between internal and external events, it may make sense to set up multiple Knative Brokers to enable managing the different event scopes. In Figure 6-2, each component runs a local Broker that receives and handles both internal and external events for the component. The component-local Broker then explicitly publishes external events to a cross-component Broker that manages the event-driven integration between components.

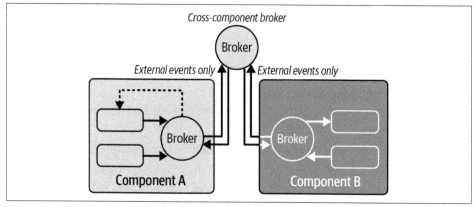

Figure 6-2. Broker hierarchies with Knative

Note that the configuration in Figure 6-2 can be implemented using one or more Kubernetes namespaces; Knative supports creating and managing multiple Broker instances in the same namespace or using Triggers to route events to targets in a different namespaces.

Now that we've talked a bit about visibility horizons for different types of events, let's talk briefly about what makes for good external events.

Building for Extension with "Inner Monologue"

In talking about externally published and internal implementation details, I hinted about a rule for publishing events externally:

> An event-integrated system should externally publish all events that describe meaningful progress or changes in the system.

This sort of publishing can be thought of as the "inner monologue" of the software. Similarly to a monologue on stage, a software inner monologue can allow us to follow along with the processes within a software system. Unlike a monologue on stage, it can be acceptable and even beneficial for an observer of a software monologue to jump in and modify the system mid-process.

This sort of behavior can be used, for example, to implement a security system that detects account hijackings by looking for unusual patterns in user logins. In this example, a user login service might publish "user logged in," "user failed to log in," and "user reset password" events including details of the user, device, and source IP that trigger the event. An event-driven system can watch these events and react to users logging in from unexpected IPs, devices, or both. By leveraging the login service's inner monologue, the account takeover defense team can build an independent microservice without needing to interrupt the login service team with direct integration support.

Event distribution provides an essential service for connecting event-driven actors. Sometimes applications need to couple event handling with state storage, which naturally lends itself to the workflow pattern.

Workflow Orchestration

Workflows allow either ad hoc or formal definitions of patterns of events that should be processed in a larger system-defined context related to a *correlation ID*. By isolating messages related to a correlation ID within a larger context, developers can control the flow of work among components and centralize the complexity of event management in workflow configuration. For this reason, workflow orchestration is often used to implement the Saga pattern, a mechanism for managing distributed transactions using messages and per-microservice transactions.[9]

In the Saga pattern, services process the distributed transaction in a specified order; if a transaction fails, a series of compensating transactions can be run to undo the effects of work already done. By isolating a set of control flows into independent units of coordination (work), workflow orchestrators can scale on correlated workflows in the same way that serverless runtimes manage code execution.

Breaking workflows into correlated sets of managed events enables the workflow system to scale horizontally by allocating independent storage and management (locking, updates, etc.) for each instance of the workflow. Because the units are independent, it's possible to handle hundreds or thousands of concurrent workflows in such a system—when a particular workflow is not actively handling events and updating the system state, it can store the current state of the system in external storage and then exit.[10] For example, the workflow indicated in Figure 6-3 takes advantage of the bounded nature of workflow execution to fan out complex messages to multiple workflow instances.

---

9 A good reference for the Saga pattern and other distributed transaction patterns is *Microservices Patterns* by Chris Richardson (Manning).

10 This looks extremely similar to the actor model of computation. In fact, workflows are a bounded implementation of this model. The benefit of bounding a model in this way is that it allows system developers to bake in best practices and optimize common use cases at the expense of uncommon use cases. It can also allow system authors to erect a barrier around problematic or frequently misused functionality.

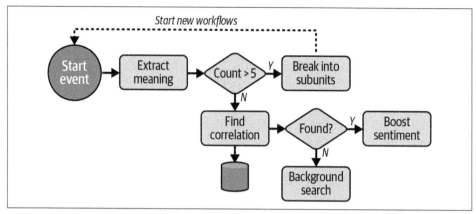

Figure 6-3. Example workflow

While this example does not aggregate the fanned-out workflows, many workflow tools provide mechanisms to wait for and aggregate multiple responses from a fanned-out event workflow. These mechanisms are sometimes named things like JOIN, AWAIT, TIMEOUT, or GATHER; some workflow systems also provide an explicit model for nesting or delegating work to subworkflows.

These sorts of tools start to look a bit like a small programming language; we'll talk more about that in "Workflow as Declarative Manifests" on page 132 after we explain *why* it makes sense to build workflows as a separate tool from general-purpose serverless runtimes.

Long-Lived Workflows, Short-Lived Compute

Workflows provide a way to manage and checkpoint the state of an application without needing to retain state in a long-running function execution. At first glance, it would be simple to implement the workflow in Figure 6-3 as code; something like the code sample in Example 6-1 would seem to have the same effect.

Example 6-1. Source code for sample workflow

```
async handle_event(event) {
  meaning = await extract_meaning(event);
  if (meaning.count > 5) {
    for (int i = 0; i < meaning.count; i += 5) {
      slice = meaning.select(i, i+4);
      submit_event(slice);
    }
  } else {
    correlation = await find_correlation(meaning)
    if (correlation.found) {
      boost_sentiment(correlation)
```

```
    } else {
      background_search(correlation)
    }
  }
}
```

In an ideal world, we could simply run this JavaScript in a process and achieve the same results as the workflow. The code is pretty simple and seems like it should be easy to write and test, requiring no special tools or management mechanisms to implement. Unfortunately, this program as written keeps all of its state *in memory*, which means that any restart of the container or host will terminate the workflow in some intermediate, unknown state. We could fix this problem by having the system store its status to a database on each `await` statement and then having a background process that checks to see whether a correlating event or timer should route to an existing program or rehydrate the process at the correct point.[11] This is what a workflow system does.

Extracting long-running processes like the previous workflow management into external systems and running compute in short-lived bursts is a standard pattern for serverless systems. Internally, those systems (like the workflow system) may also use the same short-lived bursts of compute, but their external presentation is of a long-running process per workflow. Keeping application code in a short-lived execution window is a useful strategy for managing failure and interruptions: a process that runs for 60 minutes will be interrupted at least 20 times as often as a process that takes 3 minutes to run. Furthermore, many systems offer a certain "grace period" for applications to shut down; if all requests take less than the grace period, then it's a simple matter of refusing new work and allowing the old work to complete during that shutdown window.

Because the serverless runtime is managing the graceful shutdown, application code written by the user never needs to think about the sequence of events involved in a graceful shutdown. Similarly, workflows allow users to define long-running and durable state machines for handling events without needing to bother themselves about storage, parallelism, or reentrancy of the infrastructure.

 Workflows complement short-lived serverless code execution by abstracting common storage, locking, and execution patterns for handling sequences of events related to a common entity or correlation ID.

---

11 Azure Durable Functions does, in fact, enable just this. Unfortunately, it also requires deep language hooks to be able to save and restore the state of a running application, and works for only certain patterns.

Workflow as Declarative Manifests

In Example 6-1, we expressed the desired workflow as an *imperative* set of steps in software. While many developers think about systems and software in this way, workflow systems can also be built in a declarative fashion by specifying how the components should be connected without the ceremony of variables and nested blocks. This has a few advantages over the imperative style of workflow:

- Declarative or special-purpose languages can avoid control flow (such as recursion) that could cause performance problems.
- It can be easier to store (serialize) the state if it is described as data.
- It can be easier to produce visualizations of the state from a declared manifest.
- Structural descriptions can make it easier to optimize the execution; for example, collecting a set of if/else statements into a single switch construct.

AWS Step Functions are a popular implementation of declarative serverless state machines; as described in "Long-Lived Workflows, Short-Lived Compute" on page 130, given a state machine and a mechanism for storing the intermediate state between executions, it is relatively easy to build your own workflow system.[12] In fact, one of the challenges (and the reason that Knative does not have its own workflow system) is that dozens of workflow languages and tools exist in this area, each with its own benefits and drawbacks.

Moving from this well-populated space, we'll next cover an event-driven pattern that is much more common with long-lived processes like monoliths (see Chapter 5) than for short-lived compute in serverless systems.

Event Broadcast

Broadcast is a mechanism for sending an update to every running instance of a particular application. This is commonly and frequently used to communicate about cache invalidations but can also be used to indicate that new data (such as a new machine learning model) is available or that an existing background process (such as an indexing process) should be aborted.

Serverless systems rarely use broadcast notifications—after all, if all the computational work is focused on executing a single independent task, why would you need to send information to each of those independent tasks at the same time? Generally,

---

12 While it is relatively easy to build such a system, a few "gotchas" still remain. One is handling the state of in-flight workflows when the workflow definition changes. Two generally safe strategies are either to serialize the workflow description as part of the state or to make all workflow triggers versioned and deploy the workflow as a new (tagged) serverless version.

---

this sort of cross-instance communication is a warning sign in a serverless system; your first reaction should be to ask whether there's a less internally coordinated mechanism to achieve this result. Unfortunately, sometimes there *are* good reasons (such as access revocations) to broadcast an event to all the instances of a serverless application. Unfortunately, you'll also find that this is a tricky proposition.

What's So Tricky About Broadcast?

In a traditional system, the set of broadcast recipients is known, typically because each listener registers with the broadcast system at startup. These listeners typically run for a long time and then hand off their subscription to a new instance of the same application (often with the same handle) when upgraded. This pattern works well for mostly fixed applications, but serverless applications can struggle under this type of broadcast regime.

The fundamental problem is that adding and removing members from the listener pool tends to be a somewhat heavyweight operation—the central broadcast coordinator needs to keep track of all the broadcast recipients, and a burst of adding or removing hundreds of listeners on a topic can congest the same structures used to determine which endpoints need a notification of new messages.

Fortunately, we can extend a state-management solution that is often associated with broadcast to enable serverless applications to avoid this expensive churn on the central broadcast coordination.

Broadcast in Fast-Moving Systems

So, you've gotten into a situation where you need to build a mechanism to broadcast events to all your serverless workers. The solution is to have an endpoint that serves a *log* of the current state of the world in a way that new and existing processes can easily catch up-to-date on that current state. It's no surprise that this solution looks a little bit like distributed log solutions such as Apache Kafka—distributed logs scale very well,[13] including to many readers with little server-side state. Typically, you'll want to structure the data in a log that supports read offsets as follows:

- A periodic summary record that contains all the state needed for a new instance
- Updates to the summary record for each subsequent event that happens, until the next summary record

An application instance needing to start up and load the current state can scan backward in the log (using the read offset mechanism) until it finds a summary record. It

---

13 *Distributed logs* are a particular storage system where new messages are only ever appended to a file or topic.

can load that record and then "fast-forward" through all the update events to catch up with the present moment. Once an application server is caught up, it keeps track of the last seen read offset and loads future update records from the log by attempting to perform a read starting at the last processed read offset. This pattern works for both serverless and conventional instances, but the local management of the read offset makes it scale much more smoothly than a central coordinator.

With broadcast and workflows out of the way, we'll turn our attention to a similar-sounding but quite different mechanism for managing system load: task queues.

Task Queues

In "Task Queues" on page 45, we gave a brief example of some additional background jobs that might be used to improve the latency of our dashboard rendering. In general, task queues combine event storage and scheduling capabilities to enable deferring work asynchronously to a future time. Task queues may also provide a mechanism for workers to store results for a work item that can be collected by another process in the future. Depending on the system, task queues may either operate on a *leasing system* (workers poll a central system and mark what they are currently working on) or as a *push system* (the task queue calls a separate execution platform to execute the work).

In either case, the task queue orchestrates the execution of independent units of work, which sounds a lot like our definition of serverless. Task queues are more serverless when the number of instances consuming from the task queue is automatically managed. In a leasing system, this probably means some sort of framework that automatically manages much of the leasing process and scales the number of workers based on the number of items in the queue. For a push system, the task queue simply manages traditional RPC calls to an existing serverless runtime.

Push queues work best for short-lived work, while the lease/renew mechanism of pull queues can be easier to manage for long-lived tasks. In either case, task queues will often implement a number of other quality-of-life features.

Task Queue Features

In addition to deferring work to a future date, task queues may implement several optional features:

Status queries
> In some task queue systems, the task queue will return a task ID or ticket associated with the queued task. This task ID can be used to query the task queue in the future to determine whether a task has executed, the task success or failure, and any results from the task.

Task scheduling

Some task queue systems allow specifying that a task should execute after a certain time in the future. This may be either a relative time ("10 minutes later") or at a specific date and time. Future scheduling helps stateless systems handle systems that may need a delay, such as retrying a failed work item or checking the status of a real-world process.

Completion notifications

Some task queues provide a way to notify an external service when a task completes. This could be an event ("task completed") posted back to an event-driven system or a generic webhook to a specific destination. Task completion notifications can help stitch together tasks in event-driven workflows (as described in "Workflow Orchestration" on page 129) into a comprehensive system. Task queues with completion notifications can also be used to implement a workflow system.

Task cancellation

When implementing task IDs, task queues may also support canceling work that has not yet been started or potentially even canceling a task currently in progress. This pattern can be useful in conjunction with task scheduling to implement reminders or recovery checks and then cancel the future tasks when a particular process completes.

Scaling in Time Instead of Instances

In the introduction to task queues, I described task queues as a naturally serverless paradigm. While many serverless runtimes automatically change the number of instances based on the amount of work to be done, task queues also have the option to manage bursts of work by stretching the work over *time* as well as by scaling instances, as illustrated in Figure 6-4.

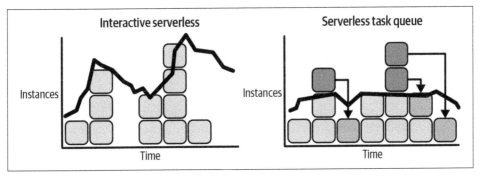

Figure 6-4. Scaling work in time rather than instances

There are several compelling reasons to shift work across time. Generally, shifting work allows for better capacity management within the application. This capacity can come in several aspects:

Hardware capacity

The task queue can either statically limit the work in-flight or react to resources available in the cluster to dynamically adjust the amount of work in-flight.

Database connections

Many databases have a fixed connection limit; a task queue can limit the number of tasks in-flight to ensure that those limits are respected.

Shifting work over time can also act as a "shock absorber," or buffer for other systems; since task queues define the set of tasks available for processing, they can implement policies such as "the number of tasks offered cannot increase by more than two times over ten minutes."

 Unlike many of the other event-driven patterns in this chapter, task queues have a controlling relation with serverless instance requirements because the queue is responsible for deciding which work is offered when to execution instances. This allows task queues to trade off capacity and latency in a way that other event patterns do not.

Summary

While event-driven architecture is not a requirement for serverless applications, most event-driven patterns naturally lend themselves to serverless execution. Debugging such an environment is a major focus of Chapter 10; at a minimum, the ability to trace event flows through the system and associate events with a unique ID are critical for debugging.[14] Both new and existing applications can take advantage of event distribution and the "inner monologue" pattern to provide asynchronous extension points; this pattern is particularly attractive when extending a monolith, as described in "Asynchronous Cleanup and Extension" on page 108. Knative Eventing provides several primitives for implementing event distribution in concert with Knative Serving.

In the next chapter, we'll dive into more depth on developing this internal monologue and build out some specific event-driven design scenarios with practical examples of event distribution, workflows, and task queues.

---

14 Fortunately, CloudEvents has clear specifications for interacting with distributed tracing frameworks.

## CHAPTER 7

Developing a Robust Inner Monologue

In "Event Distribution" on page 125, we talked a little bit about the idea of publishing the "inner monologue" of an application using events. This model (and some related ideas around active storage) form the basis of this chapter. This inner monologue can be accomplished in several ways, but the core idea is to build the integration points for your application as you build the code, rather than needing to come back in later to bolt on extension points after the original work is done.

The design techniques in this chapter apply equally to both monolithic applications as described in Chapter 5 and microservices. The patterns also apply to applications on all sorts of runtimes, from function-based serverless applications to traditional runtimes to individually stateful instances described in "Instance Addressability and Sharding" on page 166. With that said, extensions built on reacting to events published by the inner monologue will generally be well aligned with serverless principles and may benefit from running on a serverless platform. In this way, events are the razor handles of serverless, helping to sell the "blades" of serverless compute.[1]

Ambient Event Publishing

Treating event distribution as an ambient capability in the environment greatly simplifies the implementation of inner monologues and the other techniques in this chapter. When thinking about inner monologues, I find helpful comparisons with monitoring and observability instrumentation—it's possible to bolt it onto an existing application, but an application clearly benefits from having these capabilities baked in. In both cases, the application with capabilities baked in may be slightly

---

1 Or is it the other way around? Maybe serverless compute helps sell event platforms. Pricing suggests that it's probably the former, however.

more expensive to build up front but can have significantly lower cost of operations as problems can be resolved or integrations built without needing to disturb or even coordinate with the core application team.

 Design your application's event publishing the same way you would a public API, and make event publishing an intrinsic application capability like logging or monitoring. It's much easier to add an event when you're working on the code the first time than to come back later in a massive effort.

To make it attractive to bake in an event-based inner monologue, several properties of your event-distribution system make monologues cheaper and easier to implement:

Flexible event submission

Some event systems require that event topics or schemas are predeclared before events can be sent. Other systems allow event types to be mixed on a single topic, or topics to be created on the fly to support different message types. The latter systems work better for inner monologue development because they reduce the cost and rollout effort of adding a new event when developing the application. Knative Eventing supports this pattern with Brokers, where event producers can simply dump events into the Broker without needing to define separate topics for each event type.

Selective event filtering

On the flip side of easily publishing events from the application, extensions attempting to "listen in" on the application monologue need some way to control and limit the events received. A complex application may produce hundreds of types of events; a given integration may be interested in two or three of the event types (login events, for example). Rather than each extension needing to implement its own receipt and filtering of unwanted events, the event delivery system can natively provide these filters as part of the subscription process. Knative Eventing Triggers allow subscribers to define a filter on the application monologue and receive only events that match the requested attributes.

Low cost for events with no listeners

One of the properties of an inner monologue is that the event producer defines and creates events based on the important processes of the application without specifically considering the cost of transmitting the events. This helps developers determine when they should publish an event—"Is this interesting, and do I have the data to send the event?" and builds eventing as a reliable substrate. This also means that many events may be emitted that no one is *currently* integrating with.

The delivery cost for these events should be low—they can be acknowledged to the sender and then immediately discarded.[2]

Now that we've talked about how important it is to start writing your inner monologue as you develop your application, let's talk about a few "cheats" that can reduce or remove your need to write event-recording code yourself.

The Active Storage Pattern

This pattern is quite popular in the AWS serverless space, but I've never seen it named, so I call it the *active storage pattern*. This pattern covers third-party services that can be configured to emit events automatically when certain conditions occur—this is effectively an "inner monologue" for software-as-a-service (SaaS) services.

Amazon S3 is a canonical example and was actually the motivation for AWS Lambda (we'll talk about this more in "AWS Lambda" on page 211). It is possible to configure S3 to emit an event to Lambda whenever an object is uploaded, moved, or deleted in S3. This allows event-driven applications to be built around the interactions with S3—for example, a video is uploaded to S3, which triggers a function to resize the video to a standard size and then reupload the video. The second uploaded video triggers three further functions: one to summarize the video content, one to add a subtitle track, and one to check that the audio track properly mixed. This application architecture is shown in Figure 7-1.

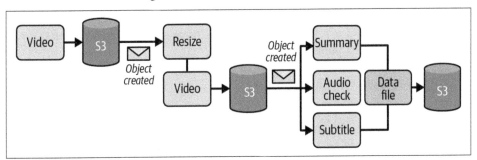

Figure 7-1. Active storage with S3 in AWS

This architecture is based on presentations from Fender guitars at ServerlessConf 2018 in San Francisco (*https://oreil.ly/M7uWK*) and others of actual serverless pipelines. In this architecture, the application's inner monologue is effectively externalized in the interactions with S3. S3 object creates, deletes, and other storage changes

---

2 If you're using an event-sourcing model, then the event log will always be listening, and this property may not be as important.

replace the need to explicitly publish state changes—the "video summarized" event is instead presented as "object uploaded to video summary bucket."

 While this section talks about using external services to extract an internal monologue from an application, it's also possible to design a service to be triggered by events from an internal monologue. For example, Amazon's Elastic Transcode service transcodes videos in one S3 bucket into another S3 bucket, but the "create job" API could also be implemented as accepting "object create" S3 events and triggering jobs directly from these notifications.

Many object stores support this pattern, but other services support this pattern as well—for example, an application could use Jira webhooks and issue updates on a rollout request ticket to coordinate the steps of rollout. Similarly, a video transcoding service might provide an event to indicate when the transcoding is complete or a key-value store could provide an event whenever a key is created or updated.

Workflows can even be seen as a manifestation of the active storage pattern. Each event that drives the workflow forward is stored in the workflow state. This way, the event-driven workflow functions as the application orchestrator as well as holder of the internal monologue. The ability to replicate events to both the workflow and external listeners by way of an event-delivery platform is particularly valuable here.

While the active storage pattern is about relying on external service APIs to publish events as a side effect of storage changes, it's also possible to turn this pattern around using the change data capture pattern to extract events from databases that aren't specifically designed to publish events.

Is Your Database Your Monologue?

Change data capture is a pattern that extracts events from database logs. Most databases use some form of transaction log, either stored as a set of committed transactions that may need to be replayed during a database restart or as a set of partially committed transactions that may need to be rolled back on failure. Additionally, many databases support some form of database replication between nodes. All of these logs can be harnessed to extract row-level update events from a running application with minimal application or database involvement.

Projects like Debezium (*https://debezium.io*) can integrate with a variety of databases by consuming their row-level replication formats; a Debezium event publisher looks from a database perspective like just another database replica. Obviously, this is a replica you wouldn't want to promote to a primary, but by hooking into the replication protocol, Debezium puts a low load on the database primary and lends itself to management with existing database tools.

This sounds very attractive—most applications use some form of database, and being able to retrofit an existing inner monologue or skip explicit development of an inner monologue seems appealing. What's the catch? Why wouldn't we want to simply use change data capture to publish our internal monologue?

 An internal monologue is an API with your integrations. Change data capture is coupled to your database schema instead of being independent of the implementation.

While change data capture or active storage may be a good way to get started quickly, these shortcuts couple the ecosystem around your application to the details of your database schema. Worse, because these integrations are asynchronous and event-driven, there's no direct application feedback that application operators can react to and realize that they've broken this API contract—it's up to the downstream extension maintainers to realize that the integration has broken and contact the application authors to roll back or adjust their integrations.

For this reason, you may want to define two horizons for your events, as described in "Internal and External Events" on page 127: an "internal system" that can consume events from change data capture and active storage and an "external system" that publishes well-documented events and acts as a more explicit contract that extension authors can rely on over time. The internal domain can use the schema-based row-change events to reconstruct domain-level events that act as an external event-based API. For example, adding an item to a shopping cart might create a row containing references to a shopping cart ID, an item ID, and a count.[3] Externally, the shopping-cart system might want to publish events about items added to carts with attributes that could be used for filtering (including the user owning the cart and item details). Just as microservices may define inbound APIs using tools like OpenAPI (*https://www.openapis.org*), external events provide a webhook-like "outbound API" for other systems to react to events happening within a microservice.

Scenarios for Inner Monologues

At the beginning of this chapter, I recommended that application authors should think about integrating inner monologue events into their applications in the same way that they integrate monitoring and observability reporting. While that is a clear statement of importance, it says very little about the *what* and *when* of event reporting—obviously, we don't want to report an event for each RPC failure or success.

---

3 This is explored in more detail in "Item added to cart" on page 148.

Now that we have some understanding of how to implement an inner monologue, let's talk about what kinds of events are useful, and the extension scenarios that can hook onto a useful inner monologue.

In addition to defining what types of events are useful for extensions, we'll describe a few antipatterns for events and message-passing systems in general. Much like monitoring and observability, indiscriminate event reporting can slow your application while snowing you under a mountain of useless events. When this happens, you'll be tempted to just shut the whole thing off and say, "Why did I bother with this to begin with?" Therefore, my first recommendation is to dabble your toes in the water of event publishing before going wild and to periodically assess your success—much like conventional API design, event publishing is as much an art as a science.

Key Events

When looking to add an inner monologue, the first thing to do is to inventory your application's functionality. What are the key workflows or user journeys for your application? Start by focusing on the most frequent or most critical interactions; for a casual online game, these key events might look like Example 7-1.

Example 7-1. Key events for an online game

- User signs up
- User starts a game
- User finishes a game (win or lose)
- User spends "points" on shop
- User spends money on shop

For each of these steps, it's probably clear that it makes sense to publish an event and what the event should contain. Given these events, it's possible for external teams to implement processes like loyalty rewards for playing the game every day for a week, without the core application needing to add this tracking information to the core database. Separating the loyalty tracking from the core application allows the customer loyalty team to experiment and make changes to the rewards system outside of the flow of the main application update.

When you're inventorying the key events in your application, remember to assess not just the frequency of the events, but also the severity or improbability of an event. For example, password resets or two-factor signups may be infrequent events, but since they control access to a user's account, they may be worth early prioritization when designing your application's internal monologue. Similarly, user support tickets may be a key target for automation, and so rise in priority compared with more frequent but less impactful events. Depending on the system used, user support tickets may also be a good candidate for either the active storage pattern (see "The Active Storage Pattern" on page 139) or for normalization behind a common abstract interface (if you expect that the user support system may change as an application scales, for example).

While you're plotting out the key events or journeys of your application's users, you'll want to pay particular attention to one type of journey for extension: workflows.

Workflows

Whether implemented through an explicit workflow management system or simply a series of steps in a UI, workflows are a natural fit for enrichment through inner monologue. While the core path through the workflow may not be suitable for asynchronous implementation, connecting these workflows to an event distribution platform allows additional workflows to choreograph themselves *around* the core workflow. Publishing an inner monologue while processing a workflow allows optional extensions to augment the workflow at each step or to connect one workflow to another in an opportunistic way.

As a concrete example of workflow extension, we can consider processing a loan application; Example 7-2 might represent the main workflow for the loan application.

Example 7-2. Loan processing workflow

1. Collect loan data from applicant

2. Collect supplemental material about a loan

3. Compute creditworthiness and loan terms

4. Loan officer reviews loan and approves/denies

5. If approved, produce loan documents for applicant to sign

6. Applicant signs loan documents

At each of these stages, it makes sense to publish an event indicating that the loan application has moved to the next step of processing. An external application could, for example, use the notification of loan application submitted to collect credit scores and other creditworthiness assessments from different APIs and attach them to the loan before the loan is sent to the loan officer for approval. Similarly, an external application could use the loan documentation complete event to contact the applicant to schedule a signing appointment without needing to extend the (possibly financially sensitive) core loan application.

While an inner monologue provides great opportunities for decoupling extension capabilities from the core workflow, event processing and inner monologue is not always the most appropriate mechanism for implementing core workflows and integrations.

Inner Monologues Versus RPCs

While asynchronous messaging and event processing work well for decoupling applications and teams, sometimes coupling is appropriate and RPCs or synchronous API calls are a better fit. As described in Table 7-1, synchronous calls can be a better integration mechanism if the data is necessary and the application should block until data is available. In general, while inner monologue is a valuable tool, RPCs can be a simple and effective way to tie two systems together if tight coupling is appropriate.

Table 7-1. Design hints for inner monologue versus RPCs

Inner monologue	Synchronous calls
Use this pattern if the integration is *optional*.	Use this pattern if the integration is *mandatory*.
Send to zero or more systems.	Calls exactly one system.
Configure the event system with recipient addresses.	Sender needs to know the address of other system.
Can proceed before the integration has responded.	Blocks until information is received.
Can be forwarded beyond the initial recipient.	

Generally, when designing an application, you'd *choose* a single synchronous and a single asynchronous implementation to standardize on. Unfortunately, depending on the existing platforms you need to integrate with, it may be necessary to support multiple protocols. While it's fairly easy to choose a different protocol for each direct (RPC) invocation, choosing a primary protocol for asynchronous integrations is a bit trickier because the same message might be delivered to different systems that each use a different messaging system. This is where a cross-messaging system protocol like CloudEvents comes in handy, as events sent using one protocol (such as AMQP) can be automatically converted to a different protocol.

Because asynchronous integrations like an inner monologue can be replicated widely (possibly beyond the known set of integrations), inner monologue events that deal with sensitive data (including data protected by regulations such as General Data Protection Regulation [GDPR]) in the EU may need special design considerations. Fortunately, an existing solution exists in the claim-check pattern from the enterprise integration space.

Sensitive Data and Claim Checks

The claim-check pattern replaces sensitive data in an event with a token that can be used to fetch the data from the original source.[4] As shown in Figure 7-2, an integration that needs access to the claim-checked data must call back to the original application to fetch the data. By requiring any integration to call back to the original application, the event sender can enforce access and audit controls even if the asynchronous event is shared widely.

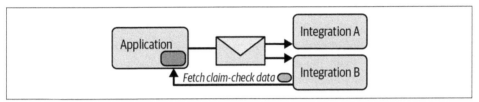

Figure 7-2. The claim-check pattern

Not every event consumer may need to fetch claim-check data from an event; for example, an "item added to shopping cart" event might claim check the customer and order ID but not the product ID; a "popular items" tracker might not need to fetch the claim-checked information and could work off only the product ID. When using the claim-check pattern, it's particularly important to ensure that any relevant routing information is extracted into plain-text attributes. For example, if hiding a customer ID with the claim-check pattern, you might want to expose an attribute indicating the "tier" of customer or whether the customer is a first-time or anonymous customer ("guest"). These types of attributes are broad enough to avoid leaking personally identifiable information (PII),[5] but can help integrations filter events to extract the "ham" from the "spam."

Now that we've got a toolkit for managing our inner monologue, let's dive into how we can extract the most value from the work we've done. This next section will hopefully provide some insight and guidance on what parts of your application to instrument first.

How to Use an Inner Monologue

In these examples, we'll learn some scalable patterns for solving problems by using events. By working through these, we'll also illustrate event properties that are useful when establishing an inner monologue. Note that these are simply illustrative

---

4 This token could be a URL, which makes it easy for the recipient to figure out which original system has the data.

5 I am not a lawyer or GDPR expert.

examples; there is a large field of event-driven architecture with further examples. While event-driven architecture is not inherently serverless, a number of event-driven principles make serverless runtimes an attractive target for event-driven architectures:

Events should represent a change in state
> Each event corresponds to a change in state. Some external system is managing the state, and each observed change corresponds to a unit of work to execute to track that particular state change.

Events should be self-contained
> A given event should have sufficient information to reconstruct the state change of the resource from the event contents. In particular, you should be able to interpret an event *independently* of processing other events.[6] This provides us with the "independent" property that allows serverless systems to manage scale automatically.

As we continue with these examples, we'll call back to these two principles when describing the events that power these scenarios.

Extending the Monolith: Workflow Decoration

A common application of event-driven architecture is customer engagement. In this example, we'll work through the process of extending an existing monolithic shopping cart application similar to Amazon, Shopify, or a WordPress plug-in like Woo-Commerce. Assuming that the existing shopping cart system has a fairly simple REST API, the only changes needed to the existing shopping cart application are to publish events as part of existing workflows—no presentation or business logic needs to be updated to enable most of these extensions and integrations.

As suggested by the example shopping cart services, one advantage of publishing an inner monologue for these types of applications is that it enables SaaS platforms to provide extension points without compromising their internal architectures or service-level agreements (SLAs). A SaaS provider may not want to manage the availability and performance implications of directly calling a customer's integration API or webhook but still allow for individual customers to extend the customer experience with their own integrations. For a SaaS provider, integrations like this tend to be "sticky"—customers need to consider the cost and feasibility of reimplementing these extensions when changing platforms.

---

6 Obviously, for some use cases, you want to sequentially process the events for a given resource, which is the event-streaming model discussed briefly in "What Does Event-Driven Mean?" on page 124. However, even in the event-streaming case, processing an event associated with one stream should be independent from processing events in other streams.

For a customizer of these platforms, these extension events provide a means to customize the checkout process, improve customer experience, and increase purchase and conversion rates. In Figure 7-3, I've highlighted three points of contact where asynchronous integrations can improve the customer experience:

1. Adding items to a shopping cart provides a signal of customer interest that can help both the current customers and future customers purchasing an item.

2. User login provides an opportunity to recognize both new and existing customers in distinct ways; deferring this to an asynchronous system makes the login flow quicker and smoother for users.

3. Selecting and entering shipping information may need to synchronously provide a shipping cost estimate, but there are additional options to improve shipping efficiency and service with additional integrations.

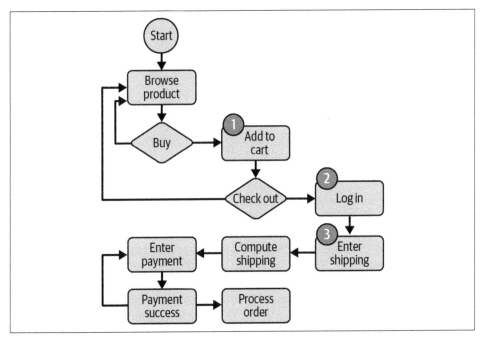

Figure 7-3. Checkout workflow

For each stage, we'll go through different event-handling functions that could all tee off the same sample event—the "functions" mode of writing serverless applications (see "Functions" on page 80) is a great match for this extension pattern because it allows each integration to be implemented and pushed independently, as described in "Top Speed: Reducing Drag" on page 84.

Item added to cart

When a user adds an item to their shopping cart, that is an indication that *someone* is interested in the product. While you want to store that indication of interest and keep the system responsive so the shopper can continue browsing, using an inner monologue event allows further system enhancement to take place simultaneously with the user's shopping session. Some of these enhancements affect or improve the current order, while others improve the long-term site quality; none of them need to be part of the core workflow of ensuring that an item is recorded in a user's shopping basket:

Item recommendations and popularity
> Many shopping sites prioritize showing items that users are more likely to buy. By moving these items toward the top of the display list, shoppers can find what they're looking for more quickly and may benefit from the knowledge and experience of other shoppers with similar tastes. These indices may be updated asynchronously and might even want to delay updating the popularity until after a logged-in user has been identified. Different types of products might also use different recommendation mechanisms—for example, books might have multiple interest categories, while staples like toothpaste might be handled much more simply.
>
> For item recommendations, the internal monologue events should include item_id, item_category, count, cart_id (or a claim-checked token) and possibly a list of interest categories (these could also be extracted within the function by looking up the user associated with the cart).

Checkout reminders
> Sometimes you start shopping for something, and then a fire alarm goes off (or there needs to be a diaper change, or...). When you get back later, you've totally forgotten what you were doing, and your shopping intent has been lost. You've probably seen companies sending a "Did you forget something?" reminder if the cart is subsequently abandoned—this can be done by using a task queue (described in "Task Queues" on page 134) that supports delayed delivery and then checking whether the cart in question still exists in a nonpurchased state and whether it still contains any items. Depending on your task queue, a completed purchase could also query and cancel any existing "reminder" tasks in the queue.
>
> For checkout reminders, the internal monologue events need only a cart_id and an event_timestamp; if the task queue supports defining the "name" of a task, reusing the cart_id as a task_id for subsequent events allows performing an "upsert" (update or insert) task operation to update the execution time of the delayed task.

Additional item suggestions

Depending on your shopping cart software, it may be possible to add "suggested items" to a particular user's session. Similar to the popularity suggestion, an asynchronous listener could enqueue additional items into a user's session that they may be interested in based on their existing cart items. This mechanism could also be used to recommend additional items to receive a bundle discount or reach a shipping threshold.

For additional item suggestions, the internal monologue events primarily need the `item_id`, `count`, and `cart_id` fields to compute any additional items to recommend.

Summarizing the necessary fields across the implementations, we find that "add item to cart" probably wants to include `item_id`, `event_timestamp`, `cart_id`, `count`, and `item_category` fields in the event, making the event fairly small (and taking advantage of the `cart_id` to act as a claim-check token). Obviously, there may be other opportunities to extend the cart-management process (including the removal of items from carts, and saving those items to "future shopping" lists), but these scenarios can also be added to an existing system without disturbing existing integrations thanks to the event-driven nature of the integrations.

In the next section, we'll talk about how login events can be similarly used to improve customer experiences; "Account Hijacking Detection" on page 152 has another scenario that also grows out of broadcasting login and other account events.

User login

At some point during the process of checking out, a user is typically associated with account credentials—they may log in when they start browsing the site to get better recommendations, or they may log in when it comes time to check out their order. Logging in provides access to the customer's saved address and billing information and also potentially allows associating their cart items with known interest categories associated with their account. Even if the user does not create an account and uses a "guest checkout," that guest checkout typically creates a temporary account for the scope of that transaction to allow the user to later return and check their shipping status, receipt, and request a return if needed.

Leveraging the knowledge of the user, the login signal can be used to trigger various incentives or discounts: new customers might have signup bonuses added to their checkout cart, or returning customers might have a loyalty code applied automatically. It's even possible to offer *different* incentives based on the customer's previous login behavior (i.e., a special reward for multiple orders in a week or for the first order in three months or more). Obviously, computing the user's login history might not be quick, so applying loyalty discounts asynchronously can be beneficial for performance as well as to decouple the customer loyalty team's processes from the checkout flow.

To compute customer loyalty discounts on login, it helps if the login event contains the user_id, an event_timestamp, and an (optional) cart_id if the user already has items in their cart.

While not all login events are related to an order checkout, each checkout has a user login. The subsequent integration steps will be more focused on checkout flows, as shipping and payment information are both specific to the checkout process. Proceeding sequentially, we'll start with receiving shipping information from the user.

Shipping

New users and existing users may have slightly different flows when choosing shipping information—typically, a new user will be asked to enter a new shipping address, while existing users can select an existing address or add a new one. A well-developed inner monologue will probably describe these orthogonally as something like "added shipping address" and "selected shipping address for order," such that existing users may fire only the second event type. We'll discuss both event types here but won't focus on getting shipping price quotes, which is a good example of the pattern we'll cover in "Scatter-Gather Advice" on page 151. Use cases for "added shipping address" and "selected shipping address" include the following:

Duplicate/fraudulent address detection
When a new address is established for a customer, it may make sense to check that address against a list of known fraudulent addresses—for example, users might create multiple accounts with different stolen credit card credentials, but ship all the purchased items to the same location for ease of pickup. Starting this check in the background even before payment information has been entered could help detect fraudulent usage early before contacting the credit card company or could simply be used as an additional check beyond the credit card fraud checks.

New address events for address checks will need an address or address_id and the cart_id of the user (to follow up on purchases deemed fraudulent). Much like customer loyalty tracking, extracting the data flows used for fraud detection to a specialized fraud team may be much simpler than having a fraud team attempt to integrate with each touch-point throughout the system.

Warehouse planning
Once a destination shipping address is chosen, the order fulfillment planning (including which items will be shipped from which warehouses) can begin. By triggering off the shipping address selection, the estimated arrival times can race with the payment completion, and it may be possible to include the estimated times in the confirmation email. Depending on implementation, the actual order

fulfillment system may also provide an inner monologue that can be used to trigger restocking orders or clearance/out-of-stock updates as orders are processed.

Computing the best shipping locations from an address selected event will need the address_id and the contents of the cart; a cart_id is probably the best way to provide this information.

While we're concluding these examples at the shipping address selected stage, event-driven extension via the inner monologue approach can also be used to enrich the order preparation and delivery process. However, event- and message-driven approaches can also be used for patterns beyond workflow extension. The next few sections will be somewhat briefer explorations of these other patterns, starting with the Scatter-Gather messaging pattern for supporting multiple information sources.

Scatter-Gather Advice

A common messaging pattern for interacting with multiple service providers is the *Scatter-Gather pattern*: the same request is sent to multiple endpoints, then the results are collected from the various providers. For example, this process could be used with the three main credit-rating agencies to determine a "median credit score" when computing a loan. This pattern works fairly well when there are a well-known set of service providers to integrate with but gets somewhat trickier as the number of providers grows. An alternative is to use an "advice event" to describe that an evaluation has started, allowing multiple (possibly unbounded) participants to register suggestions ("advice") on a decision before it is made.

In the case of deciding on a loan application, performing the Scatter-Gather request to the big three credit-reporting agencies should *also* produce a "loan evaluation" event that could be used by other teams to provide additional credit evaluations (for example, proprietary statistical models or noncredit agency data sources like employment history). Each additional data source that wanted to participate *for a particular loan application* would need to call the loan portfolio API to record its extra advice—defining the API for this additional advice would be the job of the loan portfolio team, who would then be responsible for including it in the general loan record.

Once the full set of data about the quality of the loan has been collected, it's possible to repeat the "advice event" pattern to allow multiple components or teams to offer to fulfill the loan at specified terms. Note that a key component of both the basic Scatter-Gather and the extended "advice event" pattern is setting a *timeout* for collecting advice about the decision—it's helpful to include this decide_by time as part of the event metadata so applications can use it to determine whether they have time to contribute to a given event. If an event has a decide_by time three minutes in the future and predictions have a five-minute execution time, then there's no point in attempting to handle the event. If the decide_by time is six minutes in the future, it may be worth dispatching the prediction to a dedicated or elevated queue compared with normal predictions, to allow the result to be computed before the deadline.

While advice events provide a mechanism for many systems to provide advice on a single decision, sometimes a single decision needs to be made in the context of many factors in the application. Account hijacking detection is perhaps the best example of this, but many other business processes sometimes require sifting through a haystack looking for needles—predictive maintenance, auditing, and detecting misbehavior and malfeasance (whether fraud or insider attacks) are other common uses for this "wide net" approach.

Account Hijacking Detection

While Scatter-Gather focuses on a single decision, account hijacking detection is instead an ongoing *risk assessment*: how much does the recent behavior on the account align with either normal account behavior or with common behavior seen on hijacked accounts. In this way, account hijacking may be collecting events from many stages or interactions with the application. For a social media application, this might include the following:

- Successful and failed login attempts
- Source IP addresses, platforms, and login times
- Number of new follows or followers
- Frequency of posting
- Post content (if a humor poster suddenly starts posting affiliate links, there might be a problem)
- Account settings changes

As you can see from this list, account hijacking may reach into many aspects of the application. The good news is that all of these should be easy to extract from an inner monologue, as they are all "interesting occurrences" in the application. In fact, given a robust internal monologue, it should be easy for the account hijacking team to develop and improve their controls and detection without needing to negotiate one-on-one integrations with existing teams to get the information they need.

Processing and making sense of all these events is the much trickier problem, and it's likely that most teams working on this problem will want a way to consider a window of these internal monologue events in somewhat-sorted order, even if the underlying systems don't guarantee such an order. Fortunately, stream processing systems are a great fit for these sorts of problems. While I won't cover streaming systems much in this book, it's a great example of how building an application in a serverless-friendly way can also make it easier to integrate with other technologies when it makes sense.[7]

---

7 Isn't it awesome when the veggies (serverless designs) you're being asked to eat not only taste *awesome* but also help keep you from getting sick? Someone needs to tell my kids that.

With all these events running around and being produced and consumed in different contexts over time, it can be hard to manage all the different combinations of "new code, old event" and "old code, new event" that can happen in a system. While versioning can be managed through careful rules and disciplined upgrade paths, serverless systems provide a second, simpler pattern for handling internal event upgrades.

Versioned Events, Unversioned Code

If you recall from "Top Speed: Reducing Drag" on page 84, one of the motivations for choosing serverless technologies is to reduce the maintenance cost of services. If your cost per service is low enough, it can be very cheap to launch or run a service to resolve an engineering challenge. Handling schema changes in events handled within an application is one such challenge. Many serverless platforms provide mechanisms for routing work to a particular version of the deployed code. It's possible to combine unique version numbers on events and version-specific code routing to align events between the code that sent the event and the code that receives and processes the event. This can simplify the backward- and forward-testing of internal events during schema changes: you need to test v153 events with the v153 code, but you know that v152 events will be routed to the existing (working) v152 code and v154 events will be routed to v154 code in the future.

Note that this is different from the traditional notion of semantic versioning with major/minor/patch versions—there's no expectation a v3.1.3 event would ever be handled by v3.4.1 code. Because serverless platforms will run versions only when there are events to trigger them, the resource costs of running many old versions simultaneously with the current version are very low—the triggers and revisions for v152 events can simply be left idle in the system until all v152 events have been cleared. This pattern works only when all components are released from the same pipeline, so there is a v152 release of each component with the appropriate handling code. If component releases are fully decoupled, each component would need to separately release a v154 version before any could start emitting that event format.

 Using versioned routing of events works only *within* an application with a common push process (a serverless monolith, if you will). Events *between* applications need to be versioned and evolved intentionally like any other API.

Note that this pattern *does not apply* to data stored in databases or other long-term storage. Any long-term stored data still needs to be designed with proper upgrade and downgrade paths; in particular, when using this pattern, it's *more likely than usual* that you can end up with multiple versions of code reading and storing data at the same time. In particular, old versions of database-writing code need to be careful not to destroy columns that have been added since the code was written—putting database writes behind a (synchronous) API can be a good solution for ensuring that all database paths have broad version support.

Now that we've covered a variety of reasons and techniques for building your application's inner monologue, let's explore a bit more application of these techniques. In particular, "Extending the Monolith: Workflow Decoration" on page 146 described a SaaS shopping cart application that could leverage the internal monologue pattern to enable extension. In the next section, we'll talk about how your infrastructure provider may also be letting you listen in on their internal monologue.

Clouds Have Monologues Too

As described previously, inner monologues are a great tool for providing extensibility at high reliability by allowing integrations to follow along with an application's behavior without blocking the execution of that behavior. Cloud infrastructure providers (both public clouds like Amazon, and on-premises clouds like VMware or Kubernetes) benefit from this pattern as well. While the previous sections focused primarily on integrating and automating applications, this section will show that the same techniques can also be used when managing infrastructure. This practice of automation is sometimes called DevOps, systems engineering, or platform engineering, but it's a critical piece of helping large engineering teams manage and scale running infrastructure.

Most platform engineering work is periodic (clock-driven) or *reactive* to changes in either the platform (something breaks or goes out of compliance) or the demands on the platform (user requests, capacity changes). Each of these is a small, independent unit of work that is perfect for serverless execution. Many of these actions are also event-triggered, so the ability to collect, centralize, and distribute events across the platform environment (aka event-driven architecture) is also critical. In the modern day and age, system engineering is *definitely* software engineering, and all the advantages of serverless apply to system or platform engineers as well as the product developers on top of those platforms.

Before diving into more-general cloud engineering principles, I'm going to focus on Kubernetes, for two reasons:

- Kubernetes can run in every cloud, providing a universal, consistent control plane. This was one of the reasons that Knative was built on Kubernetes—we wanted a consistent serverless platform to be available on any infrastructure.
- Kubernetes provides some clear and concrete examples of how event-driven architecture can enable large-scale automation.

Kubernetes is a fascinating platform because it was designed for extensibility around an open data model in which any component can listen to and update any other component (given the proper permissions). How to enable such radical openness? By embracing (and publishing) the inner monologue of the system as a core principle.

Kubernetes: Only a Monologue

For those not familiar with the Kubernetes architecture, Kubernetes implements cluster management and extensible container orchestration using a standardized, consistent API model implemented by a component called the `apiserver`. These APIs provide a way to record the *current* and *desired* state of various resources; the current state is then moved toward the desired state (reconciled) by external components called *controllers*. The process of reconciliation is driven by notification of changes to resource state delivered through a "watch" mechanism. As shown in Figure 7-4, every controller, including components like the container scheduler, is effectively a public and replaceable event-driven integration.

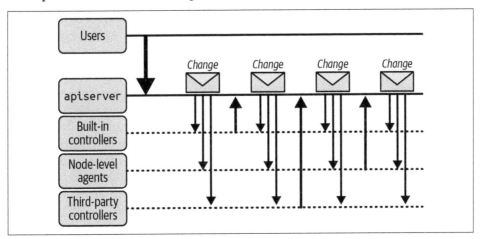

Figure 7-4. Kubernetes architecture

While the Kubernetes watch protocol is proprietary to Kubernetes, Knative provides a bridge between Kubernetes watch and CloudEvents with an event source called the ApiServerSource. This can be an easy way to extend an existing automation platform to also address Kubernetes or to implement extensions in a programming language that doesn't have strong Kubernetes API libraries.

While Kubernetes is explicitly built with an event-driven "everything on the outside" architecture, most cloud providers have a clear delineation between "public APIs" and "internal implementation." It would be nice to be able to implement the same controller model against cloud-provider APIs or even on-premises infrastructure like vSphere or Proxmox. And, it turns out that most of these providers *do* provide an API that lets you do just that.

Audit Log or Mono-Log?

While most clouds don't provide an explicit mechanism for watching changes to a resource and tracking the actual and desired state, most *do* provide an interface for logging resource changes to an audit log with a published API for reading events from that audit log. If the audit log includes actions by internal system components, it's possible to leverage this audit log to reconstruct the state changes across the infrastructure by continuously reading the audit log and converting new audit log entries into events. These events can then be used to enact either immediate controls[8] or as input to larger workflows.[9]

Some clouds, such as AWS Lambda (CloudTrail) (*https://oreil.ly/fIl1h*) and Google Cloud (Audit Logging) (*https://oreil.ly/ztMBw*) have actually documented this pattern and provide specific integration with their serverless products, but generating events from an audit log also works with on-premise software like VMware vSphere or with specialized clouds like Netlify. Much like the Knative ApiServerSource for Kubernetes, it's also possible to use API access to these audit logs to detect newly recorded events and generate general-purpose events in these systems.

Audit logs can be a rich source of events for infrastructure automation as well as security controls and mitigation. For example, the Falco community wrote a series of blog posts in 2020 (*https://oreil.ly/Memjn*) documenting various event-driven tools (including Knative) that could be used to react and terminate a detected interactive shell on an unexpected container. Much like inner monologues can be a big help to application security teams in detecting and reacting to various attack scenarios, cloud inner monologues can help platform teams ensure the security of the underlying platform.

Summary

While this chapter discussed several aspects of event-driven design, it should be clear that event-driven architecture covers a wide range of asynchronous design patterns. Events should be considered a first-class interface in the same manner as synchronous APIs, and application designers should be careful to delineate which events are

---

8 For example, ensuring that security controls are properly configured on publicly accessible resources like storage buckets. When using audit logs to trigger these workflows, it's important to monitor the latency between occurrence and event generation.

9 An example of a latency-insensitive workflow, audit log events can be used to ensure that costs of cloud resources are properly matched to engineering teams.

public interfaces and which are internal implementation details. Event distribution platforms like Knative Brokers enable loosely choreographed components to react and extend the inner monologue of existing systems; these events can also be used to trigger other event-driven components like task queues, workflows, or stream processing. It's not always necessary to manually instrument applications to achieve these benefits—the active storage and change-capture paradigms can provide tools to automatically generate an inner monologue. While serverless compute is not a necessary component for an event-driven architecture, it's a natural complement to the independent change reports provided by inner monologue and can be a compelling platform for extending both applications and infrastructure.

While event-driven architectures are generally a good match for serverless applications, the next chapter dives into some of the warning signs that serverless may *not* be a good fit for a particular solution. While serverless computing has advantages, other computing patterns are a better fit for some problems.

## CHAPTER 8

Too Much of a Good Thing Is Not a Good Thing

Starting in Chapter 1, I've been explaining the reasons and benefits for adopting serverless as a runtime architecture and design philosophy. Well-architected microservices managed through a serverless framework can definitely make application development and the long-term costs of ownership seem almost magical and fun compared with serverful architectures. Even infrastructure platforms like Kubernetes, which can delegate patching host vulnerabilities and network provisioning to platform teams behind an API, have substantially more overhead and day-to-day costs than platforms that can automatically scale and monitor applications based simply on the runtime contract those applications fulfill.

As you've probably gathered from the title of this chapter, even a serverless bed of roses can have painful thorns if taken too far. In this chapter, I'll highlight several patterns that provide early warning that serverless runtimes are not a good fit for certain corners of your application architecture. Before you flip forward to find your favorite pattern, recall that Chapters 5 and 7 include architectural tools for connecting serverless components with other architectures.

This list of patterns comes primarily from my personal experience with customers who outgrew the early Google App Engine product. As Google's first cloud infrastructure offering, many customers who saw the serverless potential of App Engine ended up trying to stretch its limits to implement patterns that would be more at home on Amazon's EC2 VM service. In many ways, the success of the early App Engine platform was a story of a vision that was bright enough to inspire people to work against these limitations; of course, the flip side of the story was that Google Cloud in 2010 did not have other options for running software, so App Engine was stretched and pressed into service in many patterns that would have been better suited to a traditional VM instance.

We'll start our journey by highlighting some application patterns that can increase the cost and difficulty of maintaining a serverless platform, and then progress to architectural challenges that represent more durable rejection of serverless principles. As we go, we'll call out serverless designs to either complement or redesign the problem patterns—handy tools to compartmentalize these challenges so that they don't spread unchecked throughout your architecture. While these patterns particularly apply when designing application architecture, they may also be of interest to platform teams that are considering what patterns are natively supported by existing clusters and which capabilities require additional engineering work.

The first challenge is work units that don't represent the same amount of work. While this may not seem important, it can cause problems for many practical implementations because it can make sizing and reserving resources for application instances unpredictable.

Different Types of Work in the Same Instance

If you view the resources needed for a request as a three-dimensional block of memory, CPU capacity, and execution time, most work destined for a single serverless service should be about the same "size," particularly in the memory and CPU capacity dimensions. Serverless platforms generally manage execution of work units on the assumption that most are around about the same size; even if one unit of work is a little larger than another, it will mostly affect the application by increasing the execution time needed for that particular unit of work.

But what happens if a work unit needs more memory or CPU capacity? Typically, serverless platforms will give each instance identical limits in these dimensions (along with a somewhat-flexible execution timeout). Instances that exceed these dimensions are terminated or blocked from executing, which can be a problem for your larger work units. The simplest solution is to increase the per-instance permitted memory or CPU, but this means that you're now paying a resource premium for *every* work unit to ensure that a small fraction have enough to complete.

This problem can affect both serverless monoliths (because everything is bundled together into one service) and microservices down to the function level (because the work done can vary based on aspects outside the request itself—like the size of a customer account). Most work will be a little lopsided, but monitoring histograms (see "Metrics" on page 194) can help diagnose when some items need 10 or 100 times the resources of other requests. While unbalanced workloads aren't a blocker for serverless implementation, they can eat away at the resource efficiency gains that serverless can offer.

Solutions

Aligned with serverless

A simple way to handle different sizes of work is to separate different work unit types to separate services. Recall that serverless makes it easy to deploy and maintain services, so you should be able to deploy the *same* application code to multiple services with different amounts of provisioned resources. If the work is delivered synchronously to the application, you may need an API gateway (see "API Gateways and Composing an App" on page 36) to route requests based on request properties. If the work is delivered as an event, it may be possible to use your existing event distribution system to route the work based on the event properties.

Independent of serverless

Another way to handle unbalanced work elements is by processing a fixed amount of work per request, and issuing an asynchronous "carryover" request to complete the rest of the work. This works for some types of applications but requires that the application code takes a more active role in balancing the work. Relatedly, you can use a two-stage process like Scatter-Gather (see "Scatter-Gather Advice" on page 151), where the first stage breaks the work into evenly sized chunks and then each stage operates on one chunk.

While unbalanced work units are mostly an operational headache, the remaining problems in this chapter represent more fundamental application architecture challenges and require deeper structural changes. Next, we'll talk about work patterns that break one of the assumptions of serverless: that work units execute and then complete.

Work Units That Don't Signal Termination

In Chapter 1, we defined *serverless* as a pattern of running distributed applications that breaks load into independent units of work that are scheduled and executed automatically. Application flows that continue to execute after completing a unit of work (for example, returning an HTTP response and then doing additional follow-on background work[1]) violate the assumption that the serverless runtime can use the boundaries of work items as an opportunity to reschedule instances to match demand. Similarly, workloads that accumulate state over time such as stream processing or stateful communications over protocols like TCP or WebSocket can make the "completion time" of a work unit hard to estimate.

---

1 See the previous sidebar for one way to convert this carry-over work to an asynchronous event.

The last case where work units may not correlate with instance idleness is when the application implements background work (either on a timer or by reading from something like a message queue in the application code). This is a common pattern for existing monoliths, but serverless systems will generally try to funnel all work units through a single interface. When a program adds "read from queue" or "read from clock" to the primary work contract, a serverless runtime that is unaware of this side work may scale the application to zero instances—at which point, there are no processes checking the clock or reading from the queue. Modeling these side inputs as explicit work units, i.e., making "read from queue" or "read from clock" explicit events to be handled the same way as "read primary event" can be an easy solution if the work units are independent.

Unlike different-sized work units in the same instance, work units without defined termination semantics can completely compromise the features offered by the serverless runtime, including scheduling, automatic monitoring, and process lifecycle management. In the case of undeclared background work, the serverless runtime can also break critical application functionality while managing concurrency based on work units—either by scaling instances to zero, or by running multiple instances when it is assumed that there is a single exclusive instance.

Solutions

Aligned with serverless

For follow-on background work after completing a synchronous response, enqueuing the background work in a task queue can provide a serverless alternative to running the follow-on work within the serverless process after work completes. This approach also works for undeclared background work—move the work off the main application into a separate service that is triggered by events or a cron-type mechanism. Many event systems include cron-type functionality for repeatedly sending events; in Knative, this is called the "PingSource," but many cloud providers have similar scheduling capabilities.

Independent of serverless

Some applications and protocols intrinsically define operations that don't have a clearly defined end. For example, an application that sends users notifications on new messages via long polling may be defined to run as long as the user has the connection open. Cache invalidations and periodic heartbeats are other operations that are often defined to occur *after* a request has completed, which can conflict with serverless work semantics. In these cases, there are three options:

1. Use a traditional (serverful) runtime. It's not required that every component of your system run serverlessly; this may be a place where running a static VM or container is appropriate.

2. Define an "end of work" signal outside the application protocol that the serverless runtime can use to recognize when an instance has completed the protocol transaction. This requires the ability to adjust either the serverless runtime or the application input to support this redefinition—while most elegant, this may also be the highest cost.

3. Change the protocol to eliminate the follow-on operations. The previous sidebar suggested a few mechanisms for deferring work to future serverless actions. It's also possible to redefine the protocol to put bounds on the work; for example, maybe long-polling for notifications will never last longer than 15 minutes; after that time, the connection will be closed and clients will need to reconnect.

In this section, we covered a few possibilities where the desired application behavior might not match the desired serverless semantics. Next, we'll talk about what happens when the serverless runtime expects a different protocol than application clients expect.

Protocol Mismatch

Most serverless runtimes are built around either HTTP requests or event-delivery protocols. In both cases, the protocol in question is well-defined, standardized, and stateless. But not all application protocols meet these criteria, and many serverless runtimes don't support other protocols that *do* meet these requirements. In some cases, application protocols such as FTP not only are stateful but also require coordinating inbound and outbound connections to transfer data. Protocols like FTP involve maintaining an implicit shared state between client and server around the session's current working directory and other settings.

While many application protocols are stateful at the small-scale level, some protocols have well-defined transactions or units of work that consist of several smaller statements chained together in well-defined ways. SMTP (the email delivery protocol) is an example of this; as depicted in Figure 8-1, delivery of an individual email occurs through a series of SMTP commands and acknowledgments, but the combination of commands can be accumulated into a single "mail delivery" message or event that can be handed off to a serverless system.

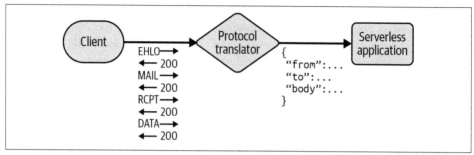

Figure 8-1. SMTP protocol gateway

Solutions

Aligned with serverless

For application protocols that can be translated into useful individual units of work, a proxy or gateway can be used to translate from the foreign protocol to the serverless application protocol. Early versions of Google App Engine provided inbound SMTP and XMPP bridges, which allowed App Engine applications to treat incoming emails or chat messages as special HTTP requests. In some cases, such as SMTP, multiple protocol exchanges might need to occur (EHLO, MAIL, RCPT, DATA) before a single consolidated request is sent from the gateway to the application.

Independent of serverless

If a gateway isn't an appropriate tool, running a standard version of the application service may be appropriate. Depending on the application, implementing an event-based inner monologue (see Chapter 7) in the traditional application may make it easier for serverless applications to react to application interactions through the existing API interfaces. For example, while implementing an FTP protocol gateway to a serverless runtime might not make sense, the standalone FTP server could emit an event each time a file is changed during an FTP session.

Protocol mismatches are a design-level challenge for serverless application architectures. Moving from the design level to the implementation level, some application implementations may also be a poor fit for serverless because of poor scaling characteristics.

Inelastic Scaling

In Chapter 1, we described serverless runtimes as scheduling and executing independent units of work. While the abstract idea of independent units of work is attractive, practical details of application implementation can limit the utility of serverless scaling. These limitations can manifest either within the application as high instance startup costs or outside the application as scalability limits in supporting services.

Some applications have a high initial cost to start an application instance. Here are three examples:

- Machine learning inference applications may need to load large (multigigabyte) models before they can perform a single analysis.

- Text-search applications may need to build extensive in-memory indexes before they are able to answer a query.

- Messaging applications may need to process a backlog of individual messages since the last checkpoint to have a current state of conversation groups to answer notifications.

In all of these cases, serverless runtimes that assume a low cost for starting or terminating application instances may cause performance or reliability problems if instances are not already available when demand increases. While it's possible to tweak some serverless runtimes to take into account higher startup latency, some applications may operate more reliably under a fixed number of instances. Some serverless platforms support this type of static scaling, but some of the advantages of serverless are lost.

Dependent services with fixed scalability limits can impose even greater architectural costs on serverless applications. These nonscalable backend services could be databases with fixed connection limits or application services with "per seat" or "per connection" billing models where opening additional connections or instances has a financial cost. As an example of financially limited scalability, some application programs charge a monthly fee for each processor where the licensed software runs. Allowing a serverless runtime to scale to 100 instances for 5 minutes could lead to licensing charges for 100 processors for the month, even if the steady-state background requirement is only 8 processors. In these cases, fixed allocations with deep task or message queues can help act as "shock absorbers" for brief spikes in demand and may be a better architectural choice than a highly scalable serverless design.

> ## Solutions
>
> Many serverless runtimes support some form of minimum and maximum instance counts on a microservice-by-microservice basis. If it's not possible to use instance startup costs as a scaling input, these maximum and minimum limits can be used to bound the number of instances running at one time. Some platforms also provide automatic termination of old instances; disabling this setting can help avoid expensive instance startups.

 While it may seem attractive to gain the other benefits of serverless services such as automatic monitoring and rollout tooling, the additional overhead of working *against* the scaling intent of a serverless system can eat into any efficiency and productivity gains from choosing a serverless solution.

While many serverless systems have mechanisms in place to work around poor application scaling behavior, serverless platforms generally make the fundamental assumption that application instances are *fungible*. That means that one application instance is just as good as another when it comes to handling a unit of work. For our last application architecture barrier, we'll examine what breaks down when units of work need to be directed to specific application instances.

Instance Addressability and Sharding

A common application pattern for handling large data sets is to *shard* the data across multiple instances. In this model, data items have a primary key (as in most databases), and that primary key is used to determine which instance[2] is responsible for the data. While the exact mechanism for mapping keys to instances varies from one system to another, if you ask the wrong instance for a data item, it will either respond with an empty answer or will forward your request to the correct instance. In all of these cases, finding the instance with the correct data requires being able to pick out a single instance from the set of otherwise identical instances in a service.

This assignment of work items to instances interferes with the fundamental premise of serverless runtimes: that the runtime itself can schedule and execute the work in a consistent way without needing to consult the application runtime. Introducing an application-specific mapping of work to instances or data assignments introduces two problems for the serverless runtime:

---

2 Or subset of instances in a replicated database.

- Needing to consult the runtime for instance assignment makes scaling difficult because there may not be a running application when the scaling decision needs to happen.

- Scaling the application by adding instances requires runtime coordination to request that existing instances release their ownership of data, which will move to the new instances. In some cases, this rebalancing may have cascading effects leading to a large amount of data movement; in other cases, avoiding data movement will lead to unbalanced work assignments as instances are added and removed.

Solutions

Some actor-based systems like Akka provide mechanisms for orchestrating this assignment of data to workers consistently across a cluster of nodes. Unfortunately, systems that are able to do this in a scalable and reliable fashion are rare and often need to impose complex data structure requirements like the use of conflict-free replicated data types (CRDTs) to guarantee data integrity. A generalized mechanism for operating instance-addressable workers serverlessly would be a very interesting development.

Needing instance addressability is a *strong* sign that an application is not a good fit for serverless. As described in Chapter 7, it's still possible to serverlessly extend an application that uses instance addressability by processing events emitted by individual instances. In fact, many applications that use the sharding or instance-addressability architectures to achieve scalability are good complements to serverless computation architectures that can scale horizontally alongside horizontally distributed data stores.

Summary

While serverless is not a universal salve for application design problems, appropriate usage of serverless can complement nonserverless platforms. In this chapter, we covered five signals that serverless may not be a good fit for particular application components along with some solutions outlined in Table 8-1.

The majority of these warning signs relate to work units that don't match serverless expectations: wide variance in capacity, unclear execution bounds, dependencies (state) between work items, or work items that must be handled by a particular instance. A few of these items also reflect the difference between the simplified model of theory and the thorny reality of practice: high instance startup costs and applications that accept work through multiple inputs.

Table 8-1. Problematic patterns and serverless solutions

Problem	Solutions
Unequal work units	Split services with different-sized requests, or split requests into equal chunks.
Unbounded work	Enqueue events for follow-on work, add bounds on clients, or use a serverful runtime.
Protocol mismatch	Use a protocol gateway to transform requests, or use events from a serverful implementation.
High scaling cost	Limit scaling bounds or use fixed (serverful) instances.
Instance addressing	Probably not a good fit for serverless.

With the theory of serverless thoroughly explored, we'll move on to the next part of the book, where we'll put the application of theory to the test and learn more about living the serverless lifestyle.

## PART III

Living with Serverless

Now that we've talked about how to apply serverless principles to your application design, let's talk a bit about what you'll experience as you continue to develop serverless applications. If you haven't run a serverless system in production, consider this a preview of the joys and challenges of running a serverless application. If you're already running serverless in production, these chapters may give you some insights into your current problems and suggest some solutions.

## CHAPTER 9

Failing at the Speed of Light

So far I've been a cheerleader for serverless technologies and systems, but this chapter will be an opportunity to explore the things that can go bump in the night when deploying and living with serverless at scale. We've talked a lot about how serverless systems built on relatively new technology scale easily and reduce the maintenance costs for developers and system administrators. The exciting thing about new technologies is that they can completely erase problems that are intractable in existing architectures. New technologies also bring new failure modes—every revolution has some winners and losers. Still, evaluating the trade-offs, many of us (including myself) will prefer serverless systems when they are available—but we'll also remember where the sharp edges are and design for them the same way we designed for the sharp edges of traditional systems.

Many of the failure modes we'll talk about in this chapter are related to the scaling capabilities of serverless runtimes. Sometimes these are problems that traditional systems also suffer from, but that fail differently when rapid scaling is a possible solution to a capacity problem. Others are side effects that occur because infrastructure realities don't match up with our theoretical models[1] or because not all infrastructure is equally serverless. In many of these cases, the solution to the problem is simply to enforce some upper limits on the system scaling, but understanding the different failure states can help you recognize when one of these limits may be hit—most complex software systems exhibit chaotic behavior, where it is difficult to calculate scaling limits ahead of time, and many variables may affect the scalability limits (for example, fast failures versus slow failures can manifest in greatly different behavior in traditional systems).

---

1 I refer to this as the "spherical cow problem." An old joke in theoretical physics suggests that a university research team is trying to optimize milk production on a farm. Their solution begins, "Assume a spherical cow..." Just as cows are not spheres, application containers have real-world properties that differ from our ideal model.

As suggested by the preceding paragraphs, our first class of failures will be system meltdowns. In general, these are failures where the entire system stops working, but we will see that even within this whole category of system failure there are multiple flavors of meltdown to consider.

Meltdown

Generally, we describe a *meltdown* as a system failing suddenly and catastrophically, often due to overheating or a malfunction of normal controls. While serverless systems can't literally cause an overheating event,[2] the normal scaling control loop could overreact and massively overprovision instances because of external factors that the control loop doesn't take into account. This can result in either a complete system failure (no work is done, and the system serves only errors) or a dramatic drop in "goodput"—the amount of effort needed to successfully resolve one unit of work.

Depending on the control loop and the architectural design, it's possible for a system to have *two* stable states:

Normal steady-state
> Work gets done, and scaling reacts usefully to load changes. For example, a system might have 2,000 requests per second that are handled by 200 instances, each of which takes 100 ms to process a request.

"Meltdown" state
> Added capacity reduces the throughput of useful work because of interactions with other system components. For example, a system in this state with 2,000 requests per second might spawn 6,000 instances, each of which takes 5 seconds to complete the work, with a 40% error rate.

> Unfortunately, the existence of the second state is often not obvious until you've tipped into it, and recovering from that state is difficult until load is reduced much below the steady state.

As a system architect, this is obviously pretty terrifying—we're looking for consistent, predictable behavior, not random excursions into a dark alley in a bad neighborhood. Fortunately, most of these dark alleys are pretty well marked and are predictable outcomes of ignoring standard architectural patterns, including the patterns in Chapter 8 or general microservice best practices. The two most common causes of scaling-related

---

2 If you've experienced a physical meltdown due to serverless scaling, *I really want to know!*

meltdowns are nonscalable backend bottlenecks and error feedback loops. Fortunately, both also have simple solutions.

Narrowest Bottleneck

As briefly described in "Instance Addressability and Sharding" on page 166, certain service patterns may require a fixed number of instances—in the worst case, a single vertically scaled instance like a primary SQL database to maintain ACID (atomicity, consistency, isolation, and durability) properties needed by the application. Because we understand how to scale instances horizontally (running many copies) better than we understand how to scale instances vertically (we can make processors only so big and so fast), instances like SQL databases can end up being a bottleneck to horizontally scaled serverless architectures. These systems might be bottlenecks to scaling based on any of your usual application resources: network throughput, connections, memory, CPU throughput, disk throughput, and I/O operations are all common causes of bottlenecks.

Narrow bottlenecks can occur even in systems that don't have an explicit primary instance—for example, distributed consensus algorithms or replicated data stores may incur more bookkeeping overhead as instances are added. Even if they provide a serverless-looking interface, dependencies between individual instances can mean that doubling the size of a cluster improves throughput by only 50%. Generally, bottlenecks tend to occur in systems that store state, particularly ones with richer and more "interesting" semantics that cross individual rows, such as indexes or multirow transactions.

In a steady state, it's relatively easy to predict the largest amount of traffic demand and to provision your bottleneck to be larger than that threshold by a comfortable margin. Unfortunately, external events can sometimes go beyond those limits or cause the limits to drop unexpectedly—flash traffic to a site due to a news event or increased disk latency due to a hardware failure can cause the traffic demand to exceed the capacity of the bottleneck. When this happens, the system may enter meltdown as the serverless components upstream of the bottleneck try to scale out and add load to the already-overloaded bottleneck.

Even if you haven't reached the limits of vertical (larger instance size) scaling, the process of scaling a single instance will either involve downtime to shut down and upgrade the instance or careful planning and cutover from an old primary instance to a new one. In the worst case, the additional load of replicating data from the primary instance to the new replica adds enough load to the older, smaller primary instance that it can trigger meltdown on its own.

The simplest way to mitigate bottleneck problems is to ensure that the services in front of the bottleneck have maximum scaling limits in place—a maximum number of instances that the platform will create that is smaller than or equal to the limit enforced by the bottleneck. The goal is to narrow the upstream components to the point where the system is more of a smooth pipe than a constricted system.

While bottlenecks can exist even in traditional systems, the assumption of infinite scalability of serverless can exacerbate existing issues. Similarly, feedback loops can affect traditional systems, but they have different symptoms and solutions in a serverless environment when compared with traditional architectures.

Feedback Loop

Feedback loops occur when application behavior degrades in the face of input in such a way that the behavior itself causes further degradation. This can combine with system bottlenecks to lead to meltdown, but feedback loops can also occur in a system without clear bottlenecks. For example, a system might use a login token cache with a token expiration time to avoid an expensive external authentication check. If the token cache is flushed, every interaction may lead to a new authentication check; the resulting slowdown in the authentication system could consume much of the expiration time, reducing the hit rate of the cache and causing the authentication system's load to remain high. Furthermore, if the client continues sending requests at a constant rate, the serverless frontend may add additional instances, each of which adds load to the authentication service, increasing the latency and reducing the effective duration of each token. Slow requests may also write older tokens over a newer token, further reducing the effective cache hit rate.

In addition to login tokens, caches may also be used to reduce the load on databases and widen a bottleneck. In general, the goal of a cache is to reduce the cost of running a system by storing the results of an expensive operation for future use. In the previous example, the login token cache was acting as both a *latency* cache and a *capacity* cache. In many cases, these caches are originally introduced to reduce latency, but over time the system scales past the point where the uncached behavior results in meltdown. As long as the cache is not flushed, it's not clear that the system is at risk of meltdown. A serverless client may further contribute to the meltdown by scaling out to more instances to handle the higher concurrent load.

 When building with automatic scaling, be careful that latency caches do not accidentally become capacity caches. One way to avoid this is to periodically test a cache flush and measure backend capacity consumed.

While caches are one place where feedback loops can occur, other patterns can also lead to feedback loops. Two of the common cases are as follows:

Error timeouts and retries

Systems that retry requests that either exceed a time limit or return an error can paper over small misbehaviors of backend systems. For small-scale errors, this can be beneficial in improving the apparent reliability of the system. When the errors are system-wide (rather than isolated incidents), retries can drive up the load on the backend system, making it harder to recover. For user-facing systems, humans can be part of the overload if they retry repeatedly, assuming the error is on their end.

Optimistic concurrency control

Many APIs (and the HTTP standard) support a pattern known as *optimistic concurrency control*, where clients write data after confirming that it hasn't changed from an earlier read.[3] This works well when the scope of a change is small and short enough that two transactions are unlikely to conflict. Unfortunately, overload situations can increase the time between the read and the subsequent write; increasing the number of instances (to maintain constant throughput in the face of increased latency) can increase the number of conflicts, leading to more work needing to be redone. The end result is that as instances are added, latency increases, and the probability of a successful write *drops*.

By increasing the time it takes to complete one operation without reducing the rate of operations, any of these failure modes causes the runtime to scale horizontally to more instances to maintain throughput. Unfortunately, in these cases (but not in other cases), adding instances actually makes the situation worse, rather than better. The short-term solution in any of these cases is to reduce the load on the system (by fast-failing requests or routing them to a different system) until the system recovers into the steady state. In the longer term, engineering processes and techniques like load testing, careful error handling, and circuit breakers can help avoid future meltdowns.[4]

Now that we've covered the most exciting failure stories that you'll tell, the next section will explore the death by a thousand cuts that is poor application latency caused by slow instance startup.

---

3 In HTTP, this can be done with If-Modified and the ETag headers.

4 Using circuit breakers is a technique that automatically fast-fails backends when they cross certain error thresholds.

Cold Start, Extra Slow

Amazingly, despite thousands of blog posts about the problem, we've gotten to this point in the book with only a few cursory mentions of the cold-start problem.[5] Because serverless systems are constantly adjusting the number of instances based on the work available, the runtime may start new instances much more often than a traditional system. Depending on the infrastructure and application runtime, these starts can result in unpredictable user-visible latency, sometimes as much as tens of seconds depending on a variety of factors.

Application startup latency can come from the following factors:

- Runtime provisioning of an instance (scheduling)
- Fetching the application code to the instance
- Runtime instance startup (container create, etc.)
- Application initialization (code loading, backend initialization)

Some of these factors are entirely controlled by your serverless runtime provider, but anything relating to application code is affected by both the serverless runtime and the actual application design and implementation. In a traditional runtime environment, applications are started rarely, so the cost and latency of starting an application is largely amortized by the long runtime of application instances. By contrast, some serverless application instances may be started to handle a single request. By understanding and analyzing the startup behavior of your application, it's possible to optimize the startup time and reduce the impact of cold starts.

The Race to Ready

The two application factors affecting startup time are application size and the process of actually initializing the application state. The first is largely dependent upon the dependencies and packaging of the application; application startup times can depend on a variety of factors, from the language runtime to waiting for backend connections to data loading and processing. In this section, we'll take a look at all these factors and how to reduce cold-start times, starting with application sizes.

As mentioned in "Functions" on page 80, many FaaS platforms implement an internal build system; for those cases, the size of your application code and dependencies

---

5 The term "cold start" derives from the problem of starting an engine below its operating temperature. In this condition, liquids have drained from the engine, and lubricants like oil may be much more viscous and less slippery than at normal operating temperature. Starting an engine cold requires additional energy than a recently shut down engine, much like starting a new process requires more computing resources than routing a request to an already-running instance.

will have a direct effect on the application size. For container-based runtimes, it's relatively easy to build a container image that includes hundreds of megabytes of development tools not needed during execution. To avoid bundling all of the build-time dependencies in the application, a two-stage process is used: the first stage builds the necessary application artifacts in a rich environment with all the necessary dependencies,[6] and then the second stage copies the artifacts to a minimal execution environment. Using a small runtime base and careful dependency pruning, a container image can be reduced from 600 to 800 MB to less than 50 MB in many cases. While this image slimming can be done by hand using multistage Dockerfiles, many tools (such as jib, ko, and CNCF Buildpacks) can automate much of these container packaging best practices.

Not all serverless runtimes benefit equally from the slimming of application images. In some cases, the application image is preprocessed or unpacked to network storage in such a way that the runtime can fetch individual files on demand, rather than needing to fetch the entire artifact before execution. Regardless of how the application code is delivered to the application, the lifecycle outlined in "Creature Comforts: Managing Process Lifecycle" on page 16 is typically the same:

1. Determine the placement of the new instance.
2. Initialize and start the instance on the worker.
3. Start the application running.
4. Indicate application readiness and process work.

Of these steps, the speed of launching a new process is entirely within the serverless runtime; the application startup is entirely within the control of the application author. Fetching the application and starting it can take tens of seconds depending on the application—which can lead to the conclusion that cold start is a major blocker to implementing a serverless architecture. While random high-latency outliers when under load is clearly a poor experience, it's possible to mitigate many of these factors with careful application design. If not, the following section will provide advice on tuning the serverless runtime to minimize the effects of large cold starts.

With the exception of a small number of languages that compile directly to binary code for a specific processor type, most languages used for serverless applications need to be interpreted at startup. Depending on the implementation, this can take 50 ms or several seconds of CPU or I/O usage—for example, JavaScript with a large number of imports (files read off disk) or Java programs with a large number of classes (JIT compilation of Java bytecode). For interpreted languages with many

---

6 Possibly including not just the language compiler and the C compiler, but additional tools in different languages.

dependencies, it's possible to precompile the dependencies into a smaller number of files; for example, using webpack for JavaScript. For Java JIT, consider switching to ahead-of-time compilation with the GraalVM compiler that produces native machine bytecode that no longer needs a JIT at startup. For large frameworks such as Spring, this can reduce startup times to hundreds of milliseconds from a JIT time of 10 seconds or more.

Once the application has started and loaded all of its dependent libraries, it can begin the process of running application startup code and initializing state. While natively serverless applications are often designed with limited initialization, existing applications may perform extended initialization before becoming ready to handle a request or unit of work. The two main culprits are establishing connections to many different backend services and loading a large amount of data, particularly over the network. Because these delays are part of the application code as written, a serverless runtime can do very little to accelerate the readiness of new instances. Instead, the application code may need to be refactored:

- Services that have been ported from a traditional runtime may establish and verify connections to many backend services that are needed for only one or two types of requests. In this case, separating those request handlers into separate microservices may make sense. Recall that in "Top Speed: Reducing Drag" on page 84, we described how serverless makes it cheaper to build and run additional microservices, which can help make running separate services for each set of backends make more sense.

- Once you've factored your microservices into units with a small common set of backends, the next step is to ensure that any backend connection establishment is happening in parallel across all the service backends and in parallel with any other setup steps required. Depending on how the system handles backend readiness, it may make sense to start the connection establishment process but not block the rest of application startup waiting for the completion of health checks. If you do move connection setup to a lazy initialization process, you'll need to make sure that the rest of the application code is prepared to handle delays or errors in the backend connection after startup.

- If your application needs to download a large amount of data (such as a machine learning model or a precomputed index), see whether the data can be lazy-loaded in chunks. Another option is to push off something like an index to an external storage system like a key-value store. This is generally an intensive option and may require deep integration with your underlying application library; you're effectively implementing the same kind of lazy-loading that the OS page cache does when an application opens a file. In some cases, loading the file from a shared filesystem mount may allow you to take advantage of the OS page cache without needing to fetch all the data locally immediately.

When none of these techniques help, and you're still wrestling with application start times that disrupt your users' experience with high latency, it's time to look at tuning your serverless runtime to reduce the frequency of cold starts. In the next section, we'll look at some of the different knobs and patterns your runtime or application may expose to improve instance reuse and limit how often a request is delayed waiting for an instance.

Avoiding Cold Starts

Assuming that you've picked all the low-hanging fruit in the previous section and still have a cold-start problem, it's time to work around the problem by tweaking the platform settings. While the previous section was about applying solid engineering principles to address a problem, this section is much more about mitigation strategies when engineering is either infeasible or too expensive. These flags and options can vary by cloud provider; we'll mainly be focusing on the relevant options in Knative; other cloud providers often expose similar control knobs.

A serverless runtime will start a new instance when it detects that there is or will soon be work to be done for which there isn't an available instance. This manifests as a cold start when the work item arrives and an instance is not available. If you read closely between the two sentences, one way to avoid cold-start work items in a serverless system is to ensure that a buffer of instances is always on hand to handle a request without blocking. At its simplest, you can request that the runtime has a buffer to handle at least N additional requests without blocking; as requests fill up this buffer, newly created instances backfill the capacity claimed by a burst of incoming requests. If the burst of incoming requests is larger than N, you'll see at least one cold start as you wait for an instance to refill the buffer. This design is sometimes called *provisioned instances* or *burst capacity*.

The drawback of guaranteed burst capacity is that it guarantees a certain amount of wastage at all times: even if there is zero traffic, instances need to be retained for up to N incoming requests. Fortunately, as a service receives more traffic, the overhead costs of provisioning for a fixed-size burst become smaller and smaller.

For low-traffic services, it may simply be sufficient to delay or disable shutting down the last instance of the application. If requests are handled quickly and at least one instance is available to handle requests, it's possible that a small burst of requests may be queued, but the existing instance is able to handle the work before the new instance is initialized. The new instance will be useful if a large burst of work is received, but for small numbers of requests, one instance may be sufficient. In Knative, users can adjust both the scale-to-zero-pod-retention-period *and* the minimum number of instances; the former does not entirely disable scale-to-zero, but extends the time before the final instance is shut down. Setting a minimum number of application instances disables scaling to zero altogether, which may be an appropriate response to a critical production application that must guarantee low latency regardless of circumstances.

A final tuning knob for runtimes that support delivering multiple requests to a single container is the target and maximum request concurrency for a single instance. By lowering the target concurrency substantially below the maximum, the autoscaler can be instructed to maintain a buffer of *1/target utilization percent* concurrent requests—for example, with a target utilization of 70% (the Knative default), the autoscaler would automatically maintain a maximum capacity of 1.4 times the current request load.

By leveraging the capacity settings alongside application optimizations, it should be possible to avoid customer-facing cold starts at the cost of some extra idle instances. It's also worth noting that it may make sense to adjust these runtime options differently across the spectrum of development versus production environments—it may be fine for a development environment to scale to zero in the evenings to save costs, while a production environment may be worth provisioning at least five replicas on an ongoing basis to avoid the poor customer experience of an expensive cold start. As we'll discuss in the next section, turning these dials too far toward over-provisioning can also lead to issues with your serverless provider.

Forecasting Is Hard

So far, we've talked about the infinite horizontal scaling benefits of serverless. But just as our theoretical models of instant instance start are foiled by real-world side effects, so too is the infinite scalability of serverless a bit of a mirage. In the real world, there are physical ("I have only so many computers!"), policy ("I won't let you use more than a certain amount of credit"), and technical (each instance introduces some load on a central component) reasons that horizontal scaling has its limits. In the small scale, serverless can let you ignore a lot of the requirements for capacity planning, resource allocation, etc. In the large scale, all of these physics of computing will come back to bite you in the bill (cost you money).

At the small scale, not having to think hard about the bill ("I know it will be less than $100/month—let it go") can be hugely enabling for teams. Large real-world applications won't achieve cost savings from scale-to-zero, though you may be able to fit lower-priority workloads in the "trough" between peak usages. For these larger-scale applications, the need to perform usage and cost forecasting may be a rude awakening—even if the serverless platform provides historical usage information that can be used to extrapolate cost, the team may not be familiar with the process of justifying its project costs.

Overall, having unprepared teams hit the cost-forecasting problem late is probably a net business benefit over early optimization for cost before the application has achieved a usage fit. The other problem occurs when you start to hit platform limits—for example, as of May 2023, AWS Lambda allows a burst of only 3,000 instances to be created, and then restricts additional instance creations to 500 per minute. On self-hosted infrastructure, the total number of allowed instances may be much lower—for example, limited by policy to the number of CPU cores available in the cluster. For serverless platform administrators, it can be helpful to set the policy limits much lower (by half or more) than the actual physical platform limits.

Because policy limits are effectively choices, teams reaching a policy limit have the option to reach out (support ticket, pull request, etc.) to get the policy limit raised. For teams that do have a separate platform team, this engagement provides the platform administrator the chance to perform proactive education about the physical limits so that application teams can plan necessary changes (application refactor, sharding, or expanding to multiple sites) without the impending doom of a site outage looming over their heads.

Scalability limits (both policy and physical) can be hit organically, but another common case of exceeding these limits is due to accidental feedback systems. While building a system that feeds back into itself can sometimes be useful, serverless can make it easy to produce an exponential blowup—and the next section will cover some strategies for mitigating that risk.

Loopback

While direct call-and-reply architectures can generate high levels of traffic when a call to one service fans out to many calls to dependent services, event-driven systems can have a near-infinite multiplier on load if the asynchronous events produce a continuous loop. This can happen by accident; for example, if a function is written to react to a compute instance being started, the act of running the function to respond to the event may cause a new compute instance to be started, causing another parallel function execution, etc. In this case, the infinite horizontal scalability of serverless becomes an Achilles' heel: rather than bottlenecking on the resources available on a single instance, serverless will add instances as quickly as the loop can execute, until policy or physical limits are hit.

While the example of watching for compute instances may be an obvious event loop, there are many other, more subtle ways of generating a feedback loop or the appearance of one. Systems that react to events by updating the originating system (for example, updating a database based on a streamed change record) need to be particularly careful to avoid generating loops; similarly, repeating a processed event back to an event broker may lead to redelivery of the new event, limited only by the latency between the two systems. While there are an infinity of means to generate an event-oriented processing loop, there are a few simple techniques for preventing or avoiding a massive bill or incident for handling the loop:

Unique IDs for events

When processing events, and particularly when generating a response event, generate a unique ID on the first observation of the event, and propagate the event ID through subsequent response events. When using CloudEvents (see "Why CloudEvents" on page 121), processors might set the source or type fields uniquely, while preserving the id field. Components can then use a small cache of previously seen event IDs to skip processing looped events.

Intentional concurrency limits

Most serverless platforms allow configuring a maximum horizontal (instance) concurrency limit. By setting this low enough to throttle runaway loopback behavior (but high enough to support day-to-day bursts), application teams can be given time to react if an event loop is accidentally formed across different components of the system.

Avoid reporting no-op changes

When sourcing events from a system using an inner monologue (see Chapter 7), the system itself should be selective when reporting events that don't result in a system change. For example, API PUT (overwrite) operations that write the same data that was already present should either not be reported or reported with a different type than PUT operations that changed the contents of a resource. By muting these no-op events, it becomes *harder* to accidentally construct a feedback loop by rewriting a resource with the same content. (This does not protect against two components "arguing" over the state of a resource or against continuously updating an existing resource—for example, with a new "last read" time.)

While event-based loopback can be a surprise architectural denial-of-service (or, for pay-as-you-go platforms, a "denial of wallet"), most teams will naturally think about these concerns and will architect to avoid them. After all, recursion (and unbounded recursion) are common concerns for application programmers. Loopback situations are also easily detected through monitoring—detecting a sudden and sustained increase in traffic is likely to be Monitoring 101 for most teams. Fixing a loopback once it is detected generally involves shunting the events to a holding queue while the initial design is fixed; in the worst case, this may involve passing them through a temporary filtering function that discards or archives unnecessary looping messages while passing valid ones on to the original destination.

In our next section, we'll talk about how hotspots can arise within serverless platforms and how to detect and handle these statistical anomalies. Hotspots provide a different challenge than event loops because most of the system is performing well under capacity, but there's a critical component that falls behind or struggles to keep up when processing events. This is usually due to some underlying state in the system but can also arise due to external factors.

Hotspots Don't Scale

Much like traditional systems, hotspots can cause serverless systems to stop scaling well before the limits described in the previous section have been reached. While "Inelastic Scaling" on page 165 and "Instance Addressability and Sharding" on page 166 outline a few of the ways that an application architecture can lead to hotspots, it's also possible to design an application that is horizontally scalable in theory where the actual system data leads to horizontal scaling issues with even a double-handful of instances.

Assuming that you haven't built a system that intentionally routes requests asymmetrically to certain instances, hotspots can still occur because of relationships among data, data size, and update frequency. We'll discuss each of these issues in turn, starting with data relationships.

Graphs and Focal Points

When building a representation of related data, it's often tempting to express the relations as a graph (possibly using GraphQL, though the same problems can arise with REST or other API patterns). When the graph is unevenly connected (think of a celebrity on a social network), interacting with heavily connected nodes can require a lot more data to be collected and processed than when interacting with a "normal" user. This additional load is *unpredictable*—since requests are routed to instances randomly, some requests may be larger and slower than other requests. These larger requests act as random hotspots across your serverless instances, particularly if two or more large requests happen to arrive at the same instance.

It can be tricky to detect that data patterns are triggering instance hotspots, though histograms from "Metrics" on page 194 can provide tools to help track down the problem. The first hint that hotspotting may be occurring is probably the distribution of request latency—if your application has a "fat tail" of high-latency requests, hotspots may be contributing to the latency problem. To delve deeper, request logs that correlate latency with specific data items can be used; another approach is to instrument the database read layer to count the number of rows read for a single application-level request.

Armed with these logged records (and possibly application traces for slow requests), you can check for a correlation between data processed and latency. Note that if you are processing multiple concurrent requests, a hotspot request may also impact concurrent requests on the instance, so the correlation between request rows and latency may not be 1:1, and it may be necessary to investigate the context around bursts of slow requests.[7]

---

7 Latency bursts can also be caused by other reasons, such as poor garbage collection tuning or OS-level issues.

Hotspots can occur on multiple layers; the patterns described apply to work units that are substantially different in size. It's also possible to have work units that are fairly uniform in size, but hotspots at the data layer, often related to "popular" database rows. "Locking" on page 185 covers storage-system hotspots in more detail.

While "Different Types of Work in the Same Instance" on page 160 has a few hints on how to handle requests that have different backend costs for the same business logic, it can also make sense to adjust the application architecture to move the heavy work out of user-affecting synchronous calls. Presentations about Twitter's architecture in 2012 (*https://oreil.ly/jydiq*) focused heavily on making reads quick and cacheable by implementing the "follow" fan-out when the tweet was written, rather than filtering it as the messages were read. By pushing these fan-out writes to an asynchronous queue, user reads and writes can both be fast at the cost of the system being eventually, rather than strongly, consistent.

When possible, taking advantage of weak consistency models can reduce hotspots in either a traditional or serverless architecture (while serverless is sometimes different, good engineering often works uniformly). In the next two sections, we'll discuss other data properties that can also introduce hotspots, starting with a broad hotspot problem associated with large data sizes.

Data Size

While "big data" has been a popular movement since the mid-2000s, large units of work can make the entire serverless system a broad hotspot. A good example of this occurred in May 2023 when Amazon Prime Video published a blog post sharing how it migrated a video-quality-monitoring system from AWS Lambda to long-running container instances (*https://oreil.ly/jaRnd*).

At the core of the issues with the serverless system was the frequency and size of the video data being processed and the interchange of data across components. Because the serverless components could not directly share any state, every few seconds of video had to be operated on independently and stored in durable storage between each step. Moving this state storage to local disk and memory cut costs by 90%, largely due to a reduction in the cost of reads and writes to S3 and AWS step functions (used to orchestrate the different functions involved). While other architectures were not discussed, it's clear that copying video data and analysis over the network five or ten times is not a very efficient means of operation.

Carefully managing network data flows is also a key component of optimizing batch execution. Batch systems like Apache Hadoop or Flink are relatively careful to transmit network data between nodes only when needed and often attempt to amortize the network traffic over a large number of data operations. As a rule of thumb, if the time required to transmit a unit of work over the network is more than one-fourth of the processing time for that data, it makes sense to select infrastructure that optimizes data transmission over the network. Most traditional serverless systems assume that units of work are fairly small and easily transmitted, though some analytics systems (like BigQuery or Snowflake) implement data transmission optimizations. In general, delivering high request-level network throughput requires careful thinking about copies, durability, and replication guarantees—an effort that is wasted for many applications that do not reach this sort of scale.

While copying large quantities of data over the network can lead to poor performance and general network hotspotting, network latency can also be a contributor to hotspots. In the next section, we'll talk about how even small data can generate hotspots in strongly consistent systems.

Locking

While it may be obvious that introducing row-level locking can introduce platform-level hotspots on frequently changed rows, it's less clear how to deal with these hotspots. Even without row-level locking, storage systems usually have an upper limit on the rate of row-level changes that can be processed. If an application needs to enforce strongly consistent semantics on an object with frequent changes, it may make sense to move the application logic next to the data storage using a nonserverless paradigm. If clients can steer their requests to the instance responsible for a key, the instance can batch requests and use an in-memory lock when processing the business logic, which can be more efficient than separate lock storage.

Storage layers with instance addressability can also choose to map hot rows to more-powerful instances than normal; this can hide the performance effects of unbalanced access as long as the access rate is within a certain range. Much like a latency cache can become a capacity cache (see "Feedback Loop" on page 174), this automatic storage-layer compensation can hide performance limits.[8]

Note that mapping specific hot storage rows to specific instances means introducing instance addressability, which will tend to conflict with serverless patterns as described in "Instance Addressability and Sharding" on page 166. Still, this can be an effective option for many applications—taken to the extreme, many interactive game services could be said to use this model for the in-game state, which is generally managed in-memory on a single instance and explicitly summarized before being synchronized over the network. Even if one part of your application needs this treatment, you may still find many other areas where serverless components can complement the stateful addressable component (including the routing and scheduling layer in *front* of those addressable instances).

---

8 I first encountered this failure mode when dealing with a hot lock on IP address allocation using BigTable. BigTable had automatically sequestered the root IP address node onto its own server because of the transaction rate during load testing.

One of the common uses cases for locking is ensuring exactly-once semantics in an asynchronous workflow. Many applications for exactly-once semantics exist in software systems, but it's important to also understand the costs involved.

Exactly Once Is Hard

As described in "Delivery Guarantees" on page 68, Knative Eventing is designed to implement at-least-once message delivery. While it's easier to build a bank transfer system with at-least-once messages than with at-most-once messages, what most developers really want is *exactly*-once delivery guarantees.

Unfortunately, implementing exactly-once delivery is a hard distributed systems problem with a few well-known and difficult answers, such as two-phase commit or consensus algorithms. At an underlying level, all of these mechanisms rely on multiple at-least-once request-reply round trips to ensure that a transaction that completes in system A will also complete in system B, and that a transaction that is canceled in system A is also canceled in system B. Implementing these distributed algorithms is complicated, expensive (in terms of latency), and subtle (prone to error). It's much simpler to implement deduplication of events at the destination using a database of previously seen events IDs and some idempotent processing.

To simulate exactly-once delivery, a serverless process can use one of the following patterns:

- Process the event in an idempotent way, such that a second invocation has no effect. This is a common solution for intermediate event-processing steps that read an event, enrich it with some additional data (or split the event, etc.), and then emit a new event with more information than the original. In these cases, the function can simply kick the can down the road by ensuring that it emits the new event before acknowledging the triggering event. If the function crashes before responding to the triggering event, it will be retried—this *might* generate a duplicate event if the function had originally sent the event and crashed before acknowledging the trigger, but crashing in this particular spot is rare, so the chance of duplication is low. *To ensure that subsequent steps can deduplicate events, it's a best practice to carry through an event ID from the triggering event to any derived events.* Knative Eventing natively supports this pattern with the "event in HTTP reply" model, but in some other event-processing frameworks, the instance may need to explicitly send the response event.

- If your system provides guarantees that at most one delivery of an event is in-flight at a time (this is a reasonable but not guaranteed property), a separate database with "seen/processed" event ID records can be used to skip processing of a previously delivered record. When processing the event, the instance should check the event ID database (which may be a time-limited cache), then process the event if it has not been previously seen. Once the record is processed, the instance then adds the triggering event ID to the "seen" database before acknowledging the triggering event. Note that this pattern still requires some thought about how to handle an instance that crashes in the middle of processing an event—there will be no record of processing the event, but some side effects of the event might be visible.

- Maintain a record of processed events alongside the records being updated, and commit the event ID alongside updates to the underlying database records in a single transaction. This is the strongest form of exactly-once processing, as the database commit that includes the event ID can be made to fail with a conflict if the triggering event has been added to the database by another instance. Unfortunately, the requirement that the only effect of the function is to do a single transaction to another database means that this pattern is often not practical.

For any of these solutions, the system in question should include system and unit-level tests for handling duplicated events. You may have noticed that the solutions to exactly-once event processing look similar to the ways that a robust and well-architected traditional system might handle event processing. This is not an accident—the stateless and ephemeral nature of serverless processing runtimes is often best handled by relying on the existing best practices built up over the decades of experience building distributed systems.

Summary

Many of the patterns described in this chapter are not unique to serverless systems or architectures; serverless does not change the fundamental "physics" of distributed systems. On the other hand, the dynamic scaling nature and stateless work routing of serverless systems *can* change the way that traditional problems manifest—transforming downtime into a scaling meltdown or making it harder to identify scalability hotspots by moving the hotspot around within the instance pool.

In the next chapter, we'll dig into some of the best techniques and tools for debugging and understanding serverless systems. While few of these systems are specific to serverless, the ephemeral and dynamic nature of serverless runtimes makes proper tooling all the more critical for maintaining and improving applications with a serverless component.

## CHAPTER 10

Cracking the Case: Whodunnit

While the last chapter focused on systemic failures that can bring an entire application to its knees, this chapter focuses on the much more common problem of debugging ordinary application-level bugs. While we'd all prefer to write bug-free code, evidence suggests that simply introducing a new runtime technology won't suddenly cause programmers to stop introducing logic errors, forgetting to initialize variables, using unvalidated input, or misusing locking schemes. Unfortunately, new runtime technologies can render certain debugging techniques no longer viable, while increasing the demand for other tools. In this chapter, we'll explore the differences between debugging live serverless programs and traditional applications, and see where new advances and cloud technologies can lead the way.

Because the first step in debugging a problem is realizing that the problem exists at all, this chapter will include some general best practices around monitoring and observability as well as traditional debugging practices like collecting stack traces or heap dumps. In a mature serverless codebase, monitoring for unexpected edge cases should be woven into the application code in the same way that exception handling or I/O is handled—and often these are the first places where you may want to collect metrics to see whether a certain exception happens. Once the unexpected has been detected, human beings can swing into action with some of the other techniques in this chapter to narrow down exactly what's happened and determine how to mitigate the issue in code.

As we've discussed in previous chapters, one of the key differences between a serverless system and a traditional application runtime is that the number of instances in the serverless system scales automatically, while the traditional system has a fixed number of instances, often on specific hosts. When it comes to monitoring and debugging issues, one traditional technique that does not carry over well into serverless is "log in to the server and poke around" (where "poke around" may include attaching a debugger or running shell commands). Even if the runtime permits you to log in remotely (which implies having a login shell and a way to interact with it through the serverless runtime), connecting to a specific instance gives no guarantee that the instance will receive further requests or continue running at all; it would be possible to keep selecting instances that were scheduled for shutdown shortly after the connection. Additionally, "log in to the server and poke around" is a good recipe for configuration chaos, as each instance subtly drifts from the initial setup through a series of well-intentioned single-instance changes. Serverless systems resist this entropy by regularly recycling instances; many of them also actively prevent out-of-band access to instances (both for resiliency and to avoid snowflake problems where individual instances become nonfungible).

One common debugging tool that motivates "log in and poke around" is the ability to collect CPU and heap profiles, as well as stack traces via debugging tools. For organizations that have already adopted tools to replace remote login for these capabilities, many of these suggestions and tools will probably look familiar. For teams that haven't yet adopted a "no logins" workflow, learning and converting to these tools may provide reliability and security benefits to both traditional and serverless workloads. Many of these tools can also simplify debugging traditional distributed applications; in many ways, serverless applications are simply a very strong form of distributed applications, so serverless provides extra incentive for adopting those best practices you've been meaning to do anyway.

In the following sections, we'll start with the three most common tools for detecting and debugging issues: logs, metrics, and traces. Combined, these three form the basis for many observability tools. While observability is its own separate topic about which a much longer book could be written,[1] I'll attempt to introduce the useful basics and highlight how these tools can complement and enhance a serverless development environment.

Log Aggregation

One of the oldest and most venerated of debugging techniques, *logging* is simply writing strings from your application to a file descriptor. Depending on your chosen format, logs may be simple newline-delimited strings, or they may be written in a structured format such as JSON or even binary formats. In any case, logs represent output (often with a timestamp) from the application to human users or other automation that are recorded in the context of the instance that emitted it.

---

1 As of 2023, I'd recommend *Observability Engineering* by Charity Majors et al. (O'Reilly); observability is still a rapidly moving target.

Aggregation is the procedure of collecting (and usually sorting and indexing) all the logs for a particular application, regardless of the instance. In a distributed system, aggregating logs can provide key insights in operations that occur across multiple instances. For example, a conflict between two instances updating a key should produce a log from one instance indicating the successful update and a second one at the same time indicating a failed update. Correlating these two logs by timestamp is helpful in understanding the sequence of events between the two instances.

Most developers are probably familiar with either commercial or open source log aggregation tools such as Splunk, Elasticsearch, or Loki (see Figure 10-1 for an example of the interface for querying these aggregated logs). Developing facility with these tools is very helpful when diagnosing serverless issues; most operate on a similar model of log lines with timestamps and associated metadata labels (instance, application, etc.).

Figure 10-1. Querying aggregated logs

In some systems that support structured log messages, the additional structured logs can also be reflected into the metadata (for instance, log severity may be represented as a key-value label). Based on this collection of metadata, log aggregation systems expose query systems supporting exact matches on metadata labels, time ranges on timestamps, and substring matches on log messages. While the underlying technology is well outside the scope of this book (Indexes! Fan-out!), the following pattern can help find relevant log records when investigating an error:

1. Find a relevant log message correlated with the error.

2. Use the log message to discover the exact time and instance on which the error occurred.

3. Expand the search to preceding and following log messages on the same instance (using the instance label and expanding the time range), looking for related messages or a clear cause.

4. If searching the log timeline for a particular instance does not provide clues, expand the search to other units of work in-flight at the same time on other instances. Depending on scale, this can generate a lot more records than the corresponding timeline search.[2] If you have appropriate structured metadata, it can often make sense to start by limiting the search to only logs related to the same record, customer, or component before casting a broader net.

5. As you are searching, if you find common log messages that don't add value to the investigation, you can typically avoid them in future queries by adding a *negative* (exclusion) query on the message content. Some interfaces provide a quick way to hide these queries without needing to update the query itself.

If you're unable to pin down additional logs to diagnose the problem, it may be time to bring in other tools to help identify the problem. Request tracing provides a different angle for extracting meaning from application behavior; rather than focusing on string messages from the application, it focuses on tagged time spans reported by the application.

Tracing

While log aggregation provides a view of all the different application events that have occurred across the system, *tracing* provides a detailed timeline of the events surrounding a particular request as it crosses different system boundaries.[3] To do this, applications need to be *instrumented* to record and propagate trace information correlated to a particular trace ID. Typically, traces contain high-resolution tagged data points associated with a parent trace ID, a start, and an end time.

Unlike logs, trace tags are generally compact and designed for efficient storage rather than direct human readability. Given a trace ID, the tracing system can provide a timeline of the recorded data points by cause, giving a much deeper understanding of performance issues and error causes. Because of the high frequency of measurements,

---

2 Log collection and retention can also end up being a major cost in distributed systems. Limiting collection and retention, along with thoughtful logging levels, can help manage these costs.

3 These events are different from those in Chapter 6, but traces of messages being sent and received are incredibly useful in understanding and visualizing the flow of data in an event-driven system.

---

trace data is often *sampled* at collection time—usually the trace/do not trace decision is made when the request is received and propagated through the system in the same way as trace IDs.

Now that we understand how tracing data works, how do we use it? Tracing data can help us understand and debug application problems in several ways:

- The original use-case for trace data was to diagnose slow application requests through multiple layers of backend systems. The detailed trace view in Figure 10-2 provides a breakdown of the request time spent for each trace. In systems where multiple operations are in-flight at once or operating asynchronously from one another, this type of detailed view can help understand the "critical path" of a slow request and provide optimization opportunities.

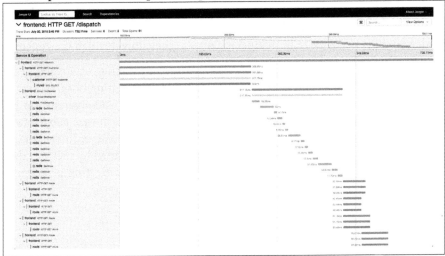

Figure 10-2. Example trace detail

- Tracing especially shines for debugging event-driven applications. While each component communicates directly with only the event distribution layer, tracing allows you to answer questions like "How long did it take to respond to this event?" or "What was the last component in this workflow that processed the event (before it disappeared)?"
- Trace data can also be processed to build visual dashboards of the flow of RPCs or events across the system. Even using sampled data, it can be easy to characterize which services send data and what corresponding systems receive the data. This can then be used to automatically draw architecture-style diagrams of data flows.

- The labels on traces can also be used to find and analyze request patterns—for example, do requests that end in a 500 correlate with timeouts talking to a particular backend? If so, it may be worth investigating the performance and behavior of a particular backend to improve the overall application reliability.

- Given a particular error, tracing data can sometimes be used to explain the error, particularly if the application has included application-level traces in addition to the process-level network call traces. For example, recording the number of rows returned or row-level timestamps from a database query can help uncover issues related to eventual consistency, where decisions might be made on stale data.

While log aggregation largely depends on the application-level effort put into logging, tracing libraries generally support a pattern of automatic trace propagation and network traffic instrumentation, providing some minimal benefit simply by linking the appropriate library. Additionally, the structured nature of tracing can help you understand the behavior of individual requests as they flow through the system.

In contrast to the sampled detail-level view provided by tracing, observability metrics aim to capture *every* occurrence at low overhead by aggregating observations within the application and presenting them as summary values. This aggregation process (collecting sums of events in-flight or over time) reduces the storage needed to collect this information, at the cost of losing details about particular occurrences and the correlations between them. Despite the reduced detail provided by metrics, this simplification provides several advantages for detecting and mitigating problems when running at scale.

Metrics

So far, all of the observability tooling we've discussed records data points that relate back to a specific occurrence. In contrast, *metrics* track numeric values that represent a sum or count of occurrences at the present moment or over the life of the process. These sums and counts can then be easily aggregated across all the instances of the application to produce totals describing the overall behavior of the system.

The most basic example of using metrics is recording the number of requests processed. When evaluated over time, this count can be used to compute the rate of requests in the system. Most metrics systems support recording additional key-value tags alongside a named metric—these key-value tags can be used to record (for example) the response code returned for a request, a latency bucket when recording histograms, or a specific backend service routed to by an application.

Because metrics gain their efficiency through aggregation, it's important that the total number of tag combinations associated with a metric (the cardinality) is relatively low—generally less than a thousand, and possibly less than a hundred. Given this low cardinality, metrics may seem like a poor debugging tool—if the number of "slow" requests goes up by 10% and the number of backend errors goes up by 5% at the same time, we can determine there is *some* sort of correlation, but we don't know (for example) how backend errors relate to slow requests, particularly since the proportion of slow requests seems higher than the backend error percentage.

In general, metrics require more context on the design and architecture of the system as a whole than other types of observability—for example, it's possible that the previous example could be explained by having only a single backend connection at a time and subsequent requests queueing up while the error is occurring. One of the most useful metric types for exploring latency is the *histogram*: looking at Figure 10-3, we can immediately see two "clumps" of latency behaviors at 2 ms and 16 ms that may merit further investigation.

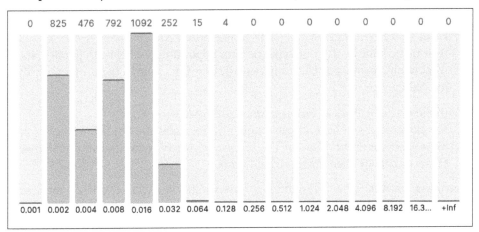

Figure 10-3. Histograms can reveal system behaviors

What metrics lack in being able to precisely explain the relationships among numbers, they make up for in illustrating broad, quick assessments of the health of applications and subsystems. Metrics are often the first point of entry for monitoring dashboards and alerting systems; a graph of latency and error rate gives an immediate overview of system health, and a threshold alert on latency or error rate can notify an operations team to take further action.

Another good use for metrics is to detect and track unexpected cases—the "this should never happen" cases can increment a metric indicating that some part of the system is not behaving as expected. An alert can then be used to raise a ticket if these expected constraints are later violated—for example, a database column expected to always contain valid IDs might be corrupted by testing data or records that failed an earlier data migration. While the metric would not indicate the exact rows affected, it can raise awareness that an investigation is warranted. Because the monitoring is continuous, it can detect issues present when the code was written, but also those introduced later, unlike a one-time query.

Much like tracing, metrics libraries support a basic level of automatic instrumentation (including runtime metrics like memory/CPU used), but even more than tracing, metrics benefit from code instrumentation to record custom metrics. Much as events in Chapter 7 provide a publishing mechanism for the application's inner monologue, metrics (and trace points) provide a publishing mechanism for the application's state. Whether or not you are implementing an event-based inner monologue, integrating metrics early and often in your development process will provide outsized benefits when heading to production. Examples of key metrics you might need to implement in application code include the following:

Conversion rate for different activities
> This is useful for detecting if a rollout has inadvertently affected user access to your business goals.

Arrival at unexpected states in your code, as mentioned earlier
> Automatic libraries can't understand your application well enough to understand what might be unexpected, but it's usually easy for a human to do, especially during code review.

Partitioning work metrics by business value, such as customer tier
> For example, if you have a large number of free users and a small number of paid users who cover the value of the service, you may be particularly sensitive to errors or latency affecting those paid users.

Metrics is the final pillar of traditional observability tools. That doesn't mean that we're done outlining tools for debugging and analyzing serverless application behavior! In the next section, we'll talk about some interesting new tools for diving deep into application behavior that might previously have been handled by logging in to a server and running a command-line tool to get instance-level insights that could hopefully be generalized. With tooling that intentionally works across a number of ephemeral instances, this data can be collected and analyzed centrally, giving additional observation power.

Live Tracing and Profiling

One of the common cases for logging in to a server is to collect a profile or debugging trace of a running application experiencing a problem. Pausing execution or changing the memory state of an individual instance is questionable in any sort of replicated service, but read-only operations like profiling (which takes passive measurements of how much time is spent in different function calls) are valid debugging tools. Historically, profiling tools operate on the scope of a single process, either locally or over a tunneled network connection from the developer's computer to the application instance.

Tools that connect from a developer machine into a specific instance again bring up the challenges of instance addressability described in "Instance Addressability and Sharding" on page 166, but recent developments have tools that instead collect profiles sent by the instance to a central collector (Google Cloud Profiler, Pixie, and possibly others). These new distributed profiling tools are an excellent match for ephemeral and interchangeable serverless instances—for example, Figure 10-4 helps visualize what code is actually executing on the live system.

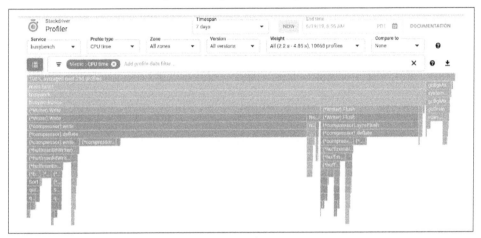

Figure 10-4. Flame chart from distributed profiling

These distributed profiling tools use OS or library-level interfaces to collect CPU and memory profiling information from agents over a network; the tool then aggregates these profiles to provide information about time spent in application and system calls, or memory allocated by object type or call location. Additionally, these monitoring tools generally run in a continuous mode where samples are periodically collected from select instances (for example, a 10-second profile every 10 minutes per instance, for about 1.6% of instance execution time being profiled). Table 10-1 highlights a few of the differences between traditional profiling tools like JProfiler and distributed tools like Pixie.

Table 10-1. Traditional versus distributed profilers

Traditional profiler	Distributed profiler
Triggered by user tool	Runs continuously
Enabled for short time	Always running
Medium overhead	Very low overhead
Exact tracking	Sampled, probabilistic
Per-language tools	Tools cover a range of languages

Of course, it's often possible to run a profiled application locally under artificial load to use a traditional profiling tool, but one of the advantages of a distributed profiling tool is that it can reveal application behavior as it actually happens in production—for example, highlighting how differences in disk performance or data size can affect system call time and overall application performance. In some cases, profiling tools can also offer snapshots of specific function argument values—a sort of "read-only breakpoint" of the application that can be helpful in debugging data-related problems in code, such as values out of bounds. These tools are sometimes also integrated into the larger suite of application debugging tools known as *Application Performance Management*, or *APM*. We'll close out our discussion of understanding and debugging serverless applications in their native environment (production) with a discussion of other features an APM agent might add, as well as some of the challenges in running an APM agent in a serverless environment.

APM Agents

APM tools combine a number of the preceding techniques into a single tool set, generally linking insights among components in an accessible manner to make it easy to transition from a trace to logs or from a metric to traces that match the pattern. In addition, they can synthesize additional insights by combining the various tools to present information in new formats.

The most common manifestation of this is an application call graph that highlights how different microservices are connected to one another by leveraging aggregated tracing data and application RPC metrics (Figure 10-5 shows the visualization in New Relic, for example). These types of visualizations both educate new team members on the structure of the application and can provide application architects validation that the actual behavior of the application matches the intended design.

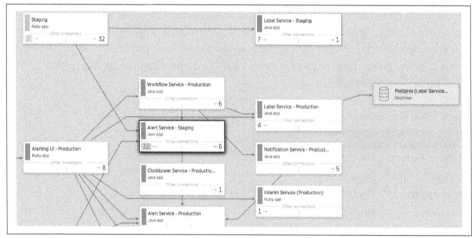

Figure 10-5. APM synthesizing an application from traces and metrics

Because they collect a variety of application data, APM tools are also well suited to extracting additional value by analyzing these data points for unexpected correlations or anomalies. For example, an APM tool monitoring database queries might be able to raise an alarm if a frequent query does not use any indexes or if the number of rows returned by a particular query changes dramatically in a short time frame. Either might be a sign of future application problems that could be hard to detect with a single tool like tracing or profiling. Additionally, APM tools provide a re-usable solution for implementing baselining and AI-driven application profiles that can augment or replace the need for humans to manually write a large number of metrics rules for a particular application.

A synthesized profile of typical application behavior can also be used by APM tools to implement automated user-level transaction probing. While the preceding sections covered open-box observability by instrumenting application processes, these obser-vations can also be turned around to perform closed-box probing. By using observa-bility inputs to build a typical profile of the operations performed by users, APM tools can build and execute synthetic user profiles that can detect changes in applica-tion behavior from a user perspective. While open-box inspection provides detailed problem diagnoses based on application internals, closed-box probing provides a high-level monitoring backstop for detecting unexpected application problems.

All of this is enabled by *agents* running alongside the application instances. These agents might be threads started by an APM library that is linked into the application, or they might be standalone processes that either instrument a single process or act as a host-level agent instrumenting all application processes on the machine. In paid cases, the APM agent may also be the unit of billing for monitoring services. While a host-level agent might make sense for a traditional application or a cloud provider's own APM services, it may be difficult to use host-level APM with serverless applica-tions, either from an installation or a billing point of view. For example, if the pro-vider charges a monthly fee per unique instance, serverless autoscaling could produce a very large bill simply by scaling the number of instances up and down on a daily basis.

If APM agents and tooling is an option, it can provide a simple, combined tool for making sense of the different angles of observing a serverless application. Even without specific APM tooling, it's still possible to understand and debug a great deal of application behavior simply by applying standard observability tools and a little bit of logic.

Summary

Observability tools have added a good deal of debugging tips and tricks even to traditional application architectures, but they become particularly critical when dealing with ephemeral runtime instances. By continually re-creating application instances and making distributed systems a first-class assumption, serverless runtimes enforce good application practice and the adoption of modern tooling approaches. These advances are driven by best practices in existing traditional systems, minimizing the risk of developing "snowflake" instances by enforcing read-only access to instance state. Serverless instances are especially resilient to snowflake-type entropy due to the ephemeral instance nature, which aligns with the observability philosophy tools like metrics, tracing, and APM agents.

At this point, we've explored all the practical aspects of living with serverless application architectures—from building to designing to debugging, with a helping of event-driven theory and a few warning signs that serverless may not be a good fit. In the final chapter, we'll explore how the serverless architecture came to be, from early inspirations to the state of the art in 2023.

## PART IV

A Brief History of Serverless

In Chapters 1 and 4, we alluded to why the serverless movement has become popular at this moment. But every advance is built on earlier insights and inventions. So in this chapter, I'm going to identify the spiritual forebears of modern serverless systems. In so doing, we'll learn more about the motivations and developments that enabled the current state of the world and maybe a little bit about the future directions of serverless.

## CHAPTER 11

A Brief History of Serverless

Those who cannot remember the past are condemned to repeat it.
—George Santayana, *The Life of Reason*

While Chapter 4 explained much of the motivation for building applications using serverless technologies and Chapter 3 covered the underlying infrastructure that made serverless systems practical in the last 10 years, this chapter will indulge in a little archaeology to understand the direction of technological advancement and predict future advancements. Technological progress is not always linear and it often spirals around common needs and goals, like a staircase on the inside of a tower. With that tower of achievement in mind, we can triangulate between different steps along the way to find the central thrust of progress.

While these may seem very high-minded and abstract, each section covers one advance toward the infrastructure and concepts used by modern serverless systems. As we progress through a series of network-software milestones starting in the 1980s, we'll see a series of progressive improvements in simplifying the work of implementing a network program by offloading capabilities onto supporting software services. As one of the founding platforms for the internet, the Berkeley Software Distribution (BSD) family of Unixes hosted many of the early networking experiments that paved the way for today's technologies. In the early 2000s, Linux took up the torch from the various other Unix vendors and continued as a platform for experimentation.

Much of the popularity of these platforms was that they were free, not only in cost but also in source code, making it easier for researchers and others to experiment with and improve them. Similarly, the mid-2010s enabled the rise of cluster-level computing systems with Mesos, Docker Swarm, and Kubernetes. While open source is not always the first instance of a popular idea, it greatly broadens the reach and appeal of ideas and acts as fertile soil for further refinements and improvements.

35 Years of Serverless

As mentioned in the last section, serverless as a mechanism for easily implementing network services was born in the mid-1980s, shortly after the birth of the internet itself in 1983 with the standardization of the TCP/IP communication protocol. While connecting a variety of computer networks together was a major achievement, implementing a network service required a lot of software plumbing. It took a few years to find common patterns to simplify offering a network service; the first was `inetd`.

inetd

The `inetd` program was introduced in 4.3 BSD in 1986 as a simpler way to implement and manage network services. Rather than implementing all the network handling for a TCP server, `inetd` uses a small configuration file to declare the network port (by name), connection type, process user, application binary, and command line for handling requests.

A declaration for the `finger` server (an early directory service) is shown in Example 11-1; the application is executed once per TCP connection as `fingerd --secure` with the `stdin` and `stdout` file descriptors connected to the TCP network socket. When the `fingerd` binary exits, `inetd` will automatically take care of closing the TCP connection. (If you're thinking this looks like "Creature Comforts: Undifferentiated Heavy Lifting" on page 13, you're correct—this is an early form of factoring common capabilities into a shared service.)

Example 11-1. Sample `inetd` service declaration

```
finger  stream  tcp  nowait  fingerd  /usr/sbin/fingerd  fingerd --secure
```

To understand the benefit of using `inetd` over implementing your own socket handling, it's instructive to look at two "echo" programs, one written to leverage `inetd`, the other as a standalone service. (We use "echo" because it's one of the simplest programs to handle input *and* output.)

The `inetd`-assisted echo in Example 11-2 is approximately 10 lines long, with relatively robust error-checking.

Example 11-2. Echo server with `inetd`

```c
#include <stdio.h>

int main(int argc, char **argv) {
  char buf[1024];
  for(int i = fread(buf, 1, sizeof(buf), stdin); i > 0; ) {
    for(int j = 0, b = 0; b >= 0 && j < i; j += b) {
```

```
    b = fwrite(buf + j, 1, i - j, stdout);
    }
  }
  return 0
}
```

By contrast, the standalone implementation in Example 11-3 is more than twice as long. Worse, it omits a large number of error checks (return values on bind, listen, and accept) and has less functionality: it can handle only one connection at a time, and the listening port is hardcoded.

Example 11-3. Echo server implemented standalone

```
#include <sys/types.h>
#include <sys/socket.h>
#include <unistd.h>

int main(int argc, char **argv) {
  int sockfd = socket(AF_INET, SOCK_STREAM, 0);
  struct sockaddr_in listen_addr;
  listen_addr.sin_family = AF_INET;
  listen_addr.sin_addr.s_addr = INADDR_ANY;
  listen_addr.sin_port = htons(7);

  bind(sockfd, (struct sockaddr)&listen_addr, sizeof(listen_addr));
  listen(sockfd, 5);
  int clientfd;
  while((clientfd = accept(sockfd, NULL, NULL)) > 0) {
    char buf[1024];
    for(int i = read(clientfd, buf, sizeof(buf)); i > 0; ) {
      for(int j = 0, b = 0; b >= 0 && j < i; j += b) {
        b += write(clientfd, buf + j, 1, i - j);
      }
    }
  }
  return 0;
}
```

Later additions to inetd included security functionality to limit server access by IP address (TCP Wrappers) and implement TLS (stunnel), all without needing to change the application code. In contrast, adding this functionality to the standalone program would add hundreds of lines of additional code and application-specific configuration (along with the opportunity to add additional errors). While inetd was a major improvement over writing the socket processing in the application itself, it did nothing to assist with implementing application protocols on top of TCP.

CGI

In the early 1990s, the HTTP protocol became increasingly common, and the National Center for Supercomputing Applications (NCSA) defined a mechanism to invoke scripts based on HTTP requests. The CGI protocol provided an interface for application authors to build dynamic web pages without needing to understand and manage the implementation details of an HTTP server. Much like inetd simplified the implementation of TCP services by handling the connection establishment and session management, CGI simplified the implementation of HTTP services by handling URL and header parsing, and content framing on the response.

While many of us today think of HTTP as a "simple" protocol to implement, fine-grained details can vary among client implementations. (RFC 1945, the original HTTP/1.0 RFC, is 59 pages without appendixes; RFC 2616 for HTTP/1.1 is 154 pages.) The CGI implementation buffers the key content (request URL, query parameters, remote host address, case-insensitive headers) from the incoming request and parses it for the program, allowing the program to focus on processing the content and producing the correct output. Most of the parsed information except the body payload of requests was parsed into environment variables, producing scripts that looked like Example 11-4.

Example 11-4. What is my IP page in Bourne shell using CGI?

```
#!/bin/sh

echo "Content-type: text/html"
echo ""
echo "<html><body><h1>"
echo "Your IP is $REMOTE_ADDR"
echo "</h1></body></html>"
```

While CGI democratized web programming by standardizing the interface between a web server and a script, it had two major failings. First, the overhead of launching a new process for each HTTP request resulted in high resource consumption per request. Second, while the CGI protocol specified the interface between a program and the web server, its scope was limited to a single machine.

Stored Procedures

While much of the arc of serverless history is connected to the web and HTTP, SQL stored procedures[1] form a parallel alternative history of serverless. Developed to enrich database APIs with procedural logic that would be applied independent of the

---

1 Introduced, as far as I can tell, by Oracle in 1992.

application client, stored procedures operate directly adjacent to the data in the database. This can allow them to operate very efficiently on data as it is fetched from the database without needing to serialize and transmit the data over the network. Popular use cases for stored procedures include data transformation and validation and fine-grained access control (for example, a stored procedure could implement privacy controls by adding noise to aggregation operations on small numbers of rows).

While stored procedures enabled interesting database capabilities (including early ship-code-to-data patterns described in "Beyond Stateless" on page 218), stored procedures also suffered from a number of drawbacks. First, the initial implementations of stored procedures (PL/SQL and SQL/PSM) were expensive and proprietary add-ons that effectively locked the implementation to a particular database vendor. Additionally, the languages available were novel and operated only in the context of the database—additional languages and tools needed to be brought to bear for the remainder of the application.

More recently, systems like Google's BigQuery and Snowflake have added support for user-defined functions implemented in standard programming languages like Python or JavaScript. As the underlying SQL engine for these systems is distributed, the arguments to these functions are serialized over the network. This provides increased flexibility in both function implementation (read and write a standard wire protocol) and tooling for testing and version management, but omits the efficiency benefits of database-stored procedures. Nonetheless, these engines retain some of the interface benefits of stored procedures even with a very different implementation. Events from change data capture triggering a general-purpose event-handling system as described in "Is Your Database Your Monologue?" on page 140 can also be seen as a successor to this technology.

Lastly, stored procedures added even more processing requirements to relational databases, which were already becoming a bottleneck as cheap datacenter networking and servers enabled a scale-out (rather than scale-up) model of hardware deployment. As the scale of the web increased, applications needed to scale beyond a single server. The late 2000s brought a series of application platforms aiming to solve the problem of distributed network applications.

Heroku

Launched in 2007, Heroku initially targeted hosting for Ruby programs but soon added support for other languages. While "VM as a service" offerings had become popular with the launch of EC2 by Amazon in 2006, Heroku offered a ready-made platform for running and scaling web applications across multiple VMs using Dynos: lightweight application containers that could be installed and managed automatically on the underlying Linux instances managed by Heroku. The addition of Dynos as a separation layer between the application and the underlying OS could be seen as a key turning point in the serverless mindset—application instances could now be managed and scaled independently of the underlying VM provisioning.

Heroku also brought about a few other changes that would persist in the serverless space for the next several years: to ensure security and reproducibility, Heroku moved the process of building the "slugs" that ran on Dynos into its own platform. Additionally, Heroku was available only as a hosted service, not as software you could install on your own hardware. Dynos were available at different RAM sizes and price points, with higher-tier services also unlocking automatic scaling and built-in logs and metrics tooling.

A relatively low entry cost and the convenience of cloud services made Heroku a popular destination for many application experiments, but difficulties with scaling to large numbers of instances and expensive costs for larger applications made it somewhat of a boutique destination. Nonetheless, Heroku became well-known for a polished and painless developer experience for new applications and a preferred environment for many authors of that era.

Behind the scenes, Heroku ran on EC2 VMs managed by the Heroku infrastructure; running on EC2 meant that it was relatively easy for applications running on Heroku to take advantage of the ever-growing set of cloud services offered by AWS with relatively few restrictions. It was also possible to "grow out" of Heroku onto EC2 with sufficient effort, though this often meant reimplementing the machine management and autoscaling capabilities. Additionally, Heroku made the buildpacks that were used by their compiler to build slugs for Dynos open source, enabling the community to help contribute language support. All of these factors made Heroku a more attractive option for many developers than the competing App Engine, despite the latter having the backing of a much more established company.

Google App Engine

Launched shortly after Heroku in April 2008, Google App Engine was conceived as a way to allow anyone to build web applications that would perform and scale the way Google applications did. While Heroku was built on EC2 VMs with autoscaling as a value-added feature, App Engine was built on Google's internal cloud (Borg) with automatic scaling and caching as default behaviors. It also shipped with bridges between email (SMTP) and chat (XMPP) and applications by translating incoming messages to HTTP requests. The "email received" and "chat received" events are the earliest event distribution patterns I'm aware of connected to the serverless space—a pattern we'll see arise with substantially more flexibility later when talking about AWS Lambda.

While Heroku was widely copied, App Engine launched with a number of limitations caused by the sandboxing model implemented at Google, which slowed the addition of new language runtimes and meant that it took nearly a year after the initial Python launch to add Java and several more years to add Go (2011), PHP (2013), and then Node.js (2018) and Ruby (2019). This sandboxing model also limited the ability of the platform to adopt new libraries in existing language runtimes, sometimes limiting developers to out-of-date versions of key libraries. As Google controlled the build and sandboxing process, it was difficult for application developers to work around these issues.

Additionally, the initial App Engine implementation did not have a robust complementary set of services and VM compute options for applications to fall back upon (in comparison to the Heroku fallback to EC2). This lead to simultaneous concerns of vendor lock-in and unsuitability of the platform for "real" workloads. These concerns were addressed over time with the development of a larger GCP, but much of the early opportunity was constrained by the surrounding platform limits.

While the reception and underlying architecture of Heroku and App Engine were substantially different, substantial similarities existed between the two environments: both abstracted application instances from underlying hardware, both defined a build and packaging process as well as a scalable runtime environment, and both provided a set of built-in capabilities that went beyond simple application execution. Altogether, these capabilities were dubbed *platform as a service* (*PaaS*), in contrast to the IaaS offered by Amazon EC2 and other VM-based services. The PaaS generation of technologies reached its culmination with the arrival of Cloud Foundry, an installable PaaS platform that adopted a number of ideas from both Heroku and App Engine.

Cloud Foundry

A few years after the launches of Heroku and App Engine, Cloud Foundry was created as an open source, multicloud PaaS to support the development and deployment of applications within an enterprise. Borrowing the idea of buildpacks from Heroku, Cloud Foundry provided both a build and run environment accessible through a simple command line.

Unlike the hosted SaaS solutions from Google and Heroku, Cloud Foundry provided all the tools needed to transform a set of VMs into a cloud. Prior to this point, cloud services had generally been proprietary or infrastructure-focused concerns; Cloud Foundry made the distinction between infrastructure and application developer concerns explicit with two haiku:

> Here is my source code,
> run it on the cloud for me,
> I do not care how.
>
> —Cloud Foundry application developer haiku

Here are my servers
make them a Cloud Foundry
I do not care how.

    —Cloud Foundry system administrator version

Cloud Foundry found a useful and valuable niche within many enterprises with a focus on developer productivity and clear affordances for both enterprise security requirements and low-touch operations from application teams. In addition to an application runtime, Cloud Foundry includes a variety of tools to present a complete application development platform:

- A Service Broker API to provision and connect applications with platform-hosted services
- Unified login services (User Accounts and Authentication [UAA])
- Log and metrics aggregation
- Organization management and permissions
- Network management
- Application storage and distribution
- URL management and request routing

In addition to these application-management features, Cloud Foundry also provides infrastructure management and scheduling features. Altogether, Cloud Foundry is a clear example of the PaaS trend from the late 2000s. Unfortunately, it is also a victim of the same trend: by building all of the preceding capabilities into a monolithic platform, the base footprint for a Cloud Foundry installation is quite large. Additionally, it's a major platform engineering challenge to replace any of the components with works-alike equivalents that might be a better fit for a particular organization either because of cost or previous adoption. This has largely limited the new adoption of Cloud Foundry in favor of more modular cloud offerings or Kubernetes, which presents a less opinionated and more flexible design.[2]

While other PaaS offerings have been built (including, for example, AWS Elastic Beanstalk), the opinionation and inflexibility of this generation of platforms ultimately led to a rejection of the "do everything" approach for serverless in favor of a more a la carte approach. AWS Lambda was the first offering to provide a platform that married fine-grained autoscaled compute with a broad suite of network services not specifically tied to the runtime platform.

---

2 And more complex!

AWS Lambda

Launched in 2014, AWS Lambda was originally conceived to provide a compact companion environment for reacting to events from Amazon storage services like S3 (object uploads), Kinesis (log records), and DynamoDB (row updates). Initially limited to JavaScript, Lambda simplified the application deployment to a single function with known arguments, removing the need to write a `main` function or other hallmarks of general-purpose programs. It also introduced a fine-grained per-request and per-CPU-second billing model that has since become a hallmark of hosted serverless offerings.

Like Heroku, App Engine, and Cloud Foundry, developers deploying to Lambda would upload their source code to AWS, which would perform a server-side build before deploying it in a scalable fashion. Like App Engine, Lambda would automatically scale instances based on the incoming traffic; unlike App Engine, Lambda would dispatch a single request per instance, which worked well in combination with the single-threaded limitations of JavaScript at the time.

The major revolution in comparison with previous serverless technologies is that Lambda contained an integrated event distribution platform (see Chapter 6). Unlike the PaaS platforms from the late 2000s, Lambda was specifically designed to handle events rather than HTTP requests; it took nearly two years for HTTP support to be added via API Gateway and almost six years to introduce a direct URL for invoking a function. In exchange for specializing in handling event-driven applications, the Lambda model reduced the required setup code for processing an event to near zero, as shown in Example 11-5.

Example 11-5. AWS Lambda function from launch blog

```
var aws = require('aws-sdk');
var s3 = new aws.S3({apiVersion: '2006-03-01'});

exports.handler = function(event, context) {
  console.log('Received event:');
  console.log(event);
  // Get the object from the event and show its content type
  s3.getObject({Bucket:event.Bucket, Key:event.Key},
      function(err, data) {
        if(err) {
          console.log('error getting object');
        } else {
          console.log('Object content type:');   console.log(data.ContentType);
        }
      });
}
```

In this way, AWS offered both more and less than platforms like Heroku: it required applications to be explicitly written for the Lambda platform, but it also enabled easy integration among existing AWS services. As noted in Chapter 2, the mantra for this pattern of application was "it's not serverless, it's serviceful." In this way, Lambda worked for cloud services much as Perl did for system administrators in the mid-1990s. This made serverless a toolkit for event-driven applications as well as a go-to mechanism for platform automation by IT departments and SREs.

The success of Lambda spawned a number of imitations from other cloud providers with much the same interface—upload code or edit directly in the web page console, and then connect it to event sources from the same cloud. While many of these services were pure imitations, Microsoft introduced an interesting way to handle state in serverless workflows with the Durable Functions feature of Azure Functions.

Azure and Durable Functions

Developed as an extension to Azure Functions in 2017, Azure Durable Functions enables programmers to define workflow orchestration using programming-language constructs that persist between individual executions (see "Workflow Orchestration" on page 129 for additional detail on this pattern). Because Durable Functions is a library running on top of Azure Functions, the underlying deployed function is still stateless, but the library adds support for orchestrating a series of function calls using deterministic function replay to drive the orchestration to completion.

While the Durable Functions library takes care of interacting with the backing state storage, the documentation is very clear that orchestration functions must be deterministic; behind the scenes the library reruns the function several times, replaying input from earlier function invocations to progress the function to the next external call. The sample code in Example 11-6 would execute at least three times: once to start the call to prepare, once after prepare completes to call service-A and service-B, and when service-A and service-B have each completed, the code will execute one more time to complete the rest of the workflow. The function may also run when one of service-A or service-B have completed, but will suspend until the second completion.

Example 11-6. Sample Durable Function with chaining and fan-out and in

```
import azure.function as func
import azure.durable_function as df

def handle_workflow(context: df.DurableOrchestrationContext):
    # "prepare" is the name of of another function that preprocesses the input
    prepared = yield context.call_activity("prepare", context.get_input())

    tasks = []
```

```
# Enqueue requests for both service-A and service-B before awaiting them both
tasks.append(context.call_activity("service-A", prepared))
tasks.append(context.call_activity("service-B", prepared))
results = yield context.task_all(tasks)

best = result[0]
if results[0].score < results[1].score:
  best = result[1]
store_result(best)  # Helper function to store the higher-value result

main = df.Orchestrator.create(handle_workflow)
```

Each time the Python function in Example 11-6 calls yield, Durable Functions has a chance to stop the execution until results from a given call are available. When new results from earlier call_activity or similar calls are available, the function is run again until further yield methods are reached. By requiring the function to be deterministic (e.g., not using time or random-number methods), the Durable Functions framework can store values from earlier invocations and replay the results in later invocations to present the user with the impression of a seamless execution.[3]

As described in "Workflow as Declarative Manifests" on page 132, an alternative model is to define an external service that manages the state of the workflow. While this is clear and straightforward to implement as a platform service, it requires developers to split their application between two languages—one programming language for the function definition and a different language for the workflow itself. Unfortunately, like many of the preceding distributed platforms, the Durable Functions approach still locks applications onto a single platform and cloud provider. While a library approach could theoretically cross platform providers, the differences in runtime behavior (e.g., function signatures in the build system and application behavior) have practically limited the library to implementation on Azure Functions. Standardizing serverless runtime behavior across different platforms was one of the primary motivations of the Knative project.

Knative and Cloud Run

Launched in 2018, Knative was introduced more extensively in Chapter 3. Shortly thereafter, Google also launched the Cloud Run managed environment, based on the same underlying runtime as App Engine but supporting the Knative runtime contract. While at Google, I worked on the Knative Serving runtime contract, with the goal of defining behavior that was compatible with both Kubernetes and the lessons learned operating a cloud-hosted serverless system at scale.

---

3 Of course, if you were to add a log message at the beginning of the function, you might see that log message printed three or four times for one complete execution of handle_workflow.

The Knative API contracts for both runtime data plane and the control APIs are explicitly defined separately from the implementation, a distinction that I believe is shared only by CGI and Cloud Foundry in this history. Additionally, the two implementations (open source Knative and Google-managed Cloud Run) share no code, making Knative and CGI the only two specification-first serverless offerings with tested compatibility across implementations.

In addition to tested portability between Knative Serving and Cloud Run, Knative aimed to provide a clean architectural separation between the three capabilities of FaaS platforms like AWS Lambda: code build, code execution, and event distribution. Initially, these three components were provided as Knative Build, Knative Serving, and Knative Eventing; in 2019, the Knative Build portion was extracted as Tekton to orchestrate software builds outside of serverless contexts. In 2022, Knative Functions was added to the project to specifically focus on the transformation of source code functions into serverless application containers.

The separation of (serverless) code build and event delivery from the core serverless runtime has since been emulated by other projects,[4] including build systems like Cloud Build and GitHub Actions and event-delivery platforms like AWS Event-Bridge and Azure Event Grid. By separating these capabilities from the FaaS runtime, serverless and traditional architectures can leverage the same enabling technologies to standardize developer workflows and interoperate between existing software platforms and greenfield applications.

Additionally, by defining an underlying open source platform built on top of standard infrastructure orchestration like Kubernetes, Knative provides a platform for academic researchers and enterprises to experiment with additional types of serverless workloads. One promising area is the combination of serverless application management with hardware accelerators such as GPUs. "AI" on page 216 provides further details on the KServe project that leverages Knative to provide a serverless AI inference platform.

Knative Serving uses the PaaS standby of an HTTP request as the defined unit of work, which allows it to handle both traditional application patterns and functions that handle event delivery over HTTP. Adopting this standard makes it simple to extend existing workloads to run on Knative, either in a fully hosted environment or on self-hosted hardware. The standardization on HTTP also aligns Knative with edge-based FaaS offerings like Cloudflare Workers and Netlify Edge.

---

4 Software builds are actually a great target for a serverless model because they run infrequently and tend to have bursty resource requirements. For some reason, few people think of remote or distributed builds as serverless systems, even if they think of job-execution systems as serverless.

Cloudflare Workers and Netlify Edge Functions

Launched in 2018, Cloudflare Workers provides a distributed, JavaScript-only sandboxed execution environment for customers who need to customize content served from the Cloudflare content delivery network (CDN). In 2022, Netlify launched a similar JavaScript-sandboxed offering aimed at application authoring and integrated with its larger application authoring suite. In contrast to general-purpose FaaS offerings, these content-delivery edge functions are specifically focused on augmenting or transforming HTTP content provided from a CDN.

Much like a traditional cloud service offering, Cloudflare and Netlify manage the distribution and scheduling of the serverless instances in a multitenant manner, packing multiple customer executions onto the same physical hardware. Unlike a traditional cloud service offering, the available resources for these content-transformation serverless platforms are exceptionally limited, often to less than 500 ms of compute time and a few hundred megabytes of memory. In exchange for these strict resource limits, application authors can deploy simultaneously to hundreds of sites around the world, providing very low latency between customers and content-enrichment functions.

This new generation of serverless infrastructure is powered by lightweight JavaScript language sandboxes originally designed for web browsers. Rather than supporting a full Linux process model, the sandbox exposes only a limited number of native JavaScript functions for performing I/O—for example, the sandbox could entirely remove the capability to write to local disk by exposing only network socket APIs or expose a network key-value store through an API that abstracts the network communication. These lightweight sandboxes have become particularly popular as a delivery target for Wasm-compiled languages, including Rust, C#, and Go.

Because these content-enrichment functions are globally distributed, they work well for enforcing application policies on content or A/B testing but are a poor fit for implementing data-intensive APIs such as GraphQL or REST interfaces on their own. Instead, the edge-content function may call back to a central API implemented using a cloud or datacenter-hosted serverless runtime that returns caching-enabled results where appropriate. Edge-content functions can also be used to enforce rate limits or to route users to their "home" datacenter without needing to change user-visible URLs.

While the arc of previous generations of serverless systems began with proprietary hosted solutions, open source options like Cloud Foundry and Knative have followed on to provide both researchers and large enterprises additional control and experimentation capabilities beyond hosted offerings. In the edge-content space, this is already occurring with Cloudflare Workers' runtime becoming open source in 2022 and the competing development of several native edge-focused Wasm runtimes in the open source community. The next several years will continue to drive advancements in both datacenter and edge serverless capabilities, with each developing their own complementary strengths.

Where to Next?

Looking at the arc of serverless as a runtime for network-distributed applications, we can see several patterns emerge:

- Initial applications are written specifically for the underlying protocols; lessons and patterns from these applications form the basis of frameworks that enable serverless technologies to reduce the repetition and toil of building protocol-specific implementations.
- Serverless platforms leverage complementary services and ecosystems—for example, Heroku, App Engine, and Cloud Foundry all benefited from the simpler hardware-provisioning model of cloud infrastructure services.
- General-purpose serverless is a trade-off between flexibility and power, labor-saving abstractions, and existing application compatibility.
- Serverless platforms begin as proprietary offerings looking to capture added value, but this markup is eroded over time as the ideas become commoditized to the point that credible open source implementations have emerged.

The safest prediction for serverless is that it will continue to spread into areas with a lot of attention. This focus will produce clear and obvious infrastructure uplifts that will start a gravitational pull toward implementation of serverless principles in the following areas: AI, distributed and edge applications, and stateful applications.

AI

In 2023, generative AI such as ChatGPT and Stable Diffusion became a hot topic, with particularly excited advocates suggesting that it will transform human labor to the same degree as the printing press. Whether or not this hype will come to pass, it's clear that all of these AI models will need infrastructure to build (train) and execute (inference) the models. Supporting services such as context and model storage and mechanisms to manage training data will also evolve as AI demands grow. Additionally, AI models need input and output translation between real-world content and the set of weighted parameters that are the lingua franca of neural network models.

As might be expected, the hyperscale cloud providers have led the way in introducing services here that take advantage of (read: sell) massive hardware resources to accelerate both training and inference. Unsurprisingly, each cloud provider has its own toolchain and format for data sets and trained models; this is further divided by the underlying tool sets (PyTorch, TensorFlow, and others), each with its own interfaces and storage formats.

Hosted providers who choose a particular opinion (say, TensorFlow and Google Cloud) will be able to produce a more coherent developer experience that hides the details of provisioning and scaling training or inference nodes, at the cost of possibly excluding interesting developments using a different library. Conversely, serverless AI platforms that do not specialize in particular libraries and frameworks might end up without sufficient labor-saving power to be useful.

Another possibility is that inference models become standardized while training remains specialized—this would match the pattern of Hadoop and other data analysis tools where the size and gravity of the application data means that engineers are explicitly designing and tuning their workloads for a specific number of instances, rather than having software that can automatically calculate the optimal parallelism for a given data set. Given the existing advances in hyperparameter tuning, model optimization, and automatic regularization, it seems possible that a future machine learning training platform could automatically determine the optimal number of training instances for a given model and data set.

Once a model has been trained, several existing toolkits can package the model plus the interpretation software into a standard OCI container that can be run on an existing container-based serverless platform. The KServe project automates this leveraging Knative as the serverless platform, including packaging the feature-recognition code as well as the model itself. A portable format for inference models makes it easier to not only run models on varied cloud resources, but also distribute models to remote physical locations.

Distributed and the Edge

Edge computing is the opposite of the trend of the last 15 years to centralize software platforms in large datacenter sites; instead, applications are distributed nearby to actual users, either humans or infrastructure such as Internet of Things (IoT) devices. While I described the application of serverless to CDNs in "Cloudflare Workers and Netlify Edge Functions" on page 215, the more general problem of distributing applications to widely distributed infrastructure is still in its infancy. General patterns have not yet been discovered and regularized for handling hundreds of small clusters of machines, possibly with partial or limited connectivity.

Ideally, a serverless edge platform might combine the ability to automatically manage compute tasks with some type of event distribution platform and a notion of application priority to enable sharing the limited hardware available at the edge. In such a system, high-priority events (or high-priority compute work) would be handled nearly immediately until completed, while lower-priority events and computation could be time delayed (or even suspended mid-process) to maintain interactive response times for high-priority events. By leveraging priorities, it might be possible to schedule (for example) 16 CPUs worth of applications onto four 4-CPU nodes, with the system able to degrade to handling critical work only if one of the three nodes were to fail.

These distributed applications would consist of dozens or hundreds of separate event-distribution and data storage systems; such a mesh of independent sites would also need to develop simple and convenient systems for managing these independent distributed data stores, including the ability to redirect or mirror data from one node to another for certain types of queries. Current serverless systems generally focus on stateless computation as the core abstraction, but a coherent distributed or edge platform would also need to treat data as a similarly serverless abstraction.

Beyond Stateless

While most current serverless systems represent each instance as identical and fungible stateless processes, some application patterns intrinsically need to support managing application state at a fine-grained scale. The Actor model provides one mechanism for managing state alongside independent units of work by using messages directed to specific data elements (addresses) as the work items, and ensuring that only a single process is spawned for a given address, even if there are multiple outstanding messages for that address—only a single message for that address will be processed at a time.

Within architectures that associate compute with storage, there are two main models: data shipping and function shipping. In the *data-shipping* model, data is copied from the authoritative store and sent over the network to the compute process handling that particular unit of data. The compute function then processes the data, transforms it if needed, and sends it back over the network to the storage layer. In contrast, the *function-shipping* model instead sends the application code to the node that hosts the data; if the function description is smaller than the data it is processing, this results in less overall network traffic and possibly better latency than a data-shipping approach. The drawback is that data storage and computation become deeply linked, introducing challenges around access fairness, sandboxing, and reliability. In either case, new serverless APIs are needed to describe the computation and its association with the underlying data.

One promising avenue for combining storage and serverless computation is the addition of user-defined functions to data warehousing products such as BigQuery and Snowflake. By adding the ability to run user-defined code written in JavaScript or Wasm to the distributed query-execution engine in these products, developers can target computation on a simple relational model and rely on the underlying platform to scale and schedule their computation at the right point in the model processing.

Another promising development in this area is Apache Flink's Stateful Functions; in this model, an existing Flink application is extended to be able to call an external function endpoint, which could be either a traditional or serverless application. When using Stateful Functions, the running Flink program will use its knowledge of the data dependencies for a particular computation to collect all the input parameters for the function calculation and ship them to the external function; the function's return is then fed back into the Flink data-processing graph and can be used like other intermediate computations.

Stateless computation with interchangeable instances is somewhat of an "easy mode" for platform designers; it greatly simplifies the implementation requirements at the cost of foreclosing on some application architectures (for example, per-instance state probably requires solving the issues raised in "Instance Addressability and Sharding" on page 166). Integrating serverless compute and storage into a broadly useful platform is much more difficult, but offers the hope of addressing many more computing problems and application architectures.

Summary

While the serverless movement has experienced a hype cycle since the growth of AWS Lambda in 2016 and onward, the forces behind serverless have a history nearly as long as the internet itself. The idea of building platforms that can abstract away much of the "undifferentiated heavy lifting" and allow developers to focus on higher-level concerns is as compelling now as it was 30 years ago. In the meantime, advances in cluster management and protocols have greatly simplified the entry bar for writing distributed applications.

At the same time, serverless is an ever-moving frontier that seeks to continue to simplify and standardize complex infrastructure and operational concerns into a standard set of computer-driven solutions. As standards and best practices form, serverless will follow shortly behind, helping developers wrangle the pile of abstractions associated with each new technology. Good serverless platforms will also accommodate old and new sitting alongside each other—no new platform completely replaces an existing one overnight, and the best ones (like many serverless platforms) bring new value and life to your existing applications and platforms.

Index

failures, 171-172
   cold starts, 176-180
   exactly-once delivery, 186-187
   feedback loops, 181-182
   forecasting, 180-181
   hotspots, 183-186
   meltdowns, 172-175
key-value storage, 42-43
limitations of, 165-166
serverless computing, 7
task queues, 45
task queues across time, 135-136
Scatter-Gather requests, 151
scheduling (in Knative), 52-53
security, serverless impact on, 97
sender, Broker Sender (in Knative Eventing),
   75-76
sensitive data, 145
Sequence (in Knative Eventing), 67
serverless computing
   benefits of, 83-84
      for event-driven architecture, 146
      micro billing, 90-94
      microservices, 84-90
   challenges in
      instance addressability/sharding,
         166-167
      protocol mismatches, 163-164
      scalability limits, 165-166
      termination of work units, lack of,
         161-163
      unbalanced work unit sizing, 160-161
   components of, 6-7
   defined, xiv-xv, 3-6
   future of, 216
      AI, 216-217
      distributed apps/edge computing,
         217-218
      state management, 218-219
   history of
      AWS Lambda, 211-212
      Azure Durable Functions, 212-213
      CGI, 206
      Cloud Foundry, 209-210
      Cloudflare/Netlify, 215-216
      Google App Engine, 208-209
      Heroku, 207-208

inetd, 204-205
      Knative/Cloud Run, 213-214
      stored procedures, 206-207
   impact of, 94-98
      on infrastructure, 97-98
      on languages, 95-96
      on sandboxing, 96
      on security, 97
      on tooling, 97
   Knative Serving (see Knative Serving)
   monoliths as, 115-118
   scaling, 7
Services (in Knative Serving), 55
serving stage (process lifecycle), 18
sharding, 43, 166-167
shipping information (inner monologue example), 150-151
shopping carts (inner monologue example),
   148-149
shutdown stage (process lifecycle), 18
SNS (Simple Notification System), 78
Sources (in Knative Eventing), 67
splitting API into components, 39-40
startup stage (process lifecycle), 18
startup times, effect on cold starts, 176-179
state management, 41-48
   future of serverless computing, 218-219
   key-value storage, 42-44
   object storage, 44-45
   task queues, 45
   timer services, 45
   workflows, 46-48
   with workflows, 130-131
static files, fetching, 31-33
status dashboard example (see application
   design example)
storage interfaces, 41-48
   Broker storage (in Knative Eventing), 72-74
   future of serverless computing, 218-219
   key-value, 42-44
   object, 44-45
   task queues, 45
   timer services, 45
   workflows, 46-48
stored procedures, 206-207
Strangler Fig pattern, 110-115
stream processing, 125

About the Author

Evan Anderson is a principal software engineer at Stacklok, where he's working to secure the software supply chains that power all modern software. Previously, he was a senior staff software engineer at VMware, where he was a technical lead on the Tanzu Application Platform and a lead on the Knative project.

Prior to VMware, he worked at Google for 15 years, including on Google Compute Engine, Google App Engine, Cloud Functions, and Cloud Run. While at Google, Evan was a founding member of the Knative project and worked on designing the Serving API and conformance specification and framework.

Outside of work, he's a parent and runner; he particularly enjoys getting away from it all on trails for multihour runs.

Colophon

The animal on the cover of *Building Serverless Applications on Knative* is a kagu (*Rhynochetos jubatus*), a mostly flightless bird native to the mountain forests of New Caledonia in the southwest Pacific.

While the kagu doesn't often fly, it still uses its wings for speedy ground movement, frightening potential predators with the dark striped pattern on its wings, or performing for other kagus. Adult kagus also sometimes utilize the "broken wing" defense, pretending to have an injured wing to draw predators away from their offspring.

Kagus are family based and territorial, with a male and female mating for many years (and sometimes for life). Each morning, the pair sings a duet to stake their territory. Since kagus are mostly flightless, their nests are on the forest floor, often near a tree or rock. The male and female both contribute to the incubation of the egg and the raising of their young. Although their young are relatively independent after 14 weeks, they sometimes live in their parents' territory for up to 6 years.

Physically, kagus are unique for their *powder downs* (waterproof and self-cleaning feathers) and *nasal corns* (structures covering their nostrils). From a diet perspective, they are carnivorous, feasting on small invertebrates such as bugs, snails, and lizards.

The current IUCN conservation status of the kagu is Endangered. Many of the animals on O'Reilly covers are endangered; all of them are important to the world.

The cover illustration is by Karen Montgomery, based on an antique line engraving from a loose plate. The cover fonts are Gilroy Semibold and Guardian Sans. The text font is Adobe Minion Pro; the heading font is Adobe Myriad Condensed; and the code font is Dalton Maag's Ubuntu Mono.

Milton Keynes UK
Ingram Content Group UK Ltd.
UKHW032122070224
437386UK00002BA/5